UNSTOPPABLE

UNSTOPPABLE

MY

LIFE

SO

FAR

MARIA SHARAPOVA

WITH RICH COHEN

SARAH CRICHTON BOOKS

FARRAR, STRAUS AND GIROUX • NEW YORK

Sarah Crichton Books

Farrar, Straus and Giroux

18 West 18th Street, New York 10011

Copyright © 2017 by SW19, Inc.

All rights reserved

Printed in the United States of America

First edition, 2017

Library of Congress Cataloging-in-Publication Data

Names: Sharapova, Maria, 1987– author.

Title: Unstoppable : my life so far / Maria Sharapova.

Description: New York : Sarah Crichton Books, Farrar, Straus and Giroux, [2017]

Identifiers: LCCN 2017017149 | ISBN 9780374279790 (hardcover) |

ISBN 9780374715311 (ebook)

Subjects: LCSH: Sharapova, Maria, 1987– | Tennis players—Russia (Federation)—

Biography. | Women tennis players—Russia (Federation)—Biography.

Classification: LCC GV994.S28 S53 2017 | DDC 796.342092 [B]—dc23

LC record available at https://lccn.loc.gov/2017017149

Designed by Abby Kagan

Our books may be purchased in bulk for promotional, educational, or business use.

Please contact your local bookseller or the Macmillan Corporate

and Premium Sales Department at 1-800-221-7945, extension 5442, or by e-mail

at MacmillanSpecialMarkets@macmillan.com.

www.fsgbooks.com

www.twitter.com/fsgbooks • www.facebook.com/fsgbooks

1   3   5   7   9   10   8   6   4   2

I know how this is. The beginning of a book. Dedication, they call it. The page we tend to skip. Next!

But this book is for you.

We might have never met, or met each other briefly. You might have never heard of me.

If you already know a little bit about my story, thank you for wanting to know more.

For trusting me with your time. For being curious. Maybe it was simply the cover that caught your eye. Thank you for taking the chance to pick it up.

Last, to the amazing number of you from all around the world who live through my victories and defeats as if they were your own. "Thank you" might not be strong enough words to show you my appreciation, but the gratitude I carry with me will forever be because of you.

Do not judge me by my successes,
judge me by how many times I fell down
and got back up again.

—NELSON MANDELA

UNSTOPPABLE

At some point toward the end of the 2016 Australian Open, a nurse asked me to pee in a cup. There was nothing unusual about this—it's just another part of the procedure, performed by the ITF, the International Tennis Federation, to drug-test athletes and keep the sport clean. I was twenty-eight years old. I'd been peeing in those cups for more than a decade, and I forgot all about the test the moment after it happened, my mind quickly returning to the matter at hand: the next leg of the tour, the next match I'd have to win to get where I still needed to go. I'd already won five Grand Slams, including the Australian Open, but the desire to be the happiest player on the last day of a big tournament never diminishes. In fact, it increases. As I neared the end of my career—in the first weeks of 2016, that's all I was thinking about—I became especially aware of time. I'd only have so many more shots at a Grand Slam title.

Serena Williams beat me in the finals in 2015. Straight sets, with a second-set tiebreaker. It's never fun to lose, but I went away optimistic, strong. I looked forward to the coming season, which would be one of my last. In fact, in those weeks, as I made my way from tournament to tournament across Asia, I was thinking less about the game than about my retirement. I knew the end was near and I wanted to go out in the perfect way. I'd take one last turn around the circuit, from the Australian Open, to the French Open, to Wimbledon. A kind of victory tour. I'd love the people and the people would love me. It would end at the U.S. Open, which I'd play just as this book hit the stores. Maybe I'd even make it to the final. Maybe Serena would be there, too.

Serena Williams has marked the heights and the limits of my career—our stories are intertwined. I approach every match against her with trepidation and respect. It was Serena whom I beat in the Wimbledon final to emerge on the international stage at seventeen, and it's Serena who's given me the hardest time since. I've beaten all the players who have beaten Serena, but it's been nearly impossible for me to beat Serena herself. There's a reason for this—she knows it and she knows that I know. It's our secret, which I'll get into in the fullness of time.

Maybe I'd find a way to beat her and my career would end as it began, with me holding the chalice beside Serena as the crowd cheered.

Well, you know what they say: Man plans, God laughs.

Three weeks into the season, I got an e-mail from the ITF. As I read it, I started to panic. That urine test I'd taken back in Melbourne? I failed it. Meldonium had been found in my urine, and in January 2016 meldonium had been added to the World Anti-

Doping Agency's list of banned substances. In other words, I was now a drug violator. I'd be suspended from competition immediately. A hearing would follow.

Meldonium?

I'd never even heard of it. This must be a terrible mistake. Sitting on my bed, I googled it. Looking at the results, my heart sank. Meldonium also goes by the name Mildronate, and that was something I had heard of. It's a supplement I'd been taking for ten years. It's used to treat many ailments, including coronary artery disease. Mildronate had been recommended to me by a family doctor back in 2006. I'd been run down at the time, getting sick very often, and had registered several abnormal EKGs. There was also a family history of diabetes. I did not think much about that pill, I just took it. I took it before any intense physical exertion, as you might take baby aspirin to ward off a heart attack or stroke. I was not the only one doing this. In Eastern Europe and Russia, Mildronate is like ibuprofen. Millions of people take it every day, including my grandmother! I had never put it on an ITF form—you're asked to list every medication or supplement you've taken in the previous seven days—because I did not take it every day and did not consider it any different from the Advil I took for pain.

How does it enhance performance?

Even the ITF can't tell you. Because it doesn't. It seems the officials banned it merely because it was being used by so many Eastern Europeans. "Well, if they're taking it, they must be taking it for a reason"—something like that. I'd missed news of the ban because it came under my radar, in a long list reached only by following a series of links included in an ITF e-mail, and I hadn't noticed anything different. That was my big mistake. I was sloppy.

And now that moment of carelessness threatened to ruin everything. I could be banned for as long as four years! Four years? That's forever to a professional athlete.

A bottomless hole opened beneath my life and in I went. Everything I'd worked for since I was four years old, that whole crazy struggle, was suddenly cast in a new, terrible, unfair light. What followed were days of disbelief and despair.

"Goddamnit," I finally screamed, rousing myself. "I'm going to fight this bullshit."

What's defined my game more than anything? Determination, tenacity. I do not quit. Knock me down ten times, I get up the eleventh and shove that yellow ball right back at you. "This will not beat me," I said. "This will not be the last word." To understand my determination, you need to know who I am, where I come from, what happened. You need to know about me and my father and the flight from Russia in the dead of night when I was six. You need to know about Nick B. and Sekou and Serena and a nice old couple from Poland. You need to know the crazy story. In other words, you need to know everything.

ONE

I've always loved to hit. From the time I was four years old. It's the one thing that can fix any problem. You've lost Wimbledon in a frustrating match and everything that might have gone right went wrong? Pick up a racket and hit. The strings and the ball, the charge that carries through your body fixes everything. Hitting returns you to the present, where the flowers bloom and the birds sing. You've gotten terrible news from the other side of the world? Your grandmother died and there is nothing but a long flight and a funeral ahead? Pick up a racket, pick up a ball. And hit. The rules changed and you did not know the rules changed and all of a sudden a pill you have taken for years has undone everything? Pick up a racket and hit!

It's one of my first memories. I was four years old. My father, who had taken up tennis a year or two earlier because his brother had given him a racket for his birthday, brought me along to the local courts where he played in Sochi. A small park with clay courts, a snack bar, and a Ferris wheel, from the top of which you could see over the apartment house to the Black Sea. That day, because I was bored, I pulled a racket and a ball out of his bag and started to hit. Off a fence, off a wall. I went around the corner and hit where other players were hitting. I was small and young and did not know what I was doing but quickly fell into a trance, the ball leaving and returning to my racket like a yo-yo in the palm of your hand. In this way, I got my father—Yuri; this is his story as much as mine—to stop what he was doing and notice me. In this way, my life began.

I'm not sure if I remember this, or if I just remember the old, faded photographs: a tiny blond girl with the knobby knees and oversized racket. I sometimes wonder if I'm still the same person who picked up that racket. Very quickly the game changed from the simplicity of hitting to the complications of coaches and lessons, matches and tournaments, the need to win, which is less about the trophies than about beating the other girls. I can get fancy and sweet about it, but at bottom my motivation is simple: *I want to beat everyone.* It's not just the winning. It's the not being beaten. Ribbons and trophies get old, but losing lasts. I hate it. Fear of defeat is what really drives many of us. I say "us" because I can't possibly be the only person who feels this way. This might never have occurred to me had I not started writing this book. When you look, you notice patterns, connections. You see things in a new way.

I've often asked myself: Why write a book?

In part, it's to tell my story, and it's also to understand it. In many ways, my childhood is a mystery, even to me. I'm always being asked the same questions: How did I get here? How did I do it?

What went right, what went wrong? As I said, if I'm known for one thing, it's toughness, my ability to keep going when things look bad. People want to know where that quality comes from and, because everyone is hoping for their own chance, how to acquire it. I've never figured it out myself. In part, it's because of *who knows?* If you look too deeply, maybe you destroy it. It's my life and I want to tell it. I talk to reporters, but I never tell everything I know. Maybe now is the time to open up the door for more questions, and to make sense of my life and get down the early days before I forget. I hope people take away every kind of lesson, good and bad. This is a story about sacrifice, what you have to give up. But it's also just the story of a girl and her father and their crazy adventure.

TWO

Where should I begin?

How about Gomel, a city in Belarus, its muddy streets and forest paths straight out of a fairy tale? It's near the border with Russia, a short drive from Chernobyl in Ukraine. My father met my mother in school. What were they like? What were *your* parents like before you were born? It's a mystery. My father will tell you he was a genius. And charming. My mother, Yelena, will not agree. He could drive her nuts. He was the kind of student who doesn't do the reading and skips class, then strolls in and nails the test. School never was important to Yuri. He figured he'd outsmart the system, and there was no teacher who could tell him how.

Yuri was out of school fast. He was in the world by age twenty, working a job I still don't really understand. He led crews that maintained smokestacks, the sort that spew. He traveled for that job, taking planes to factories all over the country. He spent days on a scaffold, hundreds of feet off the ground, maintaining whatever had to be maintained. Had the Soviet Union survived, he would've done that until he was old enough to retire. But the Soviet Union did not survive. It was, in fact, coming apart in my toddler years. If I asked about it, my father would say, "Gorbachev didn't have the balls." My father believes a person must be tough to hold anything together—a household, a career, even a country. He knew almost nothing about America. To him, it was blue jeans and rock 'n' roll and keep the rest. Same with tennis. He did not know about it, did not care. In Russia, tennis was for deposed aristocrats. Yuri played ice hockey and loved to mountain climb, which may explain his life atop the smokestacks.

My mother is beautiful and petite, with blond hair and sparkling blue eyes. She's better educated than my father: aced high school and college, then went on to get the equivalent of a master's degree. She loves the great Russian writers (when I was little she read me stories and made me memorize passages before I could understand what they were about). By 1986 she was living with my father in a house on the edge of town. There was a yard in front and a forest in back. My grandparents were not far away. My mother's parents lived in the far north, Siberia, which will be important. When my mother and father talk about those years, it sounds like Eden. The house, the trees, and the shade under the trees, a young couple very much in love. They were poor but did not know it. The house was small and drafty but they did not know that either.

Then it happened: my uncle gave my father a tennis racket for his birthday. It was a joke. Only rich people played tennis. But a club had just opened in Gomel and my father thought, "Why not?"

He started too late to become a great player, but he's a natural athlete, and got good quickly. He fell in love with the game, read books and articles about the stars, watched the Grand Slams on TV. He was preparing himself, though he did not know it. He was in training to become that strange and exotic thing, a tennis parent.

(This is where you're supposed to laugh.)

* * *

One morning in April 1986, as she was working in the garden, my mother heard a rumble in the distance, like thunder. She was wearing a scarf on her head and no shoes, her feet in the dirt. She looked at the sky, then carried on. At first, it was no more than that—just something that makes you look up. She was soon to be pregnant with me, her only child. The rumors started that night, wild, terrifying tales. What exactly caused that rumble? There was smoke in the sky the next morning. That's when the rumors took shape. These concerned the nuclear reactor in Chernobyl. People said it had exploded, that radioactive material had been thrown into the air and would rain down on everything. As if an atomic bomb had been dropped on us. When people went to the government for information, they were told everything was fine. Still, there was panic. Families were packing up and heading off. My mother got a call from her mother, who'd been able to learn more in Siberia than my parents could forty miles from the explosion.

"We called your mother and told her to get out," Grandma Tamara told me. "Chernobyl was lethal—it killed all living organisms. It was an invisible death. We knew this because we'd met a man who'd been sent in as part of the cleanup. He said the radiation was off the scale. At first, the officials said nothing. People were not even advised to close their windows! Everyone just kept living as before. I remember this man telling us: 'The mushrooms coming up in the forest are as big as dinner plates!' When he took pictures, all the film came back overexposed. This man died at forty-five or fifty years old. All those workers did."

My parents went north. Other people stayed. My father's mother stayed. Years later, we'd go to her house on vacation. We'd be amazed by the huge forest mushrooms. Everyone said it was caused by radiation, which makes you wonder. My mother and father are not small, but are not big either. I am six foot two, not counting heels. I tower over them. So where did that height come from? My father says I grew because I needed size to compete. He's a believer in the power of human will. But my mother was about to be pregnant with me when the reactor blew, drinking the water and eating the vegetables, and continued to drink the water and eat the vegetables after she had gotten pregnant, so who knows?

When I asked my father about their escape from Gomel, he laughed. "It was a crazy, crazy time," he said. "We went to your grandparents' house because they lived in Siberia, which was as far away as we could get. We took the train, an old train jammed with people. Thirty-six hours from Gomel to Yekaterinburg, called Sverdlovsk in those days, then two more hours by air to Nyagan, close to the Arctic Circle."

My father calls Nyagan "a shitty little town." That's where I was born, on April 19, 1987. Yuri was gone by then, having left for work as soon as my mother was settled. He was back in Gomel, celebrating Easter with his parents, when he learned that he was a father.

Yuri came to see me a few weeks later. That's when he got his first good look at Nyagan, a brutal industrial outpost of apartment blocks and factories, and knew that he could never live there, nor go back to Gomel. He decided to make the best of the situation and take us to a place he'd always wanted to live: Sochi, a Black Sea resort situated between mountains and sea. Yuri had fallen in love with the place on a childhood vacation.

Sochi?

My grandparents thought he was crazy, but lent him some money anyway. He was able to trade our house in Gomel for a tiny little apartment in Sochi. We arrived there when I was two years old. Had we not moved to Sochi, I never would've taken up tennis. It's a resort and tennis is part of its life. That made it different from the rest of Russia, where the sport was unknown. If you had to pick one event that made me a player, it'd be Chernobyl.

We still own that apartment. It's on a steep side street, Vishnevaya (Cherry) Street, sixth floor, in the back of the building. When we came home, I would race up the stairs with the key, leaving my parents to trudge up the five flights behind me. I have such fond memories of the afternoons I spent there as a child, the intimate dinners, the funny conversations, the people coming and going, my grandmother sitting on the stairs, chatting entire evenings away. My earliest recollections are of looking out the window of that apartment at the boys and girls in the playground up the hill. My parents were very protective. They did not let me out much. Mostly, I was just at the window, watching other kids play.

From the start, my parents took different roles in my life. My father was practice and sports and competition—outside. My mother was school and letters and stories—inside. She made me copy the Russian alphabet again and again and again, working on each letter till it was perfect. She made me write stories and memorize Russian poems. Best was when she just let me read.

Pippi Longstocking was my favorite. I dreamed about the world of the little girl, daughter of a wealthy sailor, with money in her pocket, doing whatever she wanted, just like a grown-up. She had a horse. And she had a monkey! That book took me to the place I wanted to live.

My grandparents would visit from Nyagan. I loved spending time with Grandma Tamara. I talked to her when I was working on this book—she remembers so much I can't. She laughed when I asked about the day I nearly drowned. "There's a simple explanation, which maybe you can understand better now," she told me. "I was only forty years old when you were born. I really didn't want to be called Grandmother. When you were three or four, we'd go to the beach. I'd swim a bit, then you'd go into the water and splash. Suddenly, I'd hear you screaming, 'Grandmother! Grandmother!! Grandmother!!!' And, you see, there were young men around on the beach, and I didn't want them to know. So I pretended not to hear you. Later, I sat next to you and whispered: 'Mashenka, don't call me Grandmother in front of others!' I changed you into clean, dry underwear, I remember this well, and began wringing out your swimming panties, and suddenly you go, 'You're not a grandmother! You're a squeezer!'"

As soon as I was old enough to look after myself a bit, Yuri started taking me around. Wherever he went, I went. That's why I was at the court that day, where I picked up a tennis racket for the first time. Riviera Park. For whatever reason, I had this ability. I could hit that ball against that wall for hours. It was not my skill people remarked on. It was my concentration—that I could do it again and again without getting bored. I was a metronome. Tick, tock. Tick, tock. I attracted a crowd. People stood around, watching. This happened day after day. It got to the point where Yuri felt

he had to do something. Which is why, when I was four, he enrolled me in a tennis clinic for kids. That's how I found my first
coach, Yuri Yudkin, a playground legend, a vodka-soaked maestro.
He'd been out in the world, the big world of tennis, so he knew a
thing or two. He dazzled provincial Sochi. Tennis parents stood in
line to hear his pronouncements or, better, let him appraise and
coach their kids. A few locals had already made the big time, like
Yevgeny Kafelnikov. My father enrolled me with Yudkin. He'd
line you up the first day and watch you hit. If he paused, your
heart leaped and you hit harder. He spoke to my father at the start
and said that I seemed to be something special, unique. It was how
my eyes tracked the ball, and the way I kept at it. Whether I developed into a player would depend on my toughness.

"Does Masha have it, or not? This is what we will find out."

Maria is not my real name. I was christened Masha. But there
is no good match for Masha in English, and soon after I arrived in
America, people started calling me Marsha, which I hated—they
connected me to the Brady Bunch!—so I got out in front of that
and told people to call me Maria.

By toughness, Yudkin meant persistence, the quality that makes
you lock in and focus when asked to do the same thing a million
times. If you ask most kids to do something, they will do it once
or twice, then get restless, shut down, and walk away. To be great
at anything, Yudkin believed, you had to be able to endure a tremendous amount of boredom. That is, you had to be tough. Was
I? Time would tell.

I was soon taking private lessons on the back courts. Yudkin
was a genius at building those first strokes, and that's everything. The basics. If you don't get that right, you're going to
have problems. Like setting out on a long trip and your first step

is in the wrong direction. At the beginning, it's all you have: a simple forehand, a simple backhand. It's all you have at the end, too. Yudkin hands me a racket. "What do you do?" He hands me a ball: "And what do you do now?" He sits on the side, watching. He says, "Yes, yes, no, no, no. Not flat like that, you have to put a loop in your swing, get under the ball." He asks, "As your right hand does that, what's your left hand doing?" He'd give me a simple task, have me do it again and again. And again and again. And again. He was building my stroke, but also developing my concentration. "Get tough, Masha." The player who keeps working five minutes after everyone else has quit, who carries on late in the third set when the wind is blowing and the rain is coming down, wins. That was my gift. Not strength or speed. Stamina. I never got bored. Whatever I was doing, I could keep doing it forever. I liked it. I locked into each task, and stayed at it until I got it right. I'm not sure where that comes from. Maybe I wanted approval from Yudkin, or my father. But I think my motivation was simpler. Even then, I knew these tasks, this tedium, would help me win. Even then, I wanted to beat them all.

My father had become friendly with some of the other Sochi tennis parents, especially the father of Yevgeny Kafelnikov, a real hotshot back in the day. Yevgeny was one of the first stars of post-Soviet Russian tennis. He reached number one in the world, and won the French and Australian Opens. He was big and blond, handsome, a hero to a lot of us. I played his father one day for fun. Afterward, he gave me one of Yevgeny's rackets. It was way too big. They cut it down and it still looked ridiculous, but I played with that racket for years. Sometimes I think it made me better, sometimes worse. It was like swinging a weighted baseball bat. It forced me into helpful positions and made me strong, yet its weight forced my strokes into awkward positions, creating some bad habits. But it's all I had, so it was my only option.

The summer of 1993 was a turning point. I'd been working with Yudkin for several months. I'd become his project, but he knew I'd soon exhaust my opportunities in Sochi. When I asked my father if he remembered that moment, he laughed. "Do I remember? Like yesterday, Masha. Yudkin sat me beside the court and said, 'Yuri, we need to talk about your girl. It's important.' Yudkin was careful when he spoke. He said, 'Yuri, when it comes to this game, your little girl is like Mozart. She can be the best in the world. If you want to know, if you want to compare, that's how she compares—that's the bad situation you are in.' "

"The bad situation?" my father asked Yudkin.

"Yes, bad. Because this is not Vienna in the nineteenth century. This is Sochi in the twentieth century—if Mozart were born here, today, you'd never hear of him. Do you understand?"

"Not exactly."

"I'll put it simply," he said. "If you want to develop your daughter's talent, you have to get out of Russia. No one knows where we are going in this country. No one knows even how they'll make a living. And meanwhile, in the middle of this, you've got Masha. So it's up to you. Can you develop her talent? It's a full-time job. It will mean dedicating your life.

"In the end, the only real question is this: How tough is your daughter, really?" said Yudkin. "She is strong. I know that already. But what about in the long run? She will have to play constantly, day after day, year after year. Will she come to detest it? It's not a sprint, it's a marathon. How will she handle that, not for just one tournament, but for years? How long will she have the desire? Five years, ten years? Nobody can tell you that."

My father says he made the decision at that moment, without thinking. A gut thing. When you let your brain overrule your gut, you screw up your life. That's what Yuri believes. He knew very little about tennis and had no illusions about the obstacles, but he quickly decided that he could educate himself, learn what he needed to know. For him, it was a question of will. If you decide to do it, you can do it—end of story. In the next few weeks, he gave up everything. Quit his job, ditched his pension and plans. He dedicated himself to this one goal: his daughter would become the best tennis player in the world. If he thought about it, he'd know that it was stupid. So he did not think about it, he went to work. He started by reading everything he could find about the sport and coaching. In the end, he decided he would not be my coach but the strategist overseeing the coaches—a coach of coaches. "Behind all great careers, there's one advisor, one voice," he explained. "You can bring different people in to give you whatever you need, but there has to be that one person in control. That's not a coach. That's a person who hires and fires the coaches, who never loses sight of the big picture. It does not have to be a parent, but it usually is. If you look at the history of this game, you'll see there's almost always someone like that. The Williams sisters had their father. Agassi had his father and Nick Bollettieri. Everybody needs somebody."

* * *

What about my mom? How did she feel about this radical new plan?

My father will tell you that she was on board from the start, that she viewed the idea of him quitting everything and dedicating himself to tennis instead as just terrific. But if you ask my mom, the story is more complicated. The truth is that she did not believe in tennis, but she did trust my father. As he shared his vision, made his pitch, explained what he wanted to do, I'm sure she looked at him like he was crazy. But she loved him and believed in him and came around. "He was just so sure of it," she told me, "that I knew it was going to work."

My father quit his job—that's how it began. We spent every day together, hours and hours working toward the same goal. It could get tough—he can be hard to deal with—but there was never a moment I did not know that he loved me. We made our way by trial and error, figuring out how to train. A basic routine was soon in place. I'd wake at dawn, have breakfast, grab my racket, and take the bus to Riviera Park as the sun rose over the Black Sea. The courts were supposed to be red clay, but they were dark gray, almost black, because they were not well kept. The grime would cover your shoes and socks. We'd hit back and forth, slowly, then picking up speed. If it was damp or had rained, the ball was heavy and the pace was slow. But if the weather was good, the ball sailed through the air quickly. I loved the sound of the ball coming off the racket in the morning, when we had the courts to ourselves. I did not have to speak to my father to know what he was thinking. A lot is made of the relationships between child athletes and their parents, but a lot of the time it was just about being across from each other, thinking the same thing, which was nothing. That's about as close as you can get to another person. In a sense, my entire career is just that moment. There's the money and trophies and fame, but beneath it all I'm just practicing with my father and it's early in the morning. We'd hit for a while, then I'd stretch and watch other people practice. After that, we'd work on a specific part of my game. Backhand or serve, footwork, at the net—though I still dread coming to the net. It's as if a shark were waiting for me up there. It was my goal, from the start, to one day beat my father or beat one of his friends, one of the hotshots. I got a little closer each day.

THREE

Yuri Yudkin told my father about a Moscow clinic, a showcase for Russian youth, hosted by some local tennis organization. You know the drill: send your kids, the wannabes and strivers and champions. My father was determined to get me there. I'm not sure how he paid for the plane tickets, but he had an almost magical way of making things happen. The event was in a huge hangar-like facility filled with courts and coaches, a cacophony of rackets hitting tennis balls. There were hundreds of kids, meaning there were also several hundred tennis parents. It was dizzying. Before that, I'd believed the players in Sochi were all the players in existence and that my father and I were special among them. I now realized there were dozens and dozens of such girls, each with a father who considered his daughter destined to be the best in the world.

I stood watching them hit. It was mesmerizing and humbling

but also reassuring. I could already see that I was better than most of them, that we were not hitting the ball in the same way. The clinic was filled with tennis people, coaches and players who wandered around, watching us or giving advice. Martina Navratilova was there. It made me nervous—the greatest player ever, right in front of me. I thought we were going to get to play with the pros one-on-one, but I was only six, so I had no idea. It was more like an assembly line. You'd wait for your turn to hit two or three balls, then get back in line. On my second or third trip through, Navratilova spotted me. My arms and legs were too big for my body and my knees knocked. And I had that huge racket. In other words, I was funny-looking, which is probably why she noticed me. Then she saw that I could play. I was small, but I was already a good hitter, and so focused. When I finished, Navratilova pulled my father aside to talk. They sent for a translator, because my father didn't speak English. I'm not sure exactly what she told him, nor is he, but the basic point was this: Your daughter can play; you need to get her out of the country to a place where she can develop her game. America.

My father started making plans as soon as we were back in Sochi. He was determined to get me to the United States, as he believed that was the only place my game could be developed. He became fixated on Florida. Why? I could give you a complicated explanation, comparing this region to that region, this academy to that academy, but the fact is that Yuri is superstitious and follows signs, and he'd seen a sign that pointed to Florida. It took the form of two magazine articles. One was about the Williams sisters and how they were training at Rick Macci's tennis academy in Boca Raton. The other was about Anna Kournikova and how she was training at Nick Bollettieri's academy in Bradenton.

My father believed these articles had fallen into his hands at just this moment for a reason. He was being told where to go.

Nowadays, traveling to the United States is usually a straight-forward proposition. You get a tourist visa, call the airline, buy the ticket, go. But this was not the case in the early 1990s. The Soviet Union was falling apart. It was just about impossible to find a job, which made it just about impossible to earn a living and support a family. It was hard to do anything. Even if you had the cash, you could not just get on a plane for America. Visas were impossible to come by—awarded only to those on government business. Knowing that he'd need some sort of official backing, my father wrote to the coach of the Russian Tennis Federation's national junior team. There was no question of me playing for this team: it was for kids twelve and up, and I was six. But my father was hoping that the federation would sponsor me with an eye to the future. He explained our situation and described my talent, mentioning Yud-kin and Navratilova. It worked, or seemed to. The team happened to be practicing in Florida, preparing for an American tour. The coach replied with a letter inviting us to visit and work out with the team.

My father went to the embassy in Moscow for visas. He was twenty-eight years old, wearing his only suit, the one he wore on his wedding day. He was willing to depend on luck and fate. (There are signs to tell you what to do if you learn to read them.) He had the coach's letter and had worked out what he was going to say. He waited for hours, then finally stood across from an official. This man looked Yuri over carefully, then examined the letter and the other documents, pictures and pages with raised seals. My father was talking all the time, giving the speech, saying the words: Yudkin, Mozart, Navratilova, prodigy.

"I also have a daughter," the official said finally. "She also plays tennis. And she is good. She's eight. But I do not think she's a prodigy. Your daughter is six. How do you really know that she's better than my daughter? Maybe you're just seeing her with the eyes of a father."

"I don't know your daughter," said Yuri, "but I do know mine. What I've told you is true."

"You want to take a six-year-old girl to train in the United States?"

"Yes."

"And you have no doubt?"

"None."

He looked my father in the eyes.

"You're certain?"

"Yes."

"And you know where you'll go and what you'll do?"

"Yes."

This man gave us a three-year visa—my father would have to come back to Russia to get it renewed—but there it was, that rare, invaluable thing. A golden ticket, the freedom to come and go. It's hard for an American, or even a person in Russia today, to imagine the miracle of this. It was almost impossible to get the sort of document that Yuri scored. This man, this official, whoever he was, wherever he is, made the whole thing happen. Without him, who knows? Why did he do it? It's a question Yuri still asks himself. It was not about me, of course. It was about Yuri. He recognized something in my father, a determination. Or maybe he just felt generous. Or maybe it was just the way the sun hit the road that morning. Whatever the reason, we were lucky. So lucky. But also unlucky. As rare as that visa was, it was also limited, good for only two people: me and Yuri. Using it would mean leaving my mom behind for who knew how long. Yuri thought over what he'd say to her, how he'd get her to go along. He'd be taking me away from school and from my family and from her, and I was only six years old.

When I ask my mother about it now, she shrugs and says, "Your father knew what he was doing." Grandma Tamara is more open. "I think your mother went along with it because your father is such a good talker," she tells me. "He's convincing and your mother is so positive. It's these things together, I think, that made it happen. Maybe your mother didn't really want it to happen, but she believed that it was for your own benefit. Your father was not thinking only of you but of himself and the family. Russia was falling apart. Tennis might be something for you, but it was also a way out for the family. If he could secure your living, the entire family could live at the expense of the daughter. And he succeeded. It worked. He was very smart in that respect. But your mother didn't think about that, even if, deep down, she understood what was really going on. Or, who knows? Maybe your father did discuss it with her. Of course, for me and your grandfather it was terrible. Yuri suddenly says that he's taking our granddaughter to America? In those days, people who went to America were never heard from again."

My father gathered all the money he had, then borrowed some more—something like seven hundred dollars, wound into a roll, carried in his front pocket, so that, whenever he got nervous, he could make sure it was still there. He'd gotten tickets on an afternoon flight from Moscow to Miami, where someone from the team was to meet us. It's a blur. I don't remember what I was wearing or how I felt. I must have been sad saying goodbye to my mom, but I probably didn't realize what was happening, that I would not see her again until I was almost nine years old.

It was Aeroflot, one of those big old jets with about fifteen seats in a row. We sat next to a Russian couple. My father spoke to them the whole way. I picked up pieces of the conversation as I drifted in and out of sleep. He told them about me and tennis and our plans and the junior team and the coach and the academies. I wondered why he was saying so much. My father is normally pretty quiet. The plane refueled in Shannon, Ireland. I didn't know what to do with myself for that long period of time, in one place, in one seat. It was the first long flight of my life. I remember looking out the window at men and trucks. Then we were in America. Two or three in the morning. We went through customs, then out to the curb. I remember how the air felt that first time, like a damp hand, rich and tropical, so different than in Sochi. I remember the palm trees. I remember how dark it was. And waiting. After everyone had gone, we were still on the curb, looking for the car that was supposed to have been sent by the team coach. My father must've been panicking. He spoke no English, knew no one in the country, was alone with his six-year-old daughter in the middle of the night. But he kept his cool, resting his hand gently on my shoulder, saying, "Don't worry, Masha. Don't worry." But I'm sure his other hand was thrust in his pocket, his fingers wrapped around the money. What should we do? Hire a car? Take a bus? Even if he could find someone willing to help, they'd never speak Russian. Finally, a man and woman came by. It was the couple from the plane. My father explained the situation—"If I could just call the coach." The man told him nothing could be done in the middle of the night, "and you have a little girl that needs to sleep." He had a hotel room in Miami Beach. He offered to take us along. "Sleep on the floor," he said. "Tomorrow you can make your phone calls."

In the morning, even before I opened my eyes, I knew I was in a strange place. I could hear my father talking quickly, quietly, with frustration. He'd been up for hours. Maybe he hadn't gone to bed. He softened when he saw that I was awake, sat with me, and tried to give me a sense of what would happen next. I was just happy to be with him, far from home, on this adventure. It was us against the world. He'd not been able to reach the team coach, or our family in Russia. The lines were busy, or down, or something. The few people he had reached were not helpful. But we had our routine and we had to stick to it. I put on my tennis clothes. Sneakers. Skirt. I always practiced in a skirt to replicate a match environment. (You want to practice exactly like you play.) I tied my hair back and followed my father out the door. Of course, there was one big change in that routine: my mom was not there to give me a hug before I headed out. My father carried two rackets, his and mine, and a can of balls. The man from the plane came along, probably just to see what would happen. "What are you doing?" he asked.

"We must train," said Yuri.

We were in Miami Beach, probably on Collins Avenue. I'm also not sure what my father had in mind. Did he just assume we'd find a tennis court? This was Florida, after all, the training ground of the Williams sisters and Anna Kournikova, a tennis paradise. We walked on and on, block after block, scanning. Now and then, Yuri spotted a court—through the hedges, over a fence—grabbed my hand, and made a run for it. Each time, the Russian from the plane stopped him. "No, Yuri, you can't. That's a private court."

My father had the Soviet idea that everything belonged to everyone.

"No, Yuri. Not in America."

We kept walking, finally spotting several courts beside a swimming pool. It was a hotel, with people lounging in chairs. My father spoke to the man in charge of the pool and the courts as the man from the plane translated. He explained our situation, how he had just arrived from Moscow with his daughter, a potential member of the Russian junior national team, and she needed to practice. The man looked me over. I was really cute. He said OK. We set up on a court and went through our routine—stretched, jogged, prepared, then began to hit. Half speed at first, the ball traveling in lazy parabolas. Then we began to go at it, zinging the ball back and forth from the baseline. It was early morning and I was tiny, but I was really driving the ball. I finished each forehand with a little loop, like Yudkin had taught me. Was I already grunting at the moment of impact? Probably. It's unconscious, and has always been part of my game. It was unusual to see a kid that small hit that hard and with consistency. It was a circus act. People came over from the pool to see what was happening. Then more came. Before long, we'd drawn a crowd, a few dozen tourists who stood watching the ball go back and forth.

That was my first morning in America.

We worked out for about an hour, then sat in the shade under an umbrella, cooling off. People stood around, asking questions. There was an older Polish couple at the back of the crowd. They introduced themselves, but I don't remember their names. My father doesn't either. Funny, not remembering the names or much else about the people who would be so important in those first few hours. Without them, without the good luck of meeting them, who knows what would have happened. I'd like to tell you what they looked like, how nice they were, but honestly, I remember only one detail, and it was key. They spoke Russian. Yuri was so happy to find people he could talk to. They told him they were tennis fans, that they loved and followed the game. They said they'd seen Monica Seles and Andre Agassi when they were my age, and that I was just as good as either of them. This meant a lot to my father. They asked about his plans, where we'd go from here. My father told them the whole story—the flight from Moscow and the early morning arrival, the junior team and the coach who did not show, the hotel room floor, the phone calls. "So what're you going to do?" My father said we'd make our way, somehow, to the Rick Macci Tennis Academy in Boca Raton. "The Williams sisters were there," Yuri explained. "Once they see Masha, we'll be fine. The only problem is that I have no idea where Boca Raton is, or how to get there."

"Don't worry," said the Polish woman. "We'll drive you."

You hear a lot of bad things about the world and the people in it. When you are a kid, they warn you about strangers. When you are an adult, they warn you about criminals. But the fact is, in the early days, we were repeatedly saved by strangers. It was not part of our plan, but we were willing to depend on good luck.

We got our bags out of the hotel, said goodbye to the people from the plane, and went out to the street, where the Polish couple was waiting in some big, springy, air-cooled American car. It was Sunday morning. My father talked with the couple as I stared out the window. We crossed the causeway and drove up the coast. It was beautiful and new. People later asked what I was thinking in those first hours. Was I scared? Did I miss my mother, my home, my own bed? Not really. To me, at this point, and for a long time, it all just seemed like an adventure, a fairy tale. I was just waiting to see what would happen next.

My father still talks about how disappointed he was in the Rick Macci Tennis Academy, and how we were greeted, but think of how weird it must've been for the people at the desk. One Sunday morning, in the middle of everything, this man who speaks only Russian walks in with his six-year-old daughter, who carries an oversized racket. He is followed by a couple from Poland, offering to translate. My father asked to see Rick. He was told that Mr. Macci was away, not available. The person he was speaking to, eyeing us suspiciously from behind the desk, turned out to be Macci's wife. She sized us up, then turned away. My father asked if we could just go out to one of the courts and hit. He just wanted someone there to see me play. "If you want to use one of our courts," the woman said, "you have to sign up for a program, and that costs money."

"How much?"

"A thousand dollars. And you have to pay in advance."

At this point, we had only seven hundred dollars—that was all the money in the world to us—in a roll in my father's pocket. Yuri began to argue through the translator. He told the lady at the desk that I was special, that they'd want to see me play, that, if they turned us away, they'd regret it later. Someone happened to be walking by, an instructor. She defused the whole thing, saying, "Let me go and hit with her a bit—let's just see."

We played as my father waited. When we came back, the instructor talked to the woman at the desk. Whatever was said, her attitude changed. No final decisions could be made until Rick was back, but they said they could offer us a place to stay for a few nights while they figured things out. No promises. One problem, I later learned, was that they found Yuri's story hard to believe. That he'd come from Russia by himself with this girl, that he just walked in off the street with a world-class tennis-playing kid. They didn't buy it. They wanted to know who Yuri really was. And what was his game? And what's the story behind the story? And where's the mother? And what about school? It's something we would run into again and again. No one believed our story.

By this point, my father had soured on the whole scene. He did not like the way we were greeted, the questions, the suspicion. *"Nyet."* That's what he said when the offer of two nights was made. "We're out of here."

If one characteristic defined my father, it was his willingness to say no. He did it all the time. He said no to the easy thing because he believed a better thing would come along. It was stupidity— and faith. He believed in my ability and in his smarts. It determined what happened as much as anything. Saying no put him in a position to later say yes.

The Polish couple was confused. We'd been offered a place to stay and a session with Macci. Who knew where that would lead, but my father just walked out. They asked what he wanted to do now, where we'd go next. Yuri had only one other place in mind: the Bollettieri Tennis Academy in Bradenton, on the west coast of Florida, close to Sarasota and Tampa Bay, which he'd read about in that magazine back home. Kournikova was there, so they must understand Russians. The Polish couple said they could not drive us that far, took us to the bus station, and bought us tickets. They looked up the phone number and address at Bollettieri's and wrote them down for us on a piece of paper, then handed it to Yuri, saying, "Call this number and go to this place when you arrive." Then we said goodbye. We never saw them again.

* * *

The ride to Bradenton was dark and blurry, like something out of a Van Gogh painting. We got in at around 9:00 p.m. My father called the academy, and, however he managed it in Russian, made our situation clear enough that a shuttle was sent to pick us up from the station. It was pitch-black when we arrived. I remember blocky buildings and dark courts, palm trees swaying. A man at the gate heard us out, wrote down what we told him—a message would be delivered—then sent us away. It was Sunday night, he explained. Everyone was gone or asleep. He called a cab, which took us to the closest hotel, a Holiday Inn Express. First lesson: If there's anything worse than putting "Inn" after a hotel's name, it's adding the word "Express."

My father was very careful, very suspicious. He triple-locked our hotel room door, shut the dead bolt, and hooked the chain. When we got into bed, he took the money out of his front pocket and put it under the pillow. He was sure someone would come in at night and take everything. "This way," he explained, "the robber will have to wake me to get the money, and that will be his last mistake."

We lay in the dark, talking. I was not scared, but I was nervous. Here I was, in this strange hotel room, in this strange place, waiting only for the moment when I could go out on the court and hit. When I hit, I would relax. When other people saw me hit, everything would be OK. I knew exactly what I had to do. My part was clear, which allowed me to relax and leave the rest to others.

Yuri was in a big rush in the morning. Packing our bags, gathering our gear. We called a taxi and checked out. We were in the cab, heading back to the academy, when Yuri started to freak out. He'd felt so settled in the hotel, slept so deeply, that he'd forgotten all about the money. He started cursing in Russian. The driver had no idea what was going on. Yuri got him to turn around and race back. We pulled up right outside the room, Yuri jumping out even before the car stopped. The door was open and the cleaning cart was outside. Yuri burst through the door. The maid was in the bathroom, the bed was unmade. He turned over the pillow, and there, thank God, was the money. He slid it into his pocket, and soon we were back on Highway 41.

When I asked Yuri if he remembered this incident, he laughed, then sighed, saying, "Masha, Masha, Masha. When you think of all the crazy luck we had, some of it bad but most of it good . . . We crossed this river like people who think they are walking on logs only to learn, on the far side, it's been crocodiles the entire time."

Our message had been delivered. They were expecting us at the academy. There was even a Russian translator.

And a plan. I would be sent onto the courts with a group of girls my age. I'd do drills, hit some balls, and an assessment would be made. I felt like a freak amid all those American girls. First of all, I was younger than any of them by at least two years. Second, they stood together in a circle, laughing and gossiping, and I couldn't understand a word of it.

In a situation like that, you think whatever is being said is being said about you. And that it's not nice. These were rich girls who, for whatever reason, had been judged by their parents to have talent that could be brought out at the academy. And they paid for that. Big money. A year at Bollettieri's is probably more than a year at college. Unless you're on scholarship, you come from money, with the best rackets and best shoes and best gear. And here I was, with a single change of clothes, an oversized chopped-down racket, and shoes from a factory in Minsk. I looked weird. And they laughed. And continued laughing, right up to the moment that I got to hit. First off, it relaxed me. I calmed down, remembered why I was there. Then, almost at once, the instructor could see, "This girl is not like the others."

I spoke to that instructor about this years later. He said, "Well, you know, the deal is, I was half asleep, early morning, going through the drills, thinking about my lunch break, and you came up, smaller than everyone, and just basically knocked my head off."

He took me to an empty court so we could hit alone, me and him, back and forth, five, ten minutes. Then he went to a phone at the side of the court and made a call. (A phone on a tennis court? I had never seen anything like that.) He was calling Nick Bollettieri. He said, "Hey, boss, I got something here you need to see right away."

He walked me to center court, ground zero at the academy. At this point, we had to leave Yuri behind. That's the rule: no parents on center court. It was the first time I remember being separated from my father since we'd left Sochi. I did not like it. Then I was scared. Who were these people, where was I going, would I make it back?

It's hard to untangle my first impression of Nick from the way I came to feel about him later. He wasn't tall or short, and what you noticed was that crazy gray hair and those teeth so bright you could see them a hundred yards away. His arms were thin and sinewy and his skin so tanned it was purple and leathery. Here was a guy who'd clearly spent too much time outdoors. Nick grew up in the Bronx, New York, the youngest son in a big family. Tennis was not their sport—New York meant basketball. Nick went into the military after college, then moved to Florida. He had wanted to be a lawyer, but was at the University of Miami for less than a year. Still, that is where he picked up tennis. He played, then taught friends who wanted to play, and realized he was a better instructor than player. He began giving lessons, then made his way through the hotel circuit as a tennis pro. He saved money, honed his sales pitch, gathered investors, and opened his school.

By the time I got there, Bollettieri's academy was a campus of low-slung buildings and dorms, hard courts and clay courts, center court burning under stadium lights. It was already famous, the breeding ground for Andre Agassi and Jim Courier and Anna Kournikova, Monica Seles and Mary Pierce. Nick had become a legend, almost a cartoon tennis guru. He'd been through something like seven wives and so many players. What did he care about a little girl from Russia? He was probably signing divorce papers as I walked up. At heart, he was really just a businessman. He'd built a great industry. When you think of the tennis academies in the United States, you think of Bollettieri's. There's nothing else like it. I never thought of him as a coach. I thought of him as a teacher, even a kind of mentor.

I did not hit with Nick that day. I hit with an instructor as Nick stood in the shadows, watching. He is a great watcher, a noticer of tendencies and habits and character and other things, big and small. It's his talent. Vision. He sees the end in the first moment of the beginning. When putting together this book, I went back and spoke to people who were important in my life. I spoke to Nick in his office at the academy. He is older now, a little frail, but still 100 percent Nick. When I asked him about that first meeting—"Do you remember it?"—he laughed. "Of course, I remember it," he said. "I'd heard about you—someone had called and told me, 'There's this tiny girl from Russia, and the *way* she plays!' But, honestly, I get a call like that every few days, so usually I do not pay too much attention. Then you showed up and my instructor called and said, 'Nick, you've got to see this.' That was unusual. And I could see it, right away, as soon as I watched you hit two or three balls. You were just six years old but you were hammering it. And it was not just the power—it was your footwork, your grip. Perfect, all of it just perfect. Of course, a lot of that can be taught. The amazing thing was your concentration. You never lost focus, you could just do it again and again. You didn't have all the moves at first, you didn't have the strength, but you did have the mentality. And that can't be taught."

Nick asked to see my father. The translator came along. An offer was made. I was still too young to live at the academy—you had to be at least ten years old—but I could train there. I would have practice all day, every day. No fee. A kind of scholarship. I could eat lunch and dinner in the mess hall. Yuri could eat there, too. They'd even find us a place to stay. For a moment, the future seemed assured.

FOUR

We lived about a five-minute drive from the academy in the apartment of a middle-aged Russian woman. It had been arranged by the translator. We paid $250 a month for the use of the kitchen and bathroom, as well as the living room, giving us access to the television, which was important. That's how I learned to speak English, by watching TV. I learned more from Barney the dinosaur than I ever did in school. Our lives were mixed up with that landlord, who I think had a problem with me. One minute, she'd be giving me coloring books and presents, the next she'd be threatening to evict us to make room for a better-paying tenant. She advised us, translated for us, and schemed against us. It was up and down. From that time in my life, I learned that it's possible to at once love someone, hate them, and be indifferent to them.

The apartment was the kind you see in '80s movies about

families down on their luck, single mothers, and runaways. When I think of it now, I am sometimes not sure if it's that little complex in Bradenton I'm remembering or the apartment where Daniel lived with his mother in *The Karate Kid*, one of my favorite movies and another great teacher of English. It was two stories, in the motel style, with a courtyard behind it and doors that opened onto an exterior hallway. It was small and dark inside, with windows that looked out on a road lined with palm trees. My father and I shared the living room couch, a fold-out double bed that sagged in the middle. You had to keep your balance even in your sleep. That bed might explain the back problems that have plagued Yuri ever since. Was it strange to share a bed with my father, to be sleeping side by side like an old married couple? No. It was my life and it was good. No matter how hard things got, I always knew I had him, right there, fighting for me day and night.

We settled into a routine—there wasn't a lazy day for either of us. We were up each morning before sunrise, creeping here and there so as not to wake the old lady. My father did not need an alarm. He simply set his internal clock to the witching hour. Five a.m. He got out of bed, slipped on his shoes, and was ready to go. We ate breakfast in the dark, talking over the goals for that day. What part of my game should I be working on? Where were my thoughts? Then we went to the academy. Yuri would walk me the quarter mile or so to the front gate. It took about twenty-five minutes. As we went, the sun came up. Later on, we had a bike. Yuri pedaled, and I rode behind him. Once we were pulled over by the police because I was riding without a helmet—it seemed funny to my father, who was living a hundred miles from Chernobyl when the reactor blew up.

I was on the court by 6:30, hitting balls. Then we broke into groups for drills and lessons. You were always doing something. That was Nick's philosophy. If you were not hitting balls, you were retrieving. If you were not hitting or retrieving, you were in line, moving your feet, awaiting your turn on the baseline. At first, they put me in a group of six to eight girls. We worked together all morning, and for me this was great. It gave me a chance to really get to know these people. In many cases, these would be the girls I'd go up against my entire career—people I still play now, though we've gotten old, at least by the standards of tennis. They were from all over the world. Some were good. Some were very good. Some were great. But most were not good at all. These players, the ones who really made the academy profitable, were there because their parents could not face reality. Even the very good ones would never be good enough—even I could see that. In this world, the gap between very good and great is the Grand Canyon.

Most of these girls were spoiled brats. You could tell they didn't want to be there. You knew after two minutes that they couldn't really play. No coordination. Couldn't tell the left foot from the right hand. And they couldn't stick with anything or focus. Maybe that's why they sulked and threw tantrums. That's the way a lot of the kids at Bollettieri's behaved, and it turned me off. I remember seeing photographs taken at the end of a big junior tournament. They showed the winners next to the runners-up. Without even looking at who had the trophies, you knew right away the winners from the losers. I decided right then that you'd never be able to tell if I'd won or lost by looking at a picture.

At 12:30, we broke for lunch. Why does every cafeteria have

to be so bad? That was the first time I'd seen food delivered by conveyor belt. I closed my eyes and got it down. I knew that our bank balance depended on my eating as much as I could at the academy.

In the afternoon, we went back out and played matches. These started at 1:30 and went till 5:00 or so. That was the best time. It was when you could really see who was who and what was what. Nick went from court to court, watching. If he lingered for more than a point or two, you felt special. Everyone was after that recognition. Nick had favorites, the best players at the academy, boys and girls, who worked together in an elite group. They were like rock stars. They played together, laughed together, ate together, and looked down on everyone else. The kids in that group were different ages, but all had that elite thing in common. Todd Reid was in that group; so was Jelena Jankovic and Horia Tecau, a great doubles player. I'd join this group later, though I never did feel like I was part of it.

Anna Kournikova was a standout at the academy, and I was compared to her from the very beginning because we were both Russians, because we were both blond. In those early years, and I'm not exactly sure why, when I needed clothes, I often ended up with Kournikova's hand-me-downs, which—well, skintight animal prints are not usually my thing. These comparisons only increased as I got older, along with my dislike of these comparisons. *What bullshit!* In fact, we could not be more different. We don't look alike, don't act alike, and our tennis games are *very* different. But the only thing the public saw was hair color and country of origin. But the relationship was useful in a way, not only for the hand-me-downs but as a kind of marker. I knew I needed to get past Kournikova. When I did that, I'd be judged on my own terms. My father had his own problems with the Kournikovas, especially Anna's mother. I do not think she was thrilled about our arrival at the academy. Until then, Anna had been the cute little Russian star. Suddenly, there was competition.

FIVE

Meanwhile, we were trying to survive as immigrants and new residents of Bradenton. My lessons were paid for by the academy, the tournaments were arranged, and two meals a day taken care of, but otherwise we were on our own. Rent, spending money, food, all the rest of it—that, we had to pay. Yuri, who was learning English quickly by necessity, had to find work—anything that would pay cash. He was on a construction crew, did yard work and odd jobs, and cut lawns. It must have been a lonely time for him, but he was driven—for years, it was his will that powered both of us. He was making money, managing my career, being my father, and learning, or trying to learn, the game of tennis. One night, when I stuck my head into the living room, I saw him, in reading glasses, buried in a pile of strategy and how-to books.

When I first saw the title of the movie *Mr. Mom*, I assumed it was about my father. Yuri did everything back then. For days and days, years and years, it was just him and me. We slept in the same creaky fold-out bed, shared the same goals and plans. At times, I could not tell his dreams from my own. Or his dreams became my dreams. He woke me each morning, before first light. As I said, he did not need an alarm. Five o'clock, his eyes just opened. He made me breakfast and helped me get ready. He told me what we needed to do that day, where my attention should be focused. You have a good day, it's a good day. You put together a string of good days, you have a good career.

That's what he believed.

While I was playing, Yuri worked. Whatever he did, the work had to be flexible because he had to be back at the apartment each afternoon before I came in the door. I was dropped off by an instructor or some kid's parents. Yuri and I would sit and talk through every moment of the day as he prepared me for the day to come. He dealt with my equipment and clothes. For years, most of my clothes were hand-me-downs, skirts and shorts and shoes that once belonged to Anna Kournikova. The first thing my mom did when she finally arrived in America was go through my closet and throw all that stuff in the trash. But what did Yuri know about clothes? He fed me and dressed me and cut my hair. I remember sitting on the toilet in the bathroom as he brushed out and trimmed my bangs, straight across, like a kid in a cartoon.

Was I lonely? Was I sad? I don't know. This was my life and I had no other life to compare it to. I spoke to my mother once a week on the phone. The calls were short, because of the rates. She asked what I was doing and told me that she loved me. She still managed my education, even though she was so far away. That was what mattered to her—that I remember my Russian heritage, that

I be able to read and write Russian, that I know the Russian writers and their important books. She said I was never to forget who I was and where I came from. "If you don't know where you come from, you don't know who you are," she said. I don't really remember the conversations, but I do remember the letters. I wrote to her every day. I'd scribble at the bottom: "I love you, I love you, I love you!" One day, a Russian boy I was friends with—he had a brother and his family was rich—grabbed one of my letters and ran with it, reading it out loud. He made fun of me. "Why do you write 'I love you' so much?" he asked.

"It's my mom," I said, pleading.

"What's wrong with you?" he said. "It's so cheesy."

I remember looking at him and asking, "Don't you tell your mom you love her?"

He said, "Well, yeah, but not as many times as you do."

"Well, probably because you have your mom and I don't."

I had tears in my eyes when I said this, so maybe I was sadder than I want to admit.

When I was a little older, I took classes at a public school near the academy, but at the beginning, when I hardly knew any English, my only teacher was an old Russian lady, a tutor who came to the apartment a few times a week. She taught me the basics—math, history, English—though I learned more by watching TV. These early years toughened me up. In fact, I think they explain my character, the style of my game, my on-court persona, why I can be hard to beat. If you don't have a mother to cry to, you don't cry. You just hang in there, knowing that eventually things will change—that the pain will subside, that the screw will turn. More than anything, that has defined my career. I do not bitch. I do not throw my racket. I do not threaten the line judge. I do not quit. If you want to beat me, you are going to have to work for every point in every game. I will not give you anything. Some people, especially the sort that grew up in country clubs, on manicured lawns, are not used to a girl who just keeps coming.

Of course, this is what Yudkin was talking about, that unnameable thing, that doggedness that is so Russian. My father tells a few stories, of key moments when he realized I was a tough player. There was one time, when I was six years old, before we left for America. I woke up with a bump on my eye, like a pimple on the cornea. At first, OK, no big deal. But it started to grow. One day, I woke and it was killing me. Wow, the pain. Yuri took me to the hospital. They called for a special doctor, an eye surgeon, a woman. She looked me over, then came back and said, "We have to cut away that bump immediately. Right now." OK, said Yuri, do it. "But it's near the eyeball, which means we can't give anesthesia," she said. "I won't be able to make the eye numb. Your daughter will feel every cut." OK, OK. Just do it. She took me into a room and somehow I got through it. Twenty minutes later, we went back to see Yuri. The doctor was white and speechless. Yuri was scared. He said, "My God, what's happened?"

"Don't worry," said the doctor. "Everything is fine. I did a good job. No problem, no big deal. But something does bother me—Masha did not cry. That's not normal. That's not good. You've got to cry."

Yuri said, "What can we do?"

The doctor said, "I don't know, but it's not normal. She's supposed to be crying."

"OK," said Yuri, "we can't change her. She wants to cry, she will cry. She doesn't want to cry, you cannot push her to cry."

We took the bus back home, and I didn't say a word. When we

got into the house, and my mother embraced me, that's when I cried. Oh my God, did I cry!

Another time: We were running for a bus, late for a practice. And I fell. Hard. Very hard. The fingernail on my pinkie ripped off. Completely. I was bleeding all over the place.

"Holy shit," said Yuri, "we need to get back home."

I said, "It's OK, Pop. We've got to practice."

Meanwhile, my game was developing. It came from repetition, hitting the ball again and again. I was getting stronger. My shots were becoming harder and faster. From the start, my game was all about hitting that ball, low and flat. To put the other girls back onto their heels. I was playing in tournaments and was quickly ranked number five in Florida for age ten and under. I was developing the persona that would become such an important part of my game. I was grunting when I hit the ball. Even then, I tried to set myself apart. No emotion. No fear. Like ice. I was not friends with the other girls, because that would make me softer, easier to beat. They could have been the nicest girls in the world, and I wouldn't even have known it. I chose not to know it. I figured we could be friends later, after I retired, and they retired, when we were all older and content. But not now, not yet. My biggest edge is that persona. Why would I give it up? Before I even go out onto the court, some of the other players are intimidated. I can feel it. They know that I'm strong. I have no interest in making friends on my battlefield. If we are friends, I give up a weapon. My former coach Thomas Högstedt told me that his advice to players going against me was this: "Don't look Maria in the eyes before, during, or after the match." When I asked Nick about my early days, he said, "Well, there was your game, then there was your game. That's what people don't understand about tennis. You do not have to be the best player in the world to win. You only have to be better, on that day, than the person across from you. And that's something you understood from the start."

"You scared the shit out of the other girls," he added. "Especially Jelena and Tatiana. You intimidated them. I don't know whether you did it deliberately, but you had an air about you: this is a business and you are in my way."

✻ ✻ ✻

And then, just like that, I was kicked out of the academy. For Yuri, it was like being exiled from Eden, or slapped awake in the middle of a beautiful dream. I'd only been there for a few months, but I'd been improving, advancing, moving up the ranks. Why did they boot me? What reason could possibly be given?

It was never very clear, but it had to do with my age. I was too young to be playing with those other girls. The fact that I was beating kids three or four or five years older than me caused unhappiness. Parents paying the full fee did not like to face the limitations of their prodigies. But my father felt that it was more than that. After all, they knew my age and situation when they made the offer. Yuri did not blame Nick. He blamed Anna Kournikova's mother, Alla.

Tennis is a sport populated by fierce parents. Before my arrival, Anna had been the only Russian prospect at the academy, a cute blond prodigy. Then I turned up, just as blond, hitting just as well, but even younger. And getting better every day. Yuri came to believe Alla might possibly be floating certain ideas, mainly the notion that something was not quite right about the story we told. *This father and daughter turn up in the middle of the night, from nowhere? Does that sound plausible to you?* She seemed to suggest that I'd been kidnapped by Yuri, that he grabbed me and took off. *And what about school? Is the girl even going to school? What kind of mother lets her daughter be taken away like that? Something is funny about this.* In other words, Nick got the idea that we were trouble, and as much as he might want me to be at the academy, he would not risk a scandal.

We were told to clear out. Good luck and goodbye. Did my father freak out, or consider going back to Sochi? If he did, I saw no sign of it. Through it all, he remained steely. There was no bad news. Everything had its positive side. There was always another way to look at things. There was always a Plan B. Because this was fate. All we had to do was find the path and keep on it. "Masha, look at how far we've come! Why would we turn back now?" Yuri went to Nick and worked out terms, a gentle parting of the ways. "Come on, Nick, how can you just throw a little girl out on the street?" He agreed to let us stick around for a few more months, use the courts and the mess hall, just until the kids turned up for the autumn session. All the while, Yuri was looking around, coming up with a new plan. He finally settled on a guy named Sekou Bangoura, an African-born tennis pro who for years had worked at Bollettieri's. In the early 1990s, Sekou started his own academy, a tennis school called El Conquistador, scattered across a handful of hard courts a few miles down the road from Bollettieri's.

It was one of the innumerable Florida tennis factories fronted by a guru who cast his nets wide, hoping to snag a star and establish his name. Sekou was trying to build an empire and follow in Nick's footsteps. I did not like him. He was a screamer, a tantrum thrower. He had a sly smile that I couldn't stand. I did not trust him. But Yuri was convinced Sekou was the answer. Maybe we were just out of better choices. And money.

It started with me and Sekou hitting early one morning. He was medium-sized and athletic, a former pro player who'd never been good enough to make it on the tour. He must've been thirty-five or forty. He took my father aside afterward and they talked.

Sekou said, "Yes, yes, she can play."

"Well, do you have room for her at your academy?" asked Yuri.

"Yes," said Sekou, "but she'll have to pay. A little bit of money. Not much. Something."

"That's the whole thing," said Yuri. "We can't pay. It has to be a scholarship."

Sekou thought a moment, then said, "In that case, I need to see her play in a tournament. There's hitting on a practice court," he explained, "and then there's playing when it counts. You can't really know about someone till you've seen them compete. Some players who look great in practice fold up as soon as anything goes wrong."

There was a tournament that weekend somewhere up north, a few hours away by car. Sekou wanted to take me with some of his other students, put me in the draw, and see what happened. The catch? Yuri could not come along. No parents. This bothered my father tremendously. He thought about it and thought about it—he checked with our Russian landlord and with my Russian tutor—before finally agreeing. What choice did he have? Besides, there'd be other kids along.

I don't remember the particulars. There were so many tournaments. They bleed together. What I do remember is the look on my father's face when Sekou dropped me back at the apartment that night. We were hours late. My father had been pacing the floor, watching for headlights and checking the time. He'd handed his daughter to a man he did not really know, did not really trust. But we had a good reason for being late. I'd won! Not just a match but the entire tournament. I got a trophy. My picture was taken, then it was over. Sekou seemed pleased. He asked my father to come and see him at El Conquistador in the morning.

They met in his hot little trailer office, the roof ticking in the sun. Sekou said, "OK, she is good. We will arrange something. Just tell me how much you can pay."

Yuri explained our situation again—"We can't pay anything."

Sekou sighed his world-weary sigh, looked at my father, the old up and down, then asked, "Can you at least play tennis?"

"Yes."

"Can you really hit?"

"Yes, of course. Who do you think hits with Maria?"

"OK," said Sekou. "Here's the deal. You will work for me. You will hit with the students before they start their drills, before they play. You have to do everything I tell you—everything I say. In return for that, we will take Maria as a student on scholarship. Do you agree?"

"Yes."

Sekou had my father fill out forms. In the course of this, he asked for my father's travel documents. As I remember it, Sekou took and held on to these documents, which made my father feel helpless, as if he did not have complete control of his own life. His passport, his visa. Sekou was himself an immigrant from Africa, so he knew just how important these documents were. They were the right to be here, the ability to pursue the dream. They were everything. He told my father that he would copy the documents and give them back, but he never did. Or not for a long time. He was always just about to or didn't have the key to the safe or whatever. This was important. As long as Sekou held those documents, he controlled my father. As long as he controlled my father, he controlled me.

SIX

Yuri and I would head to El Conquistador together each morning. Sekou would drive us over, or we'd get a ride from one of his instructors. We split at the gate. Yuri went to the back courts, where he spent hours practicing with kids, or else ran errands for Sekou. Now and then, Sekou had him do something that felt like busywork to my father. If Yuri questioned a task, Sekou would snap. He could be insulting. As the boss, he'd say, he was due obedience—absolute obedience. Yuri found it humiliating, which seemed to be the point. This was about dominance. Sekou wanted Yuri to fight back, but Yuri would not. He just took it. For the greater good. My father is a believer in getting through. This was a bad time, but he knew he had to keep his head down and ignore his feelings.

In the meantime, I was on the front court, training. There were workouts, drills, games, and matches, pounding shot after shot into every corner of the court. At such times, it was actually impossible to think of tennis as a game, as a pastime, as something somewhere in the world someone was doing for fun. Tennis is not a game. It's a sport and a puzzle, an endurance test. You do whatever you can to win. It has been my enemy and my friend, my nightmare and the solace to that nightmare, my wound and the salve for my wound. Ask anyone who has made a life in this game, who was been out on the clay before they were old enough to understand the consequences of a strange early talent. I know you want us to love this game—us loving it makes it more fun to watch. But we don't love it. And we don't hate it. It just is, and always has been.

There were some things I liked about El Conquistador. I liked the low-key atmosphere of the place. It was not Bollettieri's. There was not that kind of pressure and the players were not as driven or as good. I liked the routine, the low stakes, the way the water pooled on the back courts after it rained, giving a player a rare chance for a break, five minutes staring blankly in the sun, not a thought in your head. But mostly I liked having my father there—knowing he was around, even when I did not see him. He would warm me up before the afternoon matches, hitting and talking as we worked. We would talk about home, or we would talk about tennis, or we would talk about my mother and how good it would be when she joined us in Florida. If I had a problem, if I had played badly, if I had been insulted or treated unfairly, I could run to him and he would help me.

But mostly I hated El Conquistador. Because it felt second-rate to me, shabby. Because my father was always there, which meant I could never be on my own. But my main problem was Sekou. I felt like he was using me to pump up his fledgling little academy, and I think he resented me for it. I worked like a dog—all day, every day, hitting and running and getting screamed at. And he was cheap. If we stopped for a snack on the way home from a tournament, he'd bill my father for the chicken nuggets and the Sprite.

But I was getting better, more and more confident in my game. I was learning new strategies and new techniques and never forgetting that the purpose of each new weapon was not to win tournaments, or be ranked in the top hundred, or make money. It was simply to beat them all.

This is when I really started to work on my serve with my father. I feel like I've had two different serves in my career. You can date me by them: serve one and serve two—which, for an athlete, almost always means before and after the injury that changed everything, that turned what had been instinctual and childlike and natural into something adult and learned and difficult.

I had a real whip to my serve. My arm went all the way back, nearly touching my spine before it came forward. No one had seen a shoulder so loose, so flexible. People said I was double-jointed. It turned my shoulder into a slingshot and gave me power, but it was an unnatural motion that put stress on my shoulder, the sort of stress experienced by a pitcher.

In those years, size was a big problem for me. I was just so small, often as much as a foot shorter than the kid I was playing. It was like that for years. People would ask, "Who is that blond pip-squeak running here and there with a racket she must've stolen from her father's bag?" My size affected my game. As the other girls grew, it became harder and harder for me to keep up, or to generate the kind of power I needed to hit a winner. It's the first big challenge for an athlete: What happens when the weapon you've relied on, such as speed, is neutralized by a bigger or faster player? That's when a lot of people quit, because it's not working; what had been easy is suddenly hard. But it's really an opportunity, a chance to win. And meanwhile, you just hope and pray that you will grow.

Every night, as my father read his books on tennis, I'd hang from the clothing rod in the closet. I'd do this for as long as I could stand it. Then I'd walk around the room, shaking my arms out and muttering as the blood returned. When I recovered, I'd take a deep breath, grab the rod, and do it again. I was trying to stretch my body, make myself taller. There is zero history of great height in my family. I have mentioned that my mother and father are not short, but they're not tall. If my father is five foot eleven, he's wearing thick orthotics. My mother is five foot seven. I'm proud of being six foot two. It's meant that size and power have been an important part of my game. Yuri says I should be proud because I made it happen, "by hanging from that bar in the closet." He believes that I made myself tall by force of will, that I grew because I needed to for my game. Maybe it was just luck, or a recessive gene. The point is, before I grew, I'd been preparing for life as a short player, acquiring and sharpening certain skills that turned out to be especially helpful when I turned out to be one of the tallest.

Sekou was using me as a show pony, a human advertisement that he could parade around tournaments. If I won, it was because of Sekou's academy, which means I never stopped playing: all week at the academy, all weekend at the tournaments. We traveled across Florida, then across the South, Sekou and me and a few other players in that dirty white van. In this way, I actually made some friends. I hung out with the kids; Yuri hung out with the fathers. He became especially close to a man named Bob Kane, who knew Yuri as a pro because his son Steven took lessons at El Conquistador. They would sit together at tournaments. Some men don't like my father. They think he's too driven, too tough. Some men, however, love him. He quickly forms a bond with them. He is sympathetic—not as a tennis parent but as a person, on a human level. It's the old Russian in him, the Russian of Tolstoy novels. If he likes you, he feels for you and you feel him feeling for you, and that makes you love him. That's what happened with Bob Kane.

It was always the same faces at the tournaments. It's a hundred people all pursuing the same dream. It seems like a big world, but it's tiny. Just a few of us, meeting again and again. People ask, "Was it scary when you turned pro?" That's laughable. What really happens when a tennis player turns pro? I'll tell you. You get dressed up and go out and play the same girls you've been playing all along, only now you're pros. The crowd might be bigger, the referees might be getting paid more, there are advertisements on the banners, but it's still the same girls you've been playing since you were ten. I played Tatiana Golovin when I was eight at Bollettieri's, and I played her again eleven years later at the U.S. Open.

I kept winning those tournaments. At first, I was a seven-year-old playing in the under-nine division. Then I was an eight-year-old playing in the under-ten division. I was small and not very fast but I had laser focus and hit hard, and my ranking kept climbing. By my ninth birthday, I was among the best under-twelve players in America. This is how I got back on Bollettieri's radar. He'd kicked us out for whatever reason, but how could he forget me?

I kept beating his best players.

* * *

In the fall of 1995, things were going well. Too well. I was set up at El Conquistador, Yuri was earning money, my mother was making progress on her visa, and I was winning.

Which meant something had to give—something had to go wrong.

Sekou called my father into his trailer one afternoon.

"I'm sorry, my friend, but you can't work here anymore."

Sekou was firing my father? Why?

Sekou told Yuri that his presence at El Conquistador was disruptive. Because, in addition to being my father, Yuri was supposed to be a tennis pro, and the other girls were jealous that my father was one of the instructors. Yuri spent more time with me, showed more concern. Girls had complained to their parents, and the parents had complained to Sekou. That's what Sekou told Yuri, anyway.

He gave my father a second reason for the firing, and I think it was closer to the truth. With Yuri around, Sekou said it was hard to control me—well, that's not the word Sekou used; the word Sekou used was *coach*—as my father's presence constantly undermined Sekou's authority. When Sekou went to me, I went to Yuri. Even if I did not mean to undercut him, Sekou said, I did. Even if I did not say anything, he could see it in my eyes. As long as Yuri was around, I'd belong more to him than to Sekou.

Looking back, it seems obvious this was about power. I had demonstrated my worth as a player. I had won tournaments. I had climbed the rankings. It was clear, to anyone who had spent time around the junior tour, that before too long I would turn pro.

After that, money would start coming in. Sekou had to attach himself to me now, while I was still at this early stage, if he wanted to be a part of the team later, if he wanted to hook on to a percentage of the big reward. For a person in his position, this would mean getting between the player and the parent. Sekou said that if I wanted to stay at El Conquistador, my father would have to find another place to work.

Seeing as my father would no longer be working at the school, Sekou said we'd have to start paying just like everyone else. I'd be picked up and driven to El Conquistador each morning, taken to events and tournaments, then dropped back at the apartment each night. Yuri would be billed once a month, the amount determined by just how much Sekou and his staff worked with me, which was even worse. Not knowing how much we'd have to pay made it impossible for us to plan or prepare. Even worse, Sekou was also still holding Yuri's visa and passport. He just kept finding reasons not to give them back. As long as he hung on to them, we were trapped. I don't know what was in his mind, of course, but it seemed as if Sekou was trying to make us feel insecure and off balance, as if he were ripening Yuri like an apple on a tree, preparing him for the harvest.

In other words, Yuri had to find work again. Immediately. He went here and there, before finally bringing the problem to our landlady, the Russian woman who rented us her living room and part of her kitchen. She had an obvious interest in my father's financial security: come the first of every month, we owed her $250. Meanwhile, she was dating a man who was a kind of contractor, a big guy who owned a landscaping company. He rode around in a clanking white pickup truck, dropping off and picking up his crew of workers, guys who weeded and planted and cut grass and fertilized flower beds in parks and at country clubs—the sort of work my father had done before. The man offered my father a place on his crew. My father jumped at the job. He needed money to keep me in shoes and tennis rackets, and to keep both of us housed and fed.

The work started at once. It must have been so hard for my father. He'd wake each morning at 4:00 a.m. and get dressed in the dark, make me breakfast, and leave it on the table with a note, just a few words, a bit of instruction. On those days when he had to leave for work especially early, he'd wake up, cook me rice, and put the pot under his pillow to keep it warm—that's what I would eat when I woke up. Like Yuri, the other guys on the crew were immigrants who spoke little English. Only they were not Russian, but Mexican and Honduran and Guatemalan, and the language they spoke was Spanish. They were also much younger than Yuri. Ten years or so, in better shape, with better joints and better knees. But they were friendly and warm and took to my father, and he actually came to look forward to riding with them through the cool Florida dawn. He laughed at their stories in broken English and told stories of his own. He learned to swear in Spanish and came to love his little group. Among them, he was the mysterious Russian.

Most days they worked on the golf course at a big country club—a fancy place. The crew would split up when they arrived, head off in different directions. Yuri would walk the fairways and the greens, planting sod, replacing divots, weeding, whatever—I am not an expert in any of this—early in the morning, before the sun came up. It all had to be done before the first golfers teed off at around 6:00 a.m. Then he continued to work throughout the day, sometimes with other members of the crew, sometimes alone. He was back home by 5:00 each night, in time to make me dinner.

It was a weird period in our lives that went on for months and months. He was gone each morning when I woke up, then home to feed me each night, then in that fold-out couch, where he spent hours reading books about tennis and taking notes.

He'd always had trouble with his back. It started in Russia, when he was working on those smokestacks. He would forget about it for weeks or even years, then, out of the blue, the pain would return. Working on that landscaping crew was probably not the best sort of job for a man in his condition. One day, and it was very early in the morning, when he was working on a green at the country club, his back went out. It's easy for me to write that, of course. "His back went out." But I can't really understand how it felt. He said it was excruciating, the most pain he's ever experienced in his life—bolts of lightning burning through his spine. It knocked him to the ground. Literally. All he could do was lie there, flat on his back, muttering and grimacing, alone in the dark, getting wet from the dew and the sprinklers, which never let the grass dry. He does not know exactly how long he lay there. He was in a delirium, fading in and out. The sky turned pale. Then he saw the trees. Then he saw the leaves on the trees. Then the sky turned blue and it got very hot. Finally, a man spotted him— this lone figure, stretched out on the green, groaning—and raced over in a golf cart. He tried to talk to Yuri and get him up, but Yuri just muttered in Russian and could not be moved. At first, the guy assumed my father was drunk. Look what turned up on the fif- teenth green! A drunk Russian. Probably one of the oligarchs! He finally realized that Yuri was not drunk—he was in pain and ask- ing for help. The guy went and got some of the other workers from the landscaping crew. They stood around Yuri, trying to help.

They finally lifted him off the ground, put him in a cart, and brought him to the clubhouse, where he was laid out in back, moaning.

One of Yuri's coworkers called the boss. He told him that Yuri was in bad shape and needed to get to the hospital. He wanted to call an ambulance. The boss said no—ambulances are expensive. He said he'd be there soon and would take Yuri to the hospital himself. In fact, he did not show up till the end of the day. Yuri lay groaning in that back room for hours and hours.

He was in and out of the hospital in a few hours. They let him go with a bottle of painkillers, instructions for rehab exercises, and an order to stay off his feet as much as possible. I did not learn about any of this until later, when Yuri called from the hospital. It must have been 7:00 p.m. The whole time, one of the workers told me, he'd been saying, "Masha, Masha, I've got to get home to make dinner for Masha."

Yuri spent two weeks in bed. He was in the worst shape. We hid all this from my mother. When she called, we pretended everything was good, fine, perfect. Meanwhile, I was doing my best to take care of him. I did the grocery shopping, made the meals, fed him. I made breakfast before I left for El Conquistador in the morning, then came straight back to the apartment following my afternoon match. It seemed to me that what he really needed was a swimming pool. That would be the best place for him to exercise, stretch his back, and recover. I went up and down the street, knocking on doors, asking whoever answered if they had a swimming pool and could we use it. It sounds like a crazy strategy, but I finally found a nice old lady who agreed to let us use her pool several times a week. That's when Yuri finally began to recover. After three weeks rehabbing in that pool, he was good enough to stand and walk and shop and so on, but I didn't think he'd ever be able to do manual labor again.

In the meantime, we'd stopped making money. You'd think the boss of the crew, who was, after all, dating our landlady, would have at least paid Yuri for the time off, or covered some of the medical bills. After all, he'd been injured while working for this man. Nope. Nada. Nothing. In fact, my father thinks he actually prorated the day Yuri got hurt, paid him for just the two hours when he'd been pulling weeds, not the six other hours he'd been stretched out groaning. Very soon, we had to stop paying bills. That's when the landlady began looking at us in a new, unfriendly way. We stopped being tenants and started being a problem. One afternoon, she walked a strange man through our rooms, showing him around but saying nothing. A few days later, she reminded Yuri about the rent. "If you can't pay me, you and Maria will have to leave," she said. "I have another tenant ready to move in."

"How can you kick an eight-year-old girl out on the street?" asked Yuri.

"That's your fault, not mine," said the landlady.

Of course, this was the moment that Sekou picked to deliver his bill, which he must have known we'd never be able to pay. He made it his business to know our situation. In this way, he'd crank up the pressure and increase our sense of insecurity. In other words, it was harvesttime.

Yuri got himself together and went in to see Sekou, who was holding our bill in his hand. He said, "Sekou, you know I can't pay this right now. Maybe if you give me some time . . ."

"No," said Sekou, "there is no time. Either you pay what you owe El Conquistador, or Maria has to leave."

Then, as Yuri stood there, burning with anger, Sekou said, "Unless . . . well . . ."

"Unless what?"

"There may be another type of deal we can reach."

Sekou opened a drawer in his desk and handed Yuri a contract.

"If you sign this," he said, "Maria can stay and I will see to her development personally."

"What is it?"

"A very standard agreement."

"Can I take it home and read it over?"

"Yes, why not, but quickly. It doesn't really matter to me what you decide. I am being very generous. Probably too generous. I have developed a fondness for Maria. But the deal will not be on the table for very long."

My father looked through the contract as he walked back to the apartment. He read the clauses and phrases, but it was hard to follow. He was not good at reading English, and, even if he were, the pages were written in a kind of circuitous legalese you'd have to be a lawyer to untangle.

Back at home, he handed the contract to the landlady. "Can you make sense of this?" he asked.

We were not on the best terms at the moment—she'd been threatening to kick us out, after all—but she was one of the few people we could think to turn to. What's more, if it said something about a scholarship in there, or work for my father, maybe she'd lay off about the rent. She read it at the kitchen table, carefully studying each line. You could see her lips moving as she sounded out unfamiliar phrases: "in lieu of future earnings," "dependent on post-expense gross." She put away her reading glasses when she finished. Handing the pages back to Yuri, she said, "You can't sign this."

"Why? What does it say?"

"Well, for one, it seems to say, in return for a scholarship at El Conquistador, Maria will be required, for as long as she plays tennis, to give some percentage, a large percentage, of all her earnings to Sekou. If you sign this contract, that man will own your daughter."

"You've got to be wrong," said Yuri, shocked. "I've had my arguments with Sekou, but he wouldn't do that."

"That's how I read it," said the landlady. "All I'm saying is: be careful."

Yuri thought about this for a long time, sitting in the chair, staring out the window, looking at the pages, checking and double-checking the Russian–English dictionary.

What was I? Eight, nine years old? I had been playing well and it had attracted a vulture. This put my father at a crossroads. If the landlady was right, he could not sign the contract. But if he did not sign the contract, we'd be out of school and without court time or coaches, which meant I'd not stay good for long. It was a paradox. If I wanted to be good, I had to sell my soul. If I sold my soul, there was no point in being good. If I didn't sell my soul, I wouldn't stay good.

Yuri wanted another opinion, another set of eyes, someone who really knew the language and the law—the landlady was not a native English speaker—to look at the contract, but he did not have money for an attorney. Then he remembered the man he'd met at several tournaments, his sideline friend Bob Kane, whose son had played at El Conquistador. Bob was an oncologist, and he must have been a good doctor, because he was clearly wealthy. He lived in a house on the water in Venice, Florida, which is not cheap, and he drove a beautiful sports car.

Yuri tracked down a phone number, called Bob, and explained the situation.

"I'll be right there," said Bob, "and we'll get someone to look at that contract."

Bob picked us up later that day and drove us to see a friend of his, who handled these kinds of deals. It took this man about two seconds to dismiss Sekou's agreement. As he read through the pages, he kept marking them with red pen, saying, "Nah, nah, nah."

"You can't sign this," he finally told us. "It's indentured servitude."

This was the key moment. If we signed, at least we'd have somewhere to work and to train, somewhere to go. If we did not sign, we'd have no place to practice and eventually no place to live.

I give my father tremendous credit: he never lost faith, he never gave up, never took the easy way out. What saved us? What made my career possible? It was not all those times he embraced challenges and said yes. Way too much credit is given to the art or act of saying yes. It was all those times he said no that made the difference. Up to this point, yes—beyond this point, no. That was his rebellion, his revolt. He simply refused to let me be part of another person's scheme. It was me and him and it would stay that way until he found a person he could truly trust. At the moment of temptation—by which I mean the appearance of an easier path—he always said no. And he did not despair about it. Because he's determined, and because he believed. He believed that his dream for me was destined to come true. That's what he saw and that's what Yudkin had told him. All he had to do was stay on the path and take one step at a time and everything would work out. All he had to do was say no when it would be so much easier to say yes. He had a plan, after all, and it did not include selling out to Sekou.

We went to see Sekou in that little trailer on the edge of El Conquistador's courts. He had a mocking look. He knew he was putting tremendous pressure on Yuri, who was still injured and could not work. Sekou was in tennis whites and his eyes flashed and he smiled big and phony.

He got right to the matter at hand.

"Have you signed the contract?" he asked.

"No," said Yuri.

"You have to sign the contract," said Sekou. "As soon as it's signed, we can get back to business."

"I don't think so," said Yuri.

He handed the pages back, signature line blank. Sekou was irritated. Yuri ignored this and told him about the people we'd been to see and what they'd said about the contract, how Sekou would own me if Yuri signed. Sekou said the people we'd spoken to were misinformed, stupid, or lying. The contract was fair—not only fair, generous. Too generous. Yuri said he was happy to hear it and suggested we sit with the lawyer we had seen—"Me and you and this man," said Yuri—and go over the clauses and make sure we all understood them to mean the same thing. "If he's wrong, let's show him where he's wrong," said Yuri.

Sekou's eyes flashed, then went flat, blank.

"Will you sign it or not?" he asked.

"No," said Yuri. "I'm not going to sign anything."

"All right, then," said Sekou, turning cold. "You have the rest of the day to use our facilities. In twenty-four hours, you're on your own. Your daughter cannot train here unless you pay me. And, from now on, you have to pay the actual rate, which is much more than you've been paying. That will be five hundred dollars a week."

Yuri spoke to the landlady when we got back to the apartment. He told her what had happened and what it would mean. He asked if we could have a few more weeks to pay the rent—we were already behind—just long enough for Yuri to find a job, make some money, come up with a plan. She said no. Either we could pay or we could not pay. If we could not pay, we had to leave. She did not say exactly when we had to leave, but the impression Yuri got was *now*.

Yuri called Bob Kane in Venice. He told him everything that had happened.

"I'm not sure what we're going to do," said Yuri.

"Just pack up your things and wait outside," said Bob. "I'm coming to get you."

He sent a car to pick us up and bring us back to his house—a beautiful house a few miles from the beach, with a big lawn and a swimming pool and a tennis court. It was the first time I'd been in what you'd call a rich guy's house. It made me laugh. I couldn't understand it at all. Why would a person need their own tennis court? And what about all those extra rooms, what would you do with them? You can only be in one room at a time, right? I'd been in America for months and months but still didn't really understand anything.

We moved into a guest bedroom. Bob said we were welcome to stay for as long as we needed. We could take whatever we wanted from the kitchen and join the family for meals. Then he gave Yuri some cash—"for walking around, just till you're back on your feet."

"What can I do for you?" asked Yuri.

"Well, if you feel up to it and have some time, you can hit some tennis balls with my son," said Bob. "But if not, don't worry about it. You don't have to do anything."

"Why are you doing this?" asked Yuri.

"Because if I was in the same situation," said Bob, "I'd want someone to do the same thing for me."

That's just what life was like for us in those years. Salt and sugar, bad luck followed by good luck. Every now and then, some bit of greed put us up against it. When that happened, more often than not, it was some person who, for no other reason than just because, saved us with a drive, or a bus ticket, or a place to stay.

✹ ✹ ✹

We lived at the Kanes' house for close to a year. We ate dinner with the family and I played tennis with Steven when I wasn't practicing or doing drills with my father, who'd once again become my coach. This was like an oasis, a cool interlude in the middle of a long trek. It was almost like being part of a normal American family. But I never stopped working and I never stopped training. Most important, I was playing in tournaments, as many as I could qualify for and travel to. I was growing and getting stronger and my game was improving in ways that had little to do with the drills. I was coming to feel the sport, see the angles, get the game. I began to understand how each shot sets up the next shot, how you have to anticipate and plan for the kill. It's a lot like chess. Every shot should set up something else. You have to be in the moment and concentrate on this shot if you don't want to lose, but you also have to live in the twenty seconds from now if you want to win.

My mature game had begun to emerge—not completely, but on the best days you could see it. I was playing mostly from the baseline, meeting the ball on the rise, driving it back with a scream. I could hit just about as well with my backhand as my forehand, although my forehand was my weakness. I could turn every movement of my body into kinetic force. Even when I was too small to ride the roller coaster, my game was about power and depth. My serve was a work in progress, but it *was* progressing. When I could get to the net, I finished the point off with a swinging volley. I was not fast but anticipated the ball well, which made me look faster than I actually was. In other words, I was deceptive. But the best parts of my game, those things that made me hard to beat, were mental. They were my intensity, my focus. I could stay after my opponent shot after shot, game after game, never fading, never losing hope, even when I was behind. If there was still a point to play, even if I was down two breaks and facing someone twice my size, I went after it as if I were serving for the match. I'm not sure where this quality came from—my mother, my father, my crazy childhood? Maybe I wasn't that smart. Maybe, in sports, you have to be dumb enough to believe you always have a chance. And a bad memory—you need that, too. You must be able to forget. *You made an unforced error? You blew an easy winner?* Don't dwell. Don't replay. Just forget, as if it never happened. If you tried something and it did not work, you have to be dumb enough, when the same chance comes around, to try it again. And this time it will work! You have to be dumb enough to have no fear. Every time I step on a court, I believe that I'm going to win, no matter who I'm playing or what the odds say. That's what makes me so hard to beat.

This game, this sport, this life on tour, is a kind of carnival carousel—always the same horses and unicorns, always the same sad bench, always the same girls and coaches going around and around. Do I recall any of the early matches or tournaments? To be honest, most of it's a blur, but here and there a memory shines through. A perfect point on a perfect morning, the smell of the ocean, the evening sun, holding the trophy, its weight, raising it up, but just for a moment, as then it's on to the next practice, the next tournament. I was winning—that's what mattered. And it wasn't just that I was winning, but who I was beating: the best players in my age group in the world, including Nick Bollettieri's prodigies. He'd send them over; I'd dispatch them and send them back. This must have bothered Nick. It meant he'd kicked me out of his academy but could not forget me or move on, because there I was, screwing up his plans.

In the end, the best solution for Nick was just to get me back into his academy. That way, when I won a tournament, it'd be a victory for Bollettieri's. And, of course, he knew my situation; everybody knows everything in the gossipy world of tennis. He knew I was without a coach, without a school, without my own place to stay. The situation had changed for him, too. I had been too young to attend the academy when I first turned up at his gate, and definitely too young to live there. I was older now. Whether or not Nick had once been convinced there was something not quite kosher about us turning up from nowhere, all that changed, too. Now we were better than kosher. We were bagels and lox. Nick offered a scholarship. Fees would be taken care of, room and board, everything. But we still needed money, an income, so for Yuri, that meant finding a job. Which he did—he actually went back out with a landscaping crew, but was careful about lifting and straining. A person with a bad back looks at the world with an appraising eye—what are the chances?

I moved into a dorm at Bollettieri's, which I hated. More on that later. For now, it's enough to say that my suspicions were correct: I was an oddball, different from the other girls, another type altogether. Meanwhile, Yuri was living with the Kanes in Venice and working like a dog, earning money. I talked to my mother once a week and wrote her letters frequently. She was still working on her visa, trying to put together the papers so she could join us in Florida. She'd been working on this all along. Back then, it was just about impossible to get the right documents. There was a long waiting list and a lot of corruption and a lot of money that had to be paid, and if you didn't pay the right amount to just the right person, the line could get longer as you waited on it. But she was finally making real progress. Whenever Yuri had the chance, usually on the weekends, he'd visit and watch me play. He took a bus from Venice. It was sad when he left and I had to go back to my room alone. I missed him, he missed me, and the absence of my mother was becoming more intolerable by the day. I was still just a kid. I needed my family.

For me, the good things have always happened on the court. That's how I finally attracted the sort of help I needed to get to the next level. I was playing in a tournament down the coast, on the Gulf side of Florida. All the elite players were there, the coaches, too. I was probably the youngest player in the tournament—eleven years old and going up against players who were two or three years older, most of them much taller and stronger than I was. I was small for my age, knock-kneed and slight, legs too big for the rest of me, swinging from the heels. I cruised through the early rounds.

A cheer went up whenever I won a point. Hearing applause from around the court was new for me. I sat in a chair during change-over, looking to Yuri on the sidelines. He always had words for me, messages. Sometimes it was as simple as him holding up a bottle of water, which meant "Drink, Masha! Drink!" Often, in the midst of a match, I forget to drink, a fact I become aware of only at the end of the day, deep in the third set, when nausea washes over me and the world tips on its axis. *Whoa.* The bleachers around the small center court were filled. It was a typical collection of parents and siblings and, here and there, anonymous tennis fans.

Among them, unbeknownst to me, was a woman who would change my life. Her name was Betsy Nagelsen. She was in her late thirties or early forties, a handsome woman with short choppy brown hair who had retired from pro tennis not long before. She'd been a top player in the 1970s and '80s, reaching the rank of twenty-three and winning a handful of singles titles and many more in doubles. Nagelsen had played a game not unlike my own, a baseline power game. Her mom, who lived in Venice and had seen me playing on a local court, noticed the similarity and called her daughter and said, "You've got to see the tiny Russian girl. She plays just like you did at that age. It's like looking back in time."

Nagelsen worked for one of the TV networks as a commenta-tor, so had seen more players and games and can't-miss talents than she could probably remember, but still she came down. She sat there all afternoon, watching as I advanced from match to match. What most struck her, I later learned, was not merely the similarities between our games, but my doggedness, the anger with which I played, the way I chased down every ball, driving opponents to the corner of the court. At a few key moments, I have been spotted and championed by powerful women who came before me. They did not do it for a reward. In fact, they did it anonymously, just interested in giving a leg up to a girl who could play. They did it in service of the game. Navratilova sent us on our way to America. Nagelsen sent us on our way to stability.

Betsy Nagelsen was married to Mark McCormack, founder and owner of the premier sports agency in the world, the International Management Group, IMG. Not only did IMG represent the best tennis players in the world—it put on and produced some of the greatest tennis tournaments, including Wimbledon. IMG would eventually come to own Bollettieri's academy and other academies and schools involved in other sports, including football and baseball. These days, IMG is much without peer, representing some of the best athletes in the world.

McCormack, who was almost thirty years older than his wife—he was in his seventies when I came into the picture—had built the agency from scratch. It grew out of two friendships. In the 1960s, McCormack was friends with the golfer Arnold Palmer. They were among the top athletes in the world, at the peak of their sports, yet, McCormack noticed, they had trouble making real money. McCormack, who was a lawyer and a financial guy as well as a sports nut, talked it over with Palmer. He believed he could use their fame as leverage, and get them paid. It was this sort of basic transaction that built IMG in its early years. In the end, Palmer, greatly enriched by IMG, would serve as the best possible advertisement. Other athletes saw what McCormack had done for them, then came along looking for the same kind of help. And he signed them up. And IMG grew and grew until it became what it is today. It was headquartered in Cleveland, where McCormack had his office. No matter how big his firm grew, no matter how many clients he took on, it remained rooted in that first simple idea. You invest in athletes when they are young, put them on a firm footing, and let them blossom. When they succeed, IMG prospers. For every ten kids they scout and sign, only one might make it—but that's enough.

Nagelsen did not come down to meet me after the tournament, or talk to Yuri. She went home and called her husband instead. She said, "There's a girl here in Florida, a tiny little Russian girl— you've got to send someone down to see her. She's going to be a star."

McCormack contacted Gavin Forbes, the tennis guru at IMG, who had been a good player and was known for his terrific eye for talent. He could discern the great from the seemingly great player, could tell who had that extra gear, that other thing.

I've asked Gavin if he remembered the first phone call about me. He laughed and said, "Not only do I remember it—I wrote about it in my diary.

"One afternoon, Mark McCormack's wife, Betsy Nagelsen, called me out of the blue and said, 'Gavin, there's a Russian girl playing tennis down here in Florida—she's beating all of the other players. You've got to send someone to see her right away, before word gets out. She's sensational. She's going to win Grand Slams.' Betsy had been a world-class player and she knew the game inside out, so of course I took that call very seriously," Gavin told me. "But, to be honest, I get dozens of calls just like that every week. Somewhere, someone has always just discovered the next great player, and she's gonna do this, and she's gonna do that. And I get myself out of the office and go and I see them, because you never know, but ninety-eight percent of the time what you see are nice kids and good players, maybe very good players, but there's a big, big difference between very good and extraordinary.

"When I asked Betsy for more details, more information, her answer was strange," Gavin went on. "It was just different than what you normally get with the young female players. Most of them are managed by their mothers—tennis moms. But Betsy told me it was your father who worked with you, that his name was Yuri, that you'd come from Russia, just the two of you, when you were very young."

"Where's the mother?" Gavin had asked.

"She is still in Russia," said Betsy. "Come down and see this girl," she added. "You won't regret it."

"I set up a kind of audition for you at Bollettieri's academy," Gavin explained. "You would hit back and forth with some of the pros, then play a few points with another girl, an older girl we had picked out. The first thing I really remember is seeing your father walking down a little path at the back end of the academy. I introduced myself, and we started talking. Yuri kept calling me 'Mr. Gavin.' And I kept telling him my name was Gavin. 'Just plain Gavin.' I asked him, 'Yuri, how did you end up here, so far from home?' And he said, 'Well, Mr. Gavin, I will tell you. I realized, when my daughter was very young, around four, five, six years old, that she had a very special gift and a passion, and I could not ignore that. So I left everything behind and went along as she followed her dream. I have moved to the United States and I want her to be a tennis player and not just any tennis player. I want her to become the greatest tennis player in the world.' That's how it started. I said, 'OK, great. Let's go watch your daughter play.'

"I stood against the fence, in the shade. It was hot as blazes down there. I got a hitter set up, and here comes this little girl with long blond hair and clear green eyes. Your knees were bigger than your legs. That's the stage you were in. Little knobby knees and thin little legs. But your eyes! They were just so sharp, so intelligent. You were wide awake. That's what really stood out. So you got out on the court and literally did not miss a ball, not a single ball, for the first five or six minutes. I'd never seen anything like it. Five or six minutes? That's an eternity in a tennis rally. And you were always hitting the same ball. Flat and hard. And I'm watching you, thinking, 'Oh my gosh, this really is extraordinary.' I watched you play for thirty to forty minutes and I was just blown away, not only by the way you struck the ball but by your understanding of the game and the way the tennis court works. You were thinking five or six shots ahead, setting up your opponent, moving her around, using the court like a chessboard, and I don't think that kind of vision and skill can be taught. You either see that way or you don't. It was your eyes, like I said. You just understood everything that was going on, the tennis angles and all of that.

"So we come off the court and sit down and start talking. That's when I really introduced myself for the first time. You were very polite, but a little shy. But not too shy—you know? I asked you, I said, 'Maria, what is it that *you* want to do?' And you looked me right in the eye and said, 'I want to be the best tennis player in the world.'"

Gavin Forbes went back to his office in Cleveland and sat down with a bunch of colleagues from IMG. He told them all about me, how he planned to sign me and how they would need to work with me to support me. A short time later, IMG hired a young sports agent and sent him to Bradenton to work with the elite group of players. His name was Max Eisenbud. He'd been a division one college tennis player at Purdue. He was not good enough to make it on the professional tour, so he'd gone into the business side.

Max Eisenbud would become one of the most important people in my life, a reliable constant. He's one of Yuri's closest confidants, too, the one person, other than members of the family, who's been beside us for nearly the entire ride—close when things have gone right, even closer when things have gone wrong. Everyone wants to be with you when you are winning Grand Slams, but who will stick close when the whole world turns on you? That's the question.

I remember the first time I was really aware of Max. He was outside the court, just standing there, watching me play. He was impressed by my style in a way maybe only another tennis player can be. He could see through all the little details—my gender and size, the color of my hair and my age—to what was really driving me, to the core of my game. "It was all about focus," Max told me. "It was about how you locked in on that ball, stayed focused on the task. There was nothing but that ball and that shot and that game. The rest of the world just vanished. Even during the changeovers, you were locked in. You'd sit down to rest, but your feet would still be moving, your eyes staring straight ahead. If you have talent plus that kind of focus when you are a kid . . . As an agent, you have an experience like that—of walking on a court and seeing something like you at that age—maybe once in your career. If you're lucky."

Gavin Forbes made the same point: "That's the thing that really stood out," he told me. "When you walked on the court, it was one hundred percent focus until you walked off. It was beyond maturity. That level of concentration for a person your age—what were you? Ten? Eleven? The focus was just unreal."

Max sat and talked with me and my father and it clicked right away. Yuri called Gavin that night and said, "Max is our guy."

Max sat down with his colleagues a few days later and they came up with an offer, a plan. In the meantime, word got out: IMG was trying to sign this Russian girl. Just like that, I became a hot property. Agents who knew nothing about me were ready to draft a document and make a deal. Even if they'd never seen me play, IMG had, and wanted me, and that was enough. That's how the world works. My father, who'd been kicked out of El Conquistador and sent into exile a few months before, was suddenly getting phone calls from agents and managers from all over the world.

Yuri made a trip to New York to meet with a famous agent named Paul Theofanous. Yuri did not sign with Theofanous, but he was wonderful to me and gave my father a key piece of advice that got us through the coming period, which was tumultuous. His words would be a kind of guide for Yuri as our relationship changed. "Until now, it has just been you and Maria," Theofanous told my father. "But that has got to change. If your daughter becomes really big, you cannot do this all on your own. You cannot give her everything that she will need. It's impossible for one person, no matter how good that person is, to provide everything. You are going to need to step back, let go, and let others come in and help you. It will not hurt your relationship with your daughter. I promise. It will only make it stronger."

In the end, after hearing many offers, we decided to go with IMG, because they came down and paid attention first, and because they were at the time the best for us. As I said, the agency started with Mark McCormack and Arnold Palmer, and that intimate sense of partnership and "we're in this together" has never gone away. The details were worked out between Gavin Forbes and my father one afternoon. I think it was just a phone call.

Gavin said, "Yuri, tell me, what do you need?"

"Money," said Yuri. "I need money. I can do a budget for you."

"Well, what do you think it will be?" asked Gavin. "And be smart about it. You need to be realistic but you also need to make sure you can actually survive on your budget, because I need to go to my bosses and I'm going to recommend that we fully support Maria. But I only want to go to them once."

Yuri said he'd need around fifty thousand dollars. He wanted to buy a car so we could travel from tournament to tournament, and he wanted to rent an apartment near the academy. "I've already found the place," said Yuri. "I think it's very reasonable." Gavin told him he'd need more than that. For coaches and equipment, court time and travel and trainers and specialists and whatever. Altogether, the budget amounted to something like a hundred thousand dollars a year—money that IMG would get back if I ever made it as a pro.

❋ ❋ ❋

I was invited with a few other players from the academy to Mark McCormack's house soon after we signed with IMG. It was a mansion in Orlando. He worked out of Cleveland, but Florida is the capital of tennis, which is why he had a second home there. Bob Kane—that was the first time I'd ever been in a rich guy's house. Well, this was the first time I'd ever been in a *really* rich guy's house. I was mesmerized and giddy. I could not stop laughing. The size of the rooms, the garage with many doors, all those big windows, its own trail through the trees, and a guesthouse? Who'd ever heard of that? A second house on the grounds of the first and itself a bigger house than anyone could ever possibly need. It's like that house gave birth to this house but this house had decided to skip college and just live near home.

But the more important thing that happened right after signing with IMG was this: Gavin set up a showcase with the top Nike tennis executives at the time, Riccardo Colombini and Chris Vermeeren, at the back courts of the Ritz-Carlton in Miami. A few weeks later, at the age of eleven, I signed my first Nike contract for fifty thousand dollars a year, plus bonuses. I didn't realize at the time how abnormal that was—Nike was investing in an eleven-year-old girl. Like Gavin and Max at IMG, Nike believed in my talent. They were betting on me, even when I was just a kid.

Being at IMG really changed everything for us. For the first time, we did not have to worry about food and rent. If something went wrong, we could go to a doctor. If there was a tournament, we had our own means to get there, so I could focus on tennis. This money coming in—it taught me something. It was like I suddenly woke up to the truth of the world. For the first time, I sort of understood what it was all about. Tennis is a sport but it's not just a sport. It's a passion but it's not just a passion. It's a business. It's money. It's stability for my family. I got it now. You might think this would upset or disillusion me, but the opposite was true. I finally knew why I was doing what I was doing. I finally understood the stakes. It finally made sense. From that moment, my task became clear—just go out there and win.

It was the end of an era. My father and I had been living in a kind of dream. It had been me and him against the world. It made us close in a special way. We were two people who had only each other. There was no one else we could trust, or even completely understand, so we relied on each other. That changed when IMG and Max entered our lives. We were no longer alone. It was the end of the first great act of my career—the me-and-Yuri-and-no-one-else part was finished. I was happy but also sad to see it go. There were hard times, but, looking back, I can see that some of those hard times were the best times. It formed the bedrock, the basis for everything that would follow. It made me lonely, but it also made me independent and strong. When the money came in, that was over. What had been confusing became clear. What had been crooked became straight. Yuri stopped working—no more need to cut lawns or carry flower boxes. His life was now only tennis. He took to studying, really reading those tennis books. He rented the apartment he'd mentioned to Gavin. It was in the complex where we had lived with the Russian lady, only now we had a place of our own, a two-bedroom unit big enough for all of us—me, my father, and my mother, who just about had those visa issues resolved.

SEVEN

I was still living at the academy. And hating it. There might have been a great new deal, but I still had the same old life. I want to call it a prison, but I guess it was really just a tennis prison. All the academies are like that—laid out like prisons, with the stout buildings and the neat paths, the curfews and yards, the food lines, the bragging and the arguing, with the women over there and the men over here. The tennis courts and workout rooms are always very close, waiting like a row of coffins. You get up, and there they are. You lie down, and there they are. Even when you can't see them.

I lived in a suite in one of the big dorms. There was a bathroom and a living room and two bedrooms, each with two sets of bunk beds. Four girls in a room, eight girls in a suite. I kept losing roommates and getting new ones as girls cycled in and out—did well, struggled, broke down, went home. In the morning, the bed would be stripped and prepared for a new girl.

I was lonely. I barely saw my father, who had struggles of his own. Now and then, I took classes at the nearby public school. This was a requirement, probably. They'd drop a bunch of us off in vans, then pick us up late in the day. We'd sit there with the local kids, like freaks dropped from another planet, but I enjoyed it. I've always loved school, and it was an escape—something different. Life in the dorm was no fun. I was younger than the other girls—for a while, I was the youngest kid at the academy—and the others punished me for it. I went to bed earlier than the rest because I was younger and practiced longer hours and needed more sleep. They'd come in late, hopped up on candy, talking and laughing loudly on purpose, waking me up and mocking me. It was not just my age that separated me—I was on a completely different track. I was there on a mission, bound for a different kind of tennis life. These were rich kids for the most part, spoiled and sent down to live out a parental dream. I was a player—one of only a handful on scholarship—who attracted the attention of those parents and got them to fork over all that money for tuition. That was our job, how we paid back Bollettieri. We were the advertisement. We attracted the deluded, wannabe tennis parents.

These girls, they'd go through my stuff when I was out on the courts. I'd notice it when I got back—that everything had been overturned and rifled. The joke was on them: I had nothing to steal, nothing to see. *What was I?* A poor Russian girl who loved to hit tennis balls. When they weren't going after me, they were making poster-board collages. It was the thing to do at that time. Elmer's glue, cutouts of David Hasselhoff (I didn't know who that was) and Janet Jackson, and LOVE and FRIENDSHIP written in blue and yellow and pink bubble letters. If that was what it meant to have a real childhood, to be a real American girl, you could keep it. I had only one good friend in the suite. Her name was Priscilla. She was a little chubby, with the brightest American smile I'd ever seen. I think she liked me because we were both a little awkward. She didn't feel like she fit in, and I knew I didn't. We were outcasts together.

The routine never changed:

5:30 a.m. Wake up
5:45 a.m. Breakfast
6:15 a.m. Practice on Nick's court
7:30 a.m. Clinics and drills
12:30 p.m. Lunch
1:30 p.m. Practice
4:00 p.m. Fitness
5:00 p.m. Dinner
7:00 p.m. "Schoolwork"
9:00 p.m. Bed

At Bollettieri's, they never really worked on the technical aspects of my game. When I asked Nick about this, he shrugged and said something like "If it ain't broke." He said I came to them, that second time, fully formed. "Yes, there was work you could do on your serve, covering the court, but you already had that thing, that desire, that makes good players champions. We did not want to do anything to screw that up. It's like a fire. You try to light a fire. But if that fire is already going, your task is to get out of the way and let it burn, feed it maybe, but by God don't smother it and put it out!" I wasn't too sure I agreed with that philosophy.

I worked my way into Nick's "elite group," boys and girls of different ages, the best young players at the academy. There were six to eight of us at any one time. Todd Reid, Jelena Jankovic, Horia Tecau, and Tatiana Golovin were kids Nick had pegged for the pro tour, the standouts. We played with one another and against one another, ate meals at the same table, warmed one another up before matches, and traveled to tournaments together in a single van. Nick tried to make us into a team, to instill an esprit de corps, which is why he gave us the nickname: the Tigers, I think. Or maybe it was the Cougars? The fact that I can't remember it shows how little that team meant to me. He might have called us a team, but we knew, deep down, that our teammates were our competitors, not our friends. If you wanted to be number one, these were in fact the girls you would have to beat, and being friends would only make that harder. For me, it helped to turn them, in my mind, into the enemy. I imagine it's how everyone who really plays has to play, because it's how you win. Other girls just might be better at hiding it than I am. People say that I'm a bad sport because I don't seem to be friends with the other girls on the pro tour. Well, I just don't buy into that locker-room small talk. It feels forced. Fake. There are so many times when you see two players in the locker room, two girls, just chatting away like they're best friends, about personal lives and boyfriends and "I'm going on this vacation" and "I bought this dress" and "Oh my God, it was how much money?" Listening to them speak, they sound like best friends. And then, a few hours later, one of them is playing a match and the other is in the locker room watching the match on TV, looking pleased when her friend loses the point. That's how it really is.

What about the other girls in that team of elites?

We didn't spend much time together away from the courts. I was too competitive to get very close to them. They were very good. Jelena Jankovic has been in a Grand Slam final. She's been the top player in the world. I remember when we were eleven years old, we made up our first e-mail addresses together. The password to mine was Loveandpeace. I wonder if she remembers. Tatiana Golovin, almost the same age as me, was from France. Tatiana, Jelena, and I were rivals at the academy, and Tatiana was the favorite of the pack. Everyone loved her. She'd always have her hair up in just the right way, with perfect braids, and always had cute outfits, with perfectly tucked shirts. She walked Nick's daughter's dogs and wore pom-poms on her shoes. Jelena was more of a tomboy. I was in the middle. I was vanilla. I didn't think about my clothes too much, and I really didn't care about my hair. I put it up in a ponytail—done. My clothes? Usually a tennis skirt. We did some things together, activities at the academy; sometimes we'd all go out to dinner at a restaurant with a coach. That was fun but I never came back thinking, "Oh, now we're friends." I never forgot that the time would come when we'd face each other on the court, with everything on the line.

Nick's staff did not do much for me in the way of coaching. Repetition, hour after hour on a court, hitting the same shot again and again—that's what I did at the academy. If a certain part of my game needed work—and there always has been, and there always is—Yuri would call Gavin Forbes and ask him to suggest coaches, offer ideas. My father was always researching, studying, and analyzing. Many of his ideas came from articles, or from conversations he had with other parents.

"Yuri was aware of the fact that he had to have the best team around him," Gavin told me. "So he would search for the best guy for a forehand or he'd find the best guy for a serve, or he'd find the best guy for physical training. He was smart enough to realize that while he might be the director of this project, he needed the best people around you to make this thing really work. I remember one time when Yuri felt that, for some reason, you needed, number one, to be on a clay court and, number two, to work more hours than was recommended at that time for a kid of your age at the academy. And he asked me to help him get some more balls, which I did. I remember going down to meet him on Highway 41, right there in Bradenton. He'd found a clay court hidden beyond a doughnut store. He had a shopping cart with old balls and he had a guy from South America with big holes in his shoes hitting with you. This guy could hit, obviously. And they would spend an hour every morning at six with this kid. And I remember saying to Yuri, 'I've got to get this boy some new shoes!' Yuri found him on the street or something. And wow, could he hit the ball. But that was Yuri, always searching, always working."

* * *

I never thought of myself as a good tennis player, nor did I think of myself as a bad tennis player. I just did not think about it at all. I had yet to become conscious of my game in that way. I was still happily dumb to all the ways you can be valued, marked up or marked down. I was still living in the first bliss, meaning: I simply played, because it's what I'd always done and because I loved to hit. Was there a moment when this state of ignorance ended, when that bubble was pierced? Was there a moment when I realized that I was very good and that being very good would have value for those around me?

Yes, there was.

It happened at the academy one night after dinner.

I was already in bed, reading, doing homework, staring at the ceiling. One of Nick's guys called me down to center court. This was unusual. The hours and length of time we played at the academy were tightly regulated—that's why my father and I ducked out to grab an extra hour behind the doughnut shop. And this was definitely after-hours, the time of crickets and cicadas and silence. Yet center court was lit like the deck of an aircraft carrier, stadium lights blazing, and the bleachers were filled with businessmen in suits. Nick told me to warm up, then head over to the far court. One of the teachers would hit with me. So that's what I did—got out there in what felt like the dead of night, chasing and hammering, while the businessmen looked on and the mosquitoes swarmed. It was a kind of showcase. I figured this out later. These were investors thinking of putting money into the academy, and they wanted to get a look at the merchandise. In other words, Nick was the owner and I was the product. Or victory was the product and I was a machine that cranked it out.

I went back to my room and climbed into bed but never really got over it. That showcase changed my perspective. I realized how much was at stake, and it made me see the other girls in a new way. From that moment, I was on the lookout for competition, for those girls who could take my place under the lights. I knew that I liked being there. I made fun of it and dismissed it, but I liked that I was the girl Nick summoned when cash was on the line. I began looking here and there, searching for those who could challenge me. And I began searching for those I'd need to challenge. Jankovic. Kournikova. Golovin. I'd have to beat them all, beat them again and again. And as I got older, closer to the matches that really counted, I kept hearing the same names. Steffi Graf was still around. Lindsay Davenport. Monica Seles. But they were older, on their way out. Among the new generation, there were just two names: Venus and Serena, the Williams sisters. Of course, I'd heard of them before. It was in part that article about the sisters, and how they were training at Rick Macci's Tennis Academy, that convinced my father we had to make our way to America in the first place. But I had not thought about them since. I'd been living my own life. Now suddenly they were everywhere. Teenagers— only one year apart—but already the best in the world. They'd won tournaments, been crowned all around the world. They were big girls, and they hit with unbelievable power. That's what people told me. They would dominate the game for years. The more I heard about them, the more determined I became not to be beaten down, or submit. That's when the rivalry began for me. Not on a tennis court, or at some banquet, but right there, in my mind, before I'd even seen the Williams sisters.

I was twelve or thirteen—five years younger than Serena. She was already a grown woman, while I was still hanging from a chin-up bar at night, praying for inches and pounds.

Then, one day, we got the news: the sisters were coming to Bollettieri's to train. It started as a rumor and spread like wildfire. It was as if an astronaut or a movie star were visiting. The morning schedule was canceled. Everyone wanted to watch the Williamses work out, to get close and see how the magic was done. Yuri told me to watch "with clear eyes. See what they do. Learn what you can. This is who you will have to beat."

"No."

"What do you mean, 'No'?"

"I will not watch them," I said. "I'm not going to let them see me at their practice. I don't care if there are a hundred people watching and they have no idea who I am. I will never give them that satisfaction."

In truth, I did want to watch them practice, but it had little to do with tennis. I'm always fascinated by the great ones—How do they carry themselves? What are they like on the court?—but I'd never put myself in the position of worshipping them, looking up, being a fan. My father and I argued and argued about it. He said I was letting pride get in my way.

"You need to watch them," he explained.

He finally came up with a solution. The sisters were playing on court two, which had a wooden shed set up with a camera to shoot footage of each player. You were supposed to go into the shed after your session and analyze yourself on film. *Look at your feet! Look at how you dropped your shoulder!* But no one ever did that. The shed was there so Nick could put it in a brochure: "We have a film room and video facilities." It was dark and dank, filled with old equipment. Yuri got the key and snuck me in ten minutes before the sisters showed up. He rolled the camera away so I could watch through a kind of knothole—just me alone, in the dark, seeing the next twenty years of my life.

The image of the Williams sisters would eventually become iconic, and it was in the works even then. They're a force. Tall girls in tennis whites, with bright smiles and piercing, focused eyes. They began hitting, easy at first, then with terrific pace. Their father—a tennis father, parental nut, the will behind the operation, really not all that different from my own father—leaned against the fence, calling out instructions and orders. The bleachers were filled—every kid in the academy was there. They hung on each shot and followed each volley like worshippers, like fans, like sheep.

The sisters moved around the court with languid grace—Serena especially. She was younger but clearly stood out. She swung easily, but the ball smoked off her racket. Now and then, when a rally had gone one shot too long, she'd end it with a crosscourt winner. And yet, for all the power, for all the intensity of their practice, I had just one thought: I want to beat them.

* * *

In the spring of 1996, something big happened—bigger than picking up a new stroke, or developing my serve, or being signed by IMG. After years of waiting, my mom was finally granted her visa, and she joined us in Florida. She moved into the apartment in Bradenton. A few weeks later, I left the dorm and settled in the second bedroom. We were a family again. We ate meals together! And watched TV and talked together! I had not seen my mother in close to two years, but it was as if no time had passed. This was maybe the happiest time of my life. You don't realize how much you've been missing someone until you have that person back.

My mom immediately put things in order. She threw out all my Kournikova hand-me-downs, fixed my hair, confiscated Yuri's scissors. Never again would he cut my bangs. She fired my tutor. Now she and I would spend our evenings together, working on math problems, reading Russian literature. My mother, the most educated person in our family, took my education very seriously, and she was a wonderful teacher. She focused on the classics—the great Russian writers and poets—because that's what she knew and loved. She took care of the food and the shelter and the love and everything else. In a few months, I went from being a kid living a strange existence to being an athlete from a warm, stable, conventional home.

Maybe this was when my father went sort of bonkers, because suddenly there really was nothing for him to think about but my tennis. I remember one night, sticking my head into his room. He was lying there, a light shining on his lap, filling page after page with notes. I tried to back out unnoticed, but he spotted me.

"Be ready," he said.

"For what?"

"We're going to Los Angeles."

I did not believe him, but asked why anyway.

"Because that's where Robert Lansdorp lives."

"Who's Robert Lansdorp?"

"The man who's going to make you the number one player in the world."

EIGHT

Robert Lansdorp was famous for the work he'd done with Tracy Austin and Pete Sampras, but he was a lot more than that. He really deserves a book of his own. He was white-haired, gravel-voiced, moody, tough, and mean, but also sentimental and generous and kind. And a brilliant tennis coach. He does not believe in bullshit inflation. If he compliments you, you deserve it. If he says you're good, you are good. And what a story! He grew up in the Far East, in a Dutch colony that was conquered by the Japanese during World War II. His father, a Dutch businessman, was arrested and imprisoned in a concentration camp. Robert had gone back to Holland with his family, and that's where he learned to play tennis. When his father was released, the family went here and there, before heading to America in 1960.

Robert was twenty-two years old. He bought a car in New York and drove to Los Angeles, where he met up with the rest of his family. By the time he arrived, he had fallen in love with America. That's what he said. He took up tennis again and began to play on a local circuit. He was a natural athlete and astonishingly good for an untrained player. He was spotted by a coach from Pepperdine—spotted because he kept beating that coach's scholarship stars. Robert was given a scholarship of his own, went to college, and played tennis. He became an All-American player. He floated around the professional circuit afterward, but there wasn't much money in it, and he eventually took a job at a resort in Mexico. Thus began his raffish life as a hotel tennis pro. He went from job to job, resort to resort, giving lessons in the morning and drinking with socialites in the afternoon. He found his way back to L.A., where he quickly became a sought-after coach. It was not just that he was a good teacher—it was that he had a philosophy, a way of thinking about the game. He distrusted the modern reliance on trickery and spin. He believed in a steady diet of low, hard, flat shots that just cleared the net—the kind of shot it takes guts to deliver because, if you miss by half an inch, you're finished.

By the time Yuri learned about Lansdorp, he had become a fixture at the Riviera Club, a fancy spot in Beverly Hills. He charged an outrageous amount per hour for lessons and made most of his money teaching the children of movie producers and moguls. They all knew his record, the elite players he'd coached—Tracy Austin most famously. Austin and Lansdorp were a kind of team. They traveled together, became like family. She was his greatest pride, the youngest player ever to win the U.S. Open.

Lansdorp went on to coach many greats—but he never stopped talking about Tracy Austin.

Yuri learned about Robert in one of the tennis magazines. He'd been working with Lindsay Davenport, and there was a picture of them together, walking off the court. It impressed Yuri because Yuri was impressed by Lindsay. He'd seen her play at a tournament and was convinced that my game should be like her game. She was not especially fast, nor did she look very strong, but she had such tremendous power. Those hard, flat, spinless shots! According to the article, this style and those shots owed a lot to the teaching of Robert Lansdorp.

Yuri tracked down Lansdorp's phone number—probably a spare line at the Riviera—and called one afternoon. Yuri got him on about the fifteenth ring. Lansdorp was gruff.

"Who is this?"

"Yuri Sharapov."

"Who gave you my number?"

"IMG."

"Why would they do that? Bastards. What do you want?"

"I want to bring you my daughter."

"What am I supposed to do with your daughter?"

"Coach her at tennis."

"Who is your daughter?"

"Maria Sharapova."

"Never heard of her."

"Ask around. She is something special."

"Do you know my rates? You can't afford me. I am incredibly expensive."

"We're fine with the money."

"Where are you at the moment?"

"Nick Bollettieri."

"Who is Nick Bollettieri?"

* * *

We took the next plane—it felt that way, anyway. Just like that, we were in Los Angeles. My father had me call Lansdorp from the airport's pay phone. We needed directions to the club in Beverly Hills, and he figured I'd have better luck with Lansdorp on the phone. It's harder to be gruff and sarcastic to a little kid.

Lansdorp picks up. Grunts. Groans. "What?"

"Hi, this is Maria Sharapova."

"What the hell do you want?"

"I have an appointment to come and see you this afternoon."

"Yeah? So what? Is this the afternoon? Why do you people keep calling?"

"We need directions."

"What?"

"Directions."

"Take the 405. Exit at Sunset."

Bang. He hangs up.

I turned to my father and said, "Who is this monster you're taking me to see?"

"I hear he's very good," said Yuri.

This was my first time in L.A. Yuri was careful with the money we got from IMG and Nike—there were not a lot of frills in our life—so I was thrilled when we went to get our rental car and found they had mixed up our reservation: it was a sports car, a red Mustang convertible! We sat in the smog and traffic of the freeway, but

I was dazzled by the palm trees, the mansions, the distant hills, and the big broad boulevards all ending at the Pacific Ocean, which is of course the end of America.

When we finally got there and I got changed, Robert Lansdorp was sitting in a chair beside the court, all alone. He looked to me just like some mean old guy, hunched in a defensive crouch, maybe twisted up by cramps. He was talking on the phone—that's why he was all bent over—but I did not realize this at first. I walked toward him, slowly, carefully. I said, "Hello, Robert?" He didn't even look up, so I said it again, louder. "Hello, Robert?" I called out his name a few more times, put my bag down, and started to stretch, like I needed to warm up. I really didn't know what to do. That's when he finally acknowledged me. He did this by giving me one of those "Who the hell are you?" looks.

I said, "Hi, I'm Maria Sharapova. I'm here for a lesson."

"Get your ass out on the court."

That's all he said. It was our very first conversation, and yet—maybe it was his tone of voice—I knew right away it was going to work out. Robert has his way of beating you down and making you feel like nothing, but I had my way of charming grumpy older men. Always have. It's a sneaky little voice in my head that says, "I know how you are going to like me."

I picked up my racket and went to the far side of the court. It took Robert five minutes to finally get out of his chair, groaning and cursing the entire time. *Oh, fuck. Shit, fuck, shit.* My father was standing right there, but he didn't say a word. I looked at him like, "Thanks, Dad! Look at this lunatic! What a brilliant idea." Robert finally got himself situated, set up, ready. He was holding a huge wire basket with maybe five hundred balls. I was on the far service line. That's how I warmed up, by hitting balls back and forth from the service line. He scowled at me and said, "What the hell are you doing there?"

"I don't know," I said, almost laughing, because everything I did was apparently so wrong. "I thought I was warming up."

It turned out he's a coach who just feeds balls, one after another, like a machine. He doesn't hit with you, he does not volley. He just feeds and feeds and feeds and you just hit and hit and hit. He shouted at me: "Get your ass on the baseline."

OK. I got my ass on the baseline and he started feeding those perfect balls. It's this incredible gift he has. He is able to endlessly feed balls with the same pace and rhythm forever. After an hour, you feel like you can return them with the same smooth, hard stroke with your eyes shut.

I spoke to Robert while working on this book. He is currently living in a house south of L.A., and from his kitchen he can sit with a cup of coffee and look out at Long Beach harbor, which is crowded with schooners and tankers from every part of the world. It puts him in a thoughtful mood. He likes to talk, even likes to remember. He's saved memorabilia, small relics of our years together. Pictures and old rackets, even a collage that I made for him. (I guess I did do some collaging after all!) He talked about the old days calmly and happily, but of course it was not so calm and happy when it was happening. It was nuts.

I asked if he remembered the first time we met.

"Sure."

"What was your impression?"

"I thought you were a skinny little thing, but you did run well. You had a weak forehand, such a weak forehand. You couldn't hit the ball crosscourt. I remember Yuri asking me, at the end of that first practice, 'Well, Lansdorp, what do you think about my daughter?' I said, 'She's pretty good, Yuri, but her fore-hand sucks.'"

I wrote about Lansdorp in my diary. Here's one of the first entries:

> The greatest thing about Robert is that he's a no-bullshit type guy. If you suck, he tells you you suck. If you're out of shape, he tells you you're out of shape. He doesn't care if you are tired and can't do it anymore. He makes you keep going and going.

Robert's persona was really a front. It was an act, even a kind of test. If you were the sort of person who got easily offended, and couldn't take criticism, it was better to find out right away. If you couldn't take the tough words, then it wasn't going to work out with you and Lansdorp. But I knew I could work with Robert, that he could work with me. He's a weirdo but has a soft spot. He pretends to be intimidating, but that's only when you don't know him. You need to have been through a lot to really understand that guy. He's obnoxious when you first meet him and has bad moments. But ever since I was young, I could handle difficult people. It's something I developed during my childhood. I've always been able to take the best, skip the rest. It's my philosophy.

I quickly fell into a new routine. In addition to my regular schedule at Bollettieri's, I'd fly out to L.A. at the end of each month to work with Lansdorp for a week. At first, my father and I stayed in a cheap hotel near the Riviera Club. Later on, Robert asked a family whose kid he was teaching if it would be OK for me and my father to stay in their home while we were in L.A., to save a little money. The LaPortes kindly agreed. They lived in a big house in Palos Verdes and had two kids, Shane and Estelle. The first time we went to the house, a little girl with wavy-curly hair and freckles, no more than nine years old, opened the door. Her look was suspicious: Why was this blond, skinny girl and her father standing at her doorway with suitcases? But we bonded quickly. Probably because she could only play so many basketball games with her brother Shane. She became the closest thing to a younger sister I will ever have. She played some tennis, but mostly focused on school. On school days, I would patiently wait for her to wake up, then help her pick out an outfit. We would walk together for a while. She would go to her school and I would continue on to the public tennis courts behind the school to practice serves with my father. I could see her sitting in her classroom. I would wave to her and she would pretend not to notice so she didn't get in trouble with the teacher.

At the end of each day, we would jump on the backyard trampoline until it got dark, or until my father would tell me I had to stop before I tired myself out—there was always the next day's training to think about.

We made up a lot of games, pretend games. Our favorites were *Bank*, with a metal box register and handmade paper checks, and *Sherlock Holmes*, in which we staged a crime, then solved it. And when the *Harry Potter* books came out, we competed to see who could read them all the way through first.

We planned trips to Disneyland months in advance, mapping out each place we would go. Once, I asked Robert if he would give me Saturday off to go to Disneyland. He made me run side-to-sides, a hundred of them, just for *talking* about Disneyland. Then he let me go.

Eighteen years later, Estelle and I still plan our trips to Disneyland and still pick apart *Harry Potter*. It is a deep friendship. We are loyal and rely on each other. We may not be in the same city, or even in the same country, but nothing separates us.

Staying at her house made those trips fun and gave me something to look forward to—it wasn't going to be all torture. Estelle really helped me through those years. I love her, and will always be grateful.

Robert's practices were pretty much the same every time. That was the point of them. He believed in repetition. Doing the same thing again and again and again. Do it till it's second nature. No matter what, he just kept feeding those balls. Forehand to backhand. Side to side. No mercy. When you're hitting one ball, he's already feeding you the next—it's speeding toward the opposite side of the court and you have to run to get it. On some days, he was an absolute asshole. He would just pound and pound that ball until you thought you would die. He'd end each practice by feeding ten quick balls side to side, running you back and forth, back and forth. He called it "ten at the baseline." We'd do that six or seven times. Then, just as I was heading off court, he'd say, "Where do you think you're going, broad?" He loved that word, *broad*. Then he'd make you do another dozen from the baseline.

Lansdorp was not a sadist. There was a point to all that torture. Everything was done in the service of a philosophy; every drill had a reason, was taking the player somewhere. When I asked him to explain that philosophy, he laughed. "Well, you know me, Maria," he said, smiling. "I just hate spin on a tennis ball. That's what most modern players use. They hit the ball hard, then put a lot of spin on it to keep it in the court. It drops, like a sinker ball. I hate it. What I want is a good, hard, flat stroke. That's what all that repetition is teaching. A flat stroke doesn't have a lot of top-spin. Flat strokes were big in the 1970s and 1980s, into the early 1990s, then a new, terrible style came in. I think it had to do with the new rackets and new grips. It changed everything. With the new grips, it's easy to put a lot of spin on a ball. Too easy. The spin gets on there even when you don't want it to. The kids who thrive on that can be hard to beat, but when they get to be fifteen or sixteen they hit a wall, because now they have to hit the ball harder and suddenly they can't control the spin. You have to learn to hit flat when you're young because you need to be fearless to do it, and the older you get, the more fear gets into your game. That's why we did it again and again. You were learning to hit that hard, flat stroke."

Once I'd acquired what Robert considered a suitably hard, flat stroke—it was all about getting into a nirvana-like hitting groove—we began to work on my accuracy, my court placement. There was nothing high-tech or modern about his method. There were no video cameras, or lasers, or algorithms. Robert simply taped empty tennis-ball cans a few inches above the net on either side of the court and told us to hit those "targets" as many times as we could. It was like trying to drive a tennis ball through a keyhole.

"You know, you have the record," Robert told me recently.

"The record for what?"

"For hitting the target," he said. "I put them just above the net because that really gives you a sense of the sweet spot, where the zone is. You didn't like doing that in the beginning—no one does. Then, after about a year, you started getting into it. You'd actually ask me to set up the targets. That was very unusual. When you were maybe fifteen, you hit the target eight out of ten times. That's still a record. Eight out of ten forehands. Justin Gimelstob hit eight out of ten backhands. One day, Anastasia Myskina, who later won the French Open, was at the club. She had a lesson, and, Maria, you were three courts away, playing a practice match. Myskina's hitting the target, and, the way I worked, each time a player hit the target, I'd bang a tin can, ring it like a bell. One for one. Two for two. I get to four for four and you start screaming, 'I know she's not hitting the target! I know you're faking it.' Meanwhile, you never missed a beat in your own match. Crazy concentration. We were laughing so hard. You knew we were faking it—and we were! No other girl could hit that target eight for ten forehands."

These drills gave a new pace and consistency to my game. It got to where I could just drive that ball, hard and flat, over and over again. This puts tremendous pressure on opponents. The assault never stops. I did not have a lot of court speed, but these shots could make up for it. Working with Lansdorp also gave me a new attitude, a terrific confidence. Robert was so certain about what he was doing that it made you just as certain. He was a guru. You could feel his presence in your head. It was a voice that said, "This is how it should be done. There is no question and there is no doubt." And he's proved it. Lansdorp has trained three world number ones. The fact that he could be such a difficult man only made it more special. I loved him partly because I felt like I could break down that cold barrier.

Once, at the end of a long practice, as I was leaving the court, he called me back.

He said, "Hey, broad."

"What is it, Robert?"

He handed me a package.

"It's that thing you won't shut up about," he said, frowning.

That's how I got my first iPod.

"Why?" I asked.

"Well, why the hell not?" said Robert.

That's the thing about that man. He'd always surprise you.

When Robert Lansdorp celebrated his seventieth birthday, a bunch of his old students came back to pay their respects. Lindsay Davenport and Tracy Austin were there. Several of them got up to make toasts, to offer little tributes. They spoke about what they got from Robert. The ground strokes were mentioned of course, but the main thing, what people kept coming back to, was the attitude and confidence, the toughness, the determination to fight back even when everything looks bad. If you can survive Robert Lansdorp, they joked, you can survive anything.

It took two years, but Robert remade my tennis game. Or maybe *remade* is the wrong word. Maybe he just helped me find what had always been there but was dormant. I emerged from those lessons with a new confidence and a new mind. That's how I made the transition from kid to adult. By age fourteen, I was already playing the game I play now.

* * *

Those years were marked by a failed experiment that still haunts me. It's the kind of thing you dwell on late at night, asking yourself, "What if?"

Yuri believed a mistake had been made right at the beginning, when I first started playing. As I worked out with Lansdorp, as Yuri watched me hit forehand after forehand, backhand after backhand, he became convinced that I was by nature a lefty. "If you had been playing lefty from the first days, no one in the world could beat you," he said.

On a visit to Sochi, he tracked down Yudkin and asked him, "How did you miss it? Couldn't you see that she should be a lefty?"

"What do you want from me?" said Yudkin. "She came out on the court hitting the ball with her right hand. So, she was a righty. End of story. She decided that herself when she was five years old. No one knows anything better than a five-year-old knows herself."

But Yuri only became more and more convinced: "You should be playing lefty, and there's still time to fix it. It's simply a question of will."

Now and then, when I played lefty goofing around, it did feel natural. It was just so easy, so normal. It was ZING! The world humming, the gears turning, the stars lining up for the solstice. Then again, I do hold a pencil and a fork with my right hand. So maybe, or maybe not. The more I thought about it, the more confused I became.

My father asked Lansdorp: "You've been working with Maria, what do you think? Should she be playing righty or lefty?"

"I remember Yuri asking me this question," Robert told me. "And I remember my answer. I said, 'I don't know, but she probably should be a right-hander because then her backhand will be world-class.' Because you really could hit left-handed, Maria. Your ability to hit a left-handed forehand made your two-handed backhand look natural. Some people are not pure two-handers, that takes time to develop. But you were a pure two-hander from the first day I saw you. So what did I tell your father? What I tell everyone with an interesting idea: 'Why not try it?'"

A few days later, my father told me to switch to my left hand.

"Why?"

"Because Yudkin messed it all up," he said. "You really should be a lefty."

"Yeah, but I play with my right hand," I said.

"Look, Maria," said my father, "if you play left-handed, you'll be impossible to beat."

I resisted for a few days but finally decided to give it a try. A real try. At the time, my father was sort of obsessed with Monica Seles and Jan-Michael Gambill. Each of those players had a crazy method. Instead of hitting a traditional forehand and backhand, they relied on two-handed backhands from both sides. When they approached a ball on their left, they would hit a left-hand dominated backhand. When they approached a ball on their right, they would hit a two-handed forehand. Yuri wanted me to play that way. It extends your range. You get to more balls in a position of strength. That's what Yuri had in mind. He spent all his free time watching videos of Seles and Gambill.

So began this strange period when I played tennis as a lefty. Well, it was really a progression. At first, I tried playing as a pure lefty—a one-handed left-hand forehand and a two-handed backhand—but I just didn't have the arm strength. So I went with all two-handers, that is, two-handed backhands on both sides, like Seles and Gambill played. It turned out that I could do it. Robert Lansdorp was impressed, and Yuri was happy, but Nick Bollettieri and many people at the academy were irritated. They'd spent so much time working with my right-hand forehand and my two-hand backhand and now it was suddenly back to square one. And I was confused. Not in my mind, but in my body. North was south, back was front. Arms and legs, feet and hands—I did not know what to do. This went on for three or four months, endless days of my father videotaping my practices followed by endless nights of my father watching those videotapes over and over again. It exists in my memory as the time I spent in an alternate reality, in the future that never happened, on a train that never left the station. What would life have been like as a lefty? Maybe worse. Maybe better. McEnroe, Connors, Laver—all lefties. I had to decide.

One night, at the end of a practice match at the academy, playing under the big lights, a smattering of people in the bleachers, Nick Bollettieri took me and my father aside. Nick had mostly left my game alone, but now he had something on his mind. He said, "Look, I don't care what you do about this—not really. I think Maria will have great success lefty or righty. But you have to make a choice. Otherwise, she's going to be half as good at both and not nearly as good at either.

"Maria, I know this is a very hard choice," he added, looking only at me, "but you have to choose now or else it's going to be too late. It's not a choice for me, or your dad, or your mom, or Robert. It's for you—only you."

I was speechless, devastated. At that moment, I thought Nick was the meanest man on the planet. I was only twelve years old and I had to make a decision that might impact my entire future. I was crying when I got home. My mom asked me why. When I told her, she said, "Just remember which people make you cry."

It shook my father up, too. It was as if he'd been slapped awake. Was he screwing me up? Was he putting everything in jeopardy? That's the impression we got from Nick. Yuri was bugged, but he knew that Nick was right: a decision had to be made.

My father and I remember the next part differently. As I remember it, the decision, as Nick said it had to be, was left to me. Who else could know what it was like from the inside? I spent days and days going back and forth, choosing and then reversing that choice. It was one of the hardest decisions I've ever had to make. Lefty or righty? Righty or lefty? To be or not to be? My mom and dad would come out onto the court and videotape me from different angles, helping me examine the question in every possible way. In the end, I decided to stick with what I knew, with what I am, with what I've always been. I'm a righty. If I'd been seven instead of twelve years old, maybe I would have chosen differently. But if I switched hands at twelve, then I'd really have been going back to square one. I would lose all those seasons and all those years of work and development, all those hours with Yudkin, and Bollettieri, and Sekou, and Robert, all those matches on all those blistering days. I just didn't have that much strength in my left arm. I had never developed it. That was especially evident when I hit a lefty serve. I'd be taking a big step back. In the end, I just did not have the energy or desire or faith to make such a radical change. I told my father, and Nick, and Robert, "I've always been a righty. That's what I'm going to keep on being."

"Good choice," said Nick. "Now let's get back to work."

This lefty-righty adventure, even without the permanent switch, did actually affect my game. First of all, it really built up my backhand. In the old days, a coach would tie a young basketball player's right hand behind his back to develop his left. That's what it was like for me: all those weeks of playing lefty really worked up and developed my backhand. Like Robert said, it became my weapon. Backhand, down the line, my favorite shot.

My father remembers the decision being made in a different way. (At times, when we talk about the past, it's as if we've been living in two different worlds.) He says the choice was made not by me but by him. By him! "How could such an important decision be left to a child?" he asks, shrugging. He had indeed been shaken by Nick Bollettieri and what he said on the court that day—"You have to make a choice. Otherwise, she's going to be half as good at both and not nearly as good at either"—but he couldn't make up his mind. Lefty was like the moonshot—it could transform everything—but righty was logical and smart. Look at how much success I'd already had with my right hand. So he hesitated and delayed.

"What were you waiting for?" I asked.

"What I'm always waiting for," he told me. "A sign."

It finally came at the end of dinner at a friend's house—a tennis friend. Yuri held a dessert dish in one hand and a coffee mug in the other. He wandered into the living room, put the dish and cup on the coffee table, and sat on the couch to look at a stack of tennis magazines. He flipped through one at random. It fell open to the horoscope page. "Astrology Corner," he told me. "And it said, right there, in black and white, I swear, Maria, it said: 'The number one women's tennis player in the world will have the initials M. S. and she will be right-handed.'"

Yuri never mentioned my left hand again.

NINE

I started playing in big tournaments—all over the world. I was still an amateur, but I was on the road to the pro tour, a few steps away. Only the best youth players in the world make it into these tournaments. Only the best of the best make it out. It's like the eye of a needle. Just a handful get through to the next stage. It was a crucial passage that, for me, could not have come at a worse time. I was fourteen and one of my biggest dreams was about to come true. I began to grow. And grow. And grow. It seemed to happen all at once, in the course of a long summer night. You go to bed in one body and you wake up in another. Stretched out. Long and clumsy and thin—eight inches added just like that. I'd top out at six foot two.

But you know what they say about too much of a good thing. I was suddenly in possession of an entirely new body, but it was gangly and out of my control. And it hurt! Adding all those inches in such a short period of time made my bones ache. And suddenly I was looking down at everyone. I felt awkward, even embarrassed about this at first. I later came to love my height and see it as a gift. I love being tall. That's probably why I wear high heels. Also because I love the shoes. I am not going to let my height prevent me from wearing exactly what I want to wear. If you have a problem with a woman who towers over you, it's your problem—not mine. But it was not easy at first. I had a new body and had yet to figure out how to control it. I was uncoordinated, not in command of my own limbs. I could still practice with intensity, but in matches, my body would betray me, go haywire. And this was at a time when I'd started to get wild cards into the big professional tournaments. Because IMG sponsored certain tournaments, they had wild cards to give to clients. With a wild card, I could skip the qualifying rounds and jump directly to the main draw. So, bang! I was on the big, big stage, but I felt so disoriented in my body. I'd have a goal and know exactly what I had to do, but I just couldn't execute. It was as if my hands and legs, my arms and feet, were not connected to my brain.

The inevitable result was a string of embarrassing defeats, my first real losing streak. I lost, and lost everywhere. I lost in front of small crowds and big crowds. I lost in the daytime and I lost at night. I lost on hard courts and clay. I'd feel fine in practice and then go out for the match and everything would fall apart. I remember losing so many matches in a row, one after another after another. I remember walking through the halls of stadiums, hotel corridors, crying. I remember the way the other girls looked at me—less with respect than with pity, with joy disguised as compassion, looking down on someone they had once feared. I remember thinking, "What's happening?" My parents were aware of it, too. I had done so well up to this point, risen through each age group ranking, into the final rounds nearly every time. Now this! What a struggle. They tried to help me, but there is only so much another person can do. In the end, it's something you have to figure out yourself. Many promising careers have ended this way. You probably don't know their names, or their sad stories. You worry that your name will be added to that list. It was a nightmare, full of uncertainty, but, looking back, I can see that it was ultimately advantageous. Anyone can be composed and cool while winning, when everything is going according to plan. But how do you deal with a losing streak? That's the big question—that's what separates the professionals from the cautionary tales.

There really is so much more to learn from losing than from winning—about the game and about yourself. Do you get up when you've been knocked down? Do you have it in you to press ahead when your work suddenly seems pointless, when you are playing the game just for the game itself, when you worry that you are letting everyone down? Do you get up one more time than you've been knocked down? Or do you quit? That's the toughness that Yudkin had been talking about all those years before. No one really knows how they will react to disaster until the disaster is on top of them.

I never lost confidence, not entirely. I guess I was too young to fully understand confidence as a concept, to know it was a thing to be had—I just had it. There was never a match I entered not believing that I would win. Even when I lost, and I lost many times, I still believed I was moving ahead, on the path, following the plan. Just keep hitting—that's what I told myself. Flat, deep strokes, quick feet before every shot, game after game. Eventually, something will break.

I don't know exactly how long it went on like this—I could probably look it up and count the losses, but who'd want to do that, even in the spirit of being complete? It's enough to say it felt like forever. It seemed like nothing would ever change. And then, one day, it did. My brain finally began to understand my body. It didn't happen during a victory, and it didn't happen all at once. It happened during a loss. To a spectator, it would have looked like just another failure, but something important had changed. It was the kind of subtle shift you'd have to really know tennis to notice.

Robert Lansdorp can name the match, or thinks he can. We'd been working together all along. If he was worried about my losing streak—he later told me that he was—he did not say so at the time. He didn't back off either, or let me resort to the topspin that could probably have made my life a lot easier. He was like a guy whose car has overheated halfway across America: we're closer to the Pacific than to the Atlantic, so let's just keep on keeping on till we get there. "You were fourteen years old and struggling," he told me. "Your father was worried and IMG was worried and everyone was thinking, and then you got into this big tournament at this crucial moment and I just wanted to fly out there and see for myself. Was it really as bad as they all said? It was in Sarasota, your first professional event with prize money. I flew out on my own dime, which, if you know me, tells you something."

I remembered the exact tournament Robert was talking about. It was probably my first as a pro. I actually had a chance to win some money! That might seem like a big shift, but you hardly notice it when it happens. It's still the same courts and the same players and the same everything. Robert and I sat down before the match, but he did not want to talk about tennis at all. He talked about music instead, iPods, and the beach. He asked, "What do you want for your birthday?" He said it was important, now and then, to stop caring. Then he gave me a guitar. I still have it, a beautiful little acoustic guitar that I never did learn to play. And a gift certificate for lessons. He said, "That way, instead of getting yourself all wound up about a match, you can just pick up the guitar and play."

"You were playing an older girl, much older, bigger and stronger and seasoned and all of that," Robert told me. "This was on clay. I watched each point very carefully. Nowadays, someone watching those games would tell you that you played dumb, because you hit every ball just as hard as you could, low and flat, exactly like I taught you. There's a lower margin of error with all that topspin. I call it Academy Ball. It's all about the averages. 'Cause anytime you go to an academy, I don't care whose academy it is, when you hit the ball hard and low or make an error, they'll tell you to hit it high over the net with a lot of topspin, especially on clay. But you'd have none of it—you kept hitting those blazing low-margin, high-reward shots. It took guts and the kind of stubbornness that's all-important. It took the very best kind of stupidity."

I was in a funk after the match—I'd lost in three sets—but Robert was smiling when he came into the clubhouse.

He said, "Maria, if you keep playing like that, you have nothing to worry about."

I said, "What are you talking about? I lost."

He said, "You lost only because you made a few too many errors, you were slow getting up to a few balls."

"You had no fear, even at fourteen, when you were playing your first match on the professional tour, at night, on a bad clay court, and things weren't going well," he said not long ago. "You were not choking, you were not getting nervous. That loss told me more than any victory could have. Because you did not back off or give in. You did not say, 'Oh, let me hit some high balls with top-spin.' You just kept going for it and going for it. That's when I knew that Yuri was right. You were going to be the number one player in the world."

* * *

Of course, there's the spirit, then there's the body. Which is just another way of saying: yes, my attitude was important in the turn-around, but not as important as my serve. To that point, my serve was the same as it had always been. It was the same serve I'd had since I was eight or nine years old. I didn't know it, but it was about to change. This happened after a Challenger in Pittsburgh. Chal-lengers are second-tier tournaments put on by the ITF, the Inter-national Tennis Federation. If you win enough Challengers—it's all about accumulating points—you can earn a place on the WTA tour, which is the big time.

I had just turned fifteen and things were starting to fall into place. As Robert promised, my ground strokes were becoming a weapon. I'd lost in the final in Pittsburgh, and afterward, I saw a look on my father's face that could not have meant anything good. I was talking to Max when Yuri burst in, almost shouting. "Masha," he said. "You will never serve like that again."

"What are you talking about?" I asked.

"Your serve is weak," said Yuri. "It's fine for a little girl, but you are no longer a little girl. You are growing into a powerful woman and you must serve like one. Your game is not finesse. It's power."

"Why now?" asked Max.

"Because now she is strong enough to have a real serve," said my father.

In the following days, we flew back to Florida and started working on my serve with one of the academy coaches, Peter McGraw, an Australian. We worked at Bollettieri's, as the sun went down and the bugs swarmed, hitting baskets of balls. The fear of their stingers gave an urgency to the sessions. We spent hours and hours adjusting my serve—hitting the ball, then figuring out what I'd done right and what I'd done wrong by watching me on video. We made changes, then changed those changes until the serve that would define the first part of my career finally began to emerge. It was not an entirely new serve, of course. It was a refinement of the serve I'd developed with Yuri years before. But it made use of my new body—height, strength, broad shoulders and arms, flexibility. I'm strangely flexible, especially in my shoulder. This let me reach so far back when winding up to serve that my knuckles occasionally brushed against my spine. I turned into a human slingshot, arm whipping forward. It generated a kinetic energy that sent the ball whistling. I had a second serve that was slower and more certain for when I needed it, but it was that first serve that really enabled me to win. I had transformed a shot that was mediocre, neutral, into a weapon, one that I could rely on when I found myself down in a match. Struck just right, it was devastating. It meant free points. It meant starting each service point from a position of power, dictating what happened from there. It meant my service games were quicker, my matches shorter. To beat me, you had to break my serve, which did not break as easily as it had before. That's when I became dangerous. That's when all those defeats turned into victories. At age fifteen, I began to win, and win consistently. My serve propelled me into a golden era, some of the best years of my career. But I would eventually pay a price for that serve and the tremendous pressure it put on my shoulder.

* * *

My father had been waiting for a new sign—some indication that I was ready to compete in the big tournaments on the big stage of the professional tour. Technically, I was already a pro. I'd played for money. I was ranked and I was known in the world of junior tennis. But I'd yet to play in the top-tier tournaments, the majors covered by the press and followed by the fans. More money, more pressure. You fail there, it's a whole different level of complication and consequence.

The sign came on a trip we made back to Russia. It probably wasn't my first trip back, but it was the first trip I really remember. We visited Moscow and stayed in Sochi. And we traveled. We saw my grandparents, friends, and relatives. It was strange to stand in those little houses and little apartments again. Everything was so much bigger in America. I will always be Russian in my heart and in my soul, yet there is no hiding the fact that I spent many of my key early years in Florida and California, watching American TV and wanting American products. Some part of my identity will always be from the USA. It's the most comfortable culture for me, where I really feel at ease. I understood this only when I went back to Russia. That's the thing about living life on the circuit, training from such an early age—you make a dozen different hotels and apartments and countries your home, which is another way of saying you kind of live nowhere. Everything drifts by. You never let yourself get too deep or have too much fun because you know that the day after tomorrow you'll be gone. Only the tennis rackets remain, always by your side. People think it's a glamorous life. And, in a way, it is—maybe it is. I am not convinced. It can also be confusing and lonely.

I played tennis every day on that trip back to Russia. Yuri made sure of that. We had to stick to the schedule, the regimen. That meant waking up just after dawn, stretching and running, then finding a court. I've always believed that you have to train harder than you play. That's how you win—so that the match, when it comes, comes as a kind of break. And you train, in this world, not for one match or for one tournament or for one season, but for an entire career, which will continue until they make you leave the last court on the final day.

At the time, it was still just me and Yuri, out there each morning, hitting. We went back to Gomel at the end of the trip—the land of radiation. We stayed with my grandparents, walked through the streets of the little town, wandered in the park and forest. Yuri arranged a match for me at the public courts where he'd first started playing. He set me up to play against this big guy who was studying me from the far court, waving a big hand in a big greeting. I don't really remember what he looked like, but he was tall and square-jawed with a five o'clock shadow and thick black hair. I did not know it at the time, but this guy had been the standout on Yuri's old tennis scene, the unbeatable star. Yuri had been defeated by him and had seen him defeat every other good player in the area. I did not know any of this until later, much later, but this man stood as a kind of benchmark for my father, a symbol. He was to be my test. How would I stand up against this old-time hero? "If you can play with him, Masha, you are good," Yuri told me. "If you can take more than five games off him, you are ready for whatever is waiting for you."

I was fifteen years old, or close. This man must have been forty. He had an old-fashioned racket and a big ground stroke that started at his heels and ended in the sky. The court was scuffed and slow and the man grunted as we played, but I grunted louder. He was not a pushover, but he was also not all that my father remembered. I took his best shots and returned them on the rise, hitting the ball just as Robert Lansdorp would have wanted me to—hard and flat and just a whisker above the net. As the games went by, the man became agitated, then annoyed, then angry. He could not believe what was happening. Was he really losing to this kid, this girl?

We played two sets. I won them both. It was close, something like 7–5, 7–6. The angrier this man became, the happier my father got. It was as if that anger were a gauge. Yuri watched the needle climb and smiled. When it touched the red, he was fully satisfied. As we left the courts, in a dank building with weak yellow lights, echoing with the sound of balls, he put his arm over my shoulder as if to say, "Masha, you are ready."

* * *

My life as a professional tennis player really began in the spring of 2001, soon after I had turned fourteen. The first tournaments were small-time: a court on the outskirts of some medium-sized city, a few thousand to the winner. I won several of these and began to move up the ladder, to bigger showcases and larger stages. First were junior national tournaments, then the junior Grand Slams. I was flying commercial airlines all over Europe, as cheaply as possible, flying, as Yuri would say, "in the toilet." We'd also travel by train, in the rear cars, with our cash and passports safely out of reach of any potential thieves. To prepare, I would get to town a couple of days before the tournament. I was almost always playing girls who were older than me, which was really nothing new. At thirteen, I'd reached the final of the Junior Italian Open, where I lost to a seventeen-year-old.

I made my WTA debut as a fourteen-year-old in 2002. This was the Pacific Life Open, now Indian Wells. I beat Brie Rippner in the first round, 5–7, 6–1, 6–2. In the second round, I got to play Monica Seles, which was a big, big moment for me. I was fourteen, and Seles had just turned twenty-eight. She'd been the greatest player in the world. She was also a hero, less for me than for my father, who'd studied her two-handed game for hours and hours on videotape. It was close to ten years beyond the terrible stabbing she had suffered between games in Hamburg, but it was still Monica Seles—one of the best in the game. She'd won nine Grand Slams and spent months and months at number one. I could not keep my eyes off her. It was so strange, being on the same court. It was almost like I had fallen into the television set. I was surprised to find myself on the wrong side of the screen! I was dazzled, too, which might help explain the beating I took, 6–0, 6–2. I won only two games that afternoon. But there were moments when I forgot who she was and who I was and just played. It was a huge match for me because it taught me two important things: one, that I could in fact play with the best of them; and two, that I belonged. It also showed me just how far I still had to go, how much better I still had to become. Seles made it to the semifinals of that tournament, losing just a handful of games along the way. She lost to Martina Hingis in the semis, who then lost to Daniela Hantuchová in the final. There were so many levels, so many people to beat. I don't remember much about that match except the score line and Mary Joe Fernández giving me a hug in the locker room after the match when she saw me crying.

I spent most of 2002 and 2003 as a junior because there were only a limited number of pro tournaments I was allowed to play. I was still too young to play a full WTA schedule. By the end of the season, I was number six in the junior ranks. People were starting to know my name. Coaches would show up at my matches to watch me play and search for weaknesses. They devised strategies to beat me. My big weakness at that time? I was slow and not powerful enough to make up for that lack of speed. I needed to get stronger. I needed to mature.

As I became known, so did Yuri. This is just the way of things on the tennis tour, especially in the juniors. It's the mothers and the fathers you remember, the tennis parents, each of whom seems to stand for their kid. Yuri struck many people as a typical crazy Russian father, hypercontrolling and iron-willed. This was not true, or not entirely true. It was just a caricature that came across in newspaper stories.

Yes, my father did pace on the sidelines. He did whisper in my ear as I came out of the stadium tunnel. He did sit in the stands, giving me signals, which pissed off everyone—coaching is not allowed during games, especially not from the stands. But he *wasn't* coaching from the stands, not at all. He was giving me reminders. I'd get so caught up and focused during matches that I'd forget to drink and eat, and my blood sugar would crash and I'd get dehydrated. By late in the second set, the world would start to reel and my stomach heave. So, during the changeover, when I looked up at the stands to see my father, he might hold up a bottle of water, which meant "Drink," or a banana, which meant "Eat." For the most part, my father was just a classic tennis parent. And, the fact is, you probably need someone like that if you're going to make it to the top. Maybe that's the case with every sport, but it seems especially true of the non-team sports, those games to which you have to dedicate your life when you are still too young to really know anything. It usually takes a strong parent. Who else is going to get out there day after day and make the kid work when the kid only wants to go back to sleep or play video games? No seven-year-old in the world will do that on her own, and no twelve-year-old will stay with it when things go bad, as they always sometimes do, unless someone is right there cheering them along. In other words, you might not like all the antics and the TV time of the tennis parent, but, without those parents, you would not have the Williams sisters or Andre Agassi or me. The tennis parent is the will of the player before the player has formed a will of her own.

✳ ✳ ✳

When I look back, it's the big moments that stand out, the turning points. The rest of it fades into a kind of gray wash—statistics on a scorecard, numbers on a page. For me, the first big marker—it stands like the entry gate to my adult career—was the 2002 Australian Open.

I was playing in the junior tournament. I did not go in with a spotlight on my back. I was very young and skinny and people did not expect much from me on a stage that big. They knew I was good, but considered me more of a prospect than a threat. I still seemed to be about two or three years away. But I knew something that the sportswriters and tennis people did not. I knew that something had happened to me, something had changed. It was a deep-down thing, like the gears had shifted in the dark and I woke up in the morning thinking, "My God, I can beat anyone."

This was my first Grand Slam in the juniors, one of the four major tournaments you must win to be at the very top of the game. (The others are the French Open, Wimbledon, and the U.S. Open.) It was the first time I'd experienced the electric atmosphere of the big time. All those people and all those reporters and all those players, the best in the sport, gathered together for a week of the roughest sort of competition. I loved it. It made me nervous and it made me excited. And happy, because I knew I was exactly where I belonged. My early matches flew by like a dream. It seemed as if I won them all in straight sets, though that can't be true—I can't remember the last time I got through a tournament without a three-set match. But there was a lot of winning, and it left me with a lot of time to explore and soak up the atmosphere. Between matches, I watched the best games of the main draw, the pros. I loved the energy of center court ten minutes before the start of a big contest. Jennifer Capriati, Kim Clijsters, and Monica Seles. But even then, a million years ago, the dominant players—*here they are again!*—were Venus and Serena Williams. The sisters. But even if I watched them play, which I hardly ever did—unless I was on the other side of the net—it was in an abstract way, not all that interested. I looked at their game the way you might look at a tough math problem that somebody else has to solve. I'd yet to realize that all these players, all these problems, were my problems. It was personal. I'd have to solve every one of them if I wanted to get where I needed to go.

I kept winning my matches, that was the main thing. A week went by and just like that, I was in the final. I later learned that, at fourteen years and nine months, I was the youngest player to ever make it to any final in the Australian Open.

* * *

I played Barbora Strýcová in the final. Not only did she beat me, but she was dating my first-ever junior crush, Philipp Petzschner. I didn't like that—at all. Barbora was a tough Czech who'd later climb as high as number nine in the world. She was a whirlwind, coming at me from every part of the court, returning every flat, hard ground stroke with a little dink that grew maddening as she won more and more points. It's amazing. You spend months and years getting yourself into a match, and then, if you don't slow down the world and really grab hold of the moment, it's over before you know it.

I did not win a game in the first set. As I walked back to the baseline after the water break, I heard my father yell to me in Russian: *Do you know what you're losing? You're losing a fifty-thousand-dollar Nike bonus!* It was the first time I had ever heard my father speak about earnings. I managed to fight back and take five games in the second set, but it didn't matter. Or, if it did matter, it was only for my self-respect. But even with this disappointing finish, I knew it had been a great tournament for me. The youngest player to ever reach the final! There was a feeling that I was already so much further along than I was expected to be, that I was years ahead of schedule.

But the highlight of the year—and it's not even close—was Wimbledon. That tournament had always felt special to me, though I'd never actually been there. It stood above and beyond all the others—probably because my father never stopped talking about it. It was the ultimate prize and the ultimate place. It glowed in his imagination. The Australian Open, the U.S. Open, the French Open? Yes, they were all Grand Slams and all mattered, but Wimbledon mattered more. The others were sporting events, money and crowds. Wimbledon was something grander. It was the Queen and her retinue. It was aristocrats. It was the red coats of the royal guard, the lush grounds and epic battles on the green grass. It was history and empire. It was England. If you grew up in a poor Belorussian town, like my father did, if you watched that tournament (if you could watch it at all) on a flickering black-and-white TV set, if your eyes chased Borg and McEnroe all over the screen, then Wimbledon stood out. Yuri had conveyed this specialness to me from the time I was small. Every match mattered, every tournament deserved my full attention and best effort, but Wimbledon was—still is—of another order. It's the soul of the game. It's everything.

This year, 2002, was my first experience of that special place. Was I excited? Of course. It was a story I'd been listening to my entire life; now I got to walk into its pages. My mother came along, which was unusual. Wimbledon itself is a suburb in south-west London. There's a main street and outskirts, ancient trees and shady places, bed-and-breakfasts and a few hotels, but most players rent a house for the two weeks that they will—*hopefully!*—be playing.

We rented a tiny cottage that first year, right in the village. I loved it from the first day. It was all that I had imagined. I'd wake up with the sun streaming into my tiny room, or cover myself with the heavy quilt against the chill of another gray morning. Then I'd head down the stairs, open the door, and there, on the cute little front porch, just waiting for me, was a chilled bottle of fresh milk! What a great break from the usual round of hotels and locker rooms. The village was jammed with boutiques and cafés and bakeries. It was a fantasy of another life, how I might have lived had I been born in a different place, at a different time. One of the restaurants—this little Thai place—kept catching my eye. It was always packed, always had a wait. We never went, but I kept it in mind: if—*when*—I was back in Wimbledon, I was going to try it.

The clubhouse was filled with gossipy players. Reporters waited outside the door. This was a new experience for me. Who cared what I had to say? The lockers were small and the bathrooms were . . . yuck. When I joked about this, one of the other girls told me that the top sixteen seeded players are put in another locker room, a dream place of plush velvet where the porcelain shines. Capitalism! The West! They always give you something practical to play for beyond just the prestige and money. You are not playing only for cash. You are playing for a locker room with private bathtubs! And fresh plump strawberries! And a decent place to hang your jacket!

It was a great tournament for me. I did not lose until I reached the junior final, where I was beaten, in three sets, by another

Russian, Vera Dushevina. But that's not what sticks in my mind. What sticks in my mind is what happened after, as I was changing in front of my dank little locker. I'd tossed my stuff in a bag and was about to head back to the cottage, but just as I was leaving, a tournament official handed me an invitation. It turned out that all those players—men and women, juniors and pros—who make it to the final are invited to the Wimbledon Ball, a big gala right out of a storybook (or so I thought), where the Duke of This and the Lady of That are trailed by retinues and dance with the winners and losers as an orchestra plays a mazurka and the moon swells over England.

The woman who gave me the invitation was just standing there, hovering, watching as I read, and, here's the key thing, *not leaving.*

I looked up at her, smiled, and said, "It sounds nice."

"Will you be attending, madam?"

"I'd like to go," I told her, "but I don't have a dress."

She said, "That will be taken care of," and snapped her fingers, or gave a signal of some sort, and out of nowhere a man appeared with a huge selection of gowns, which he spread out on a table. I chose a long one, covered in beads, and left.

The grounds of Wimbledon were deserted as I headed back to the cottage. Fog crept along the pathways. The tournament was over. Just about all the other players had packed up and left. It's a strange thing that happens when you start to get deep into tournaments. You suddenly find yourself in a lot of empty spaces, empty halls and empty locker rooms. The crowds of players and families and coaches begin to disappear. By the quarterfinals of a tournament, only a handful of survivors remain. The better you do, the smaller the world becomes. I remember having this strange feeling that night as I left. It was déjà vu in reverse. I remember turning around and looking at the buildings in the fog and having a feeling that I'd be there again. And not just as a junior.

Yuri was reading the newspaper when I got in. He did not notice the gown, which I hung up in a hall closet. Without looking up at me, he said, "What do you want to do for dinner? I'm thinking we should try that Indian place."

"Sorry," I told him. "But I've got plans."

"What plans?"

My mother helped me get dressed. We had a special moment looking at each other in a big mirror in that little cottage, laughing and telling jokes. That was easily the best moment of the night. The ball itself was highly disappointing.

There is one thing I do remember, though. Everyone came into the big room together—everyone except the men's and women's singles champions, who made their appearance only after all the others had been seated. They came in one at a time, each making a grand entrance through huge, ornate doors and between the tables as those in the room gasped, then cheered. I was at the juniors' table, which was like the kids' table at a wedding. We were set up right beside the entrance. Just as I started to relax, I heard the clapping, that thunderous applause. Serena Williams had won the championship that year. She did it by beating her sister Venus in the final. She'd already started to separate herself from all the other players, and had begun that crazy run of dominance. She squeezed every bit of glory out of her grand entrance, head held high, shoulders back, beaming. Cheers and cheers and cheers. People started getting to their feet. It was a standing ovation.

The girl next to me, whoever that was—I can't remember—banged me on the shoulder and said, "Get up! Get up! It's Serena Williams!" I wanted to get up, but my body just would not let me. It was as if I were stuck in that chair, staring at Serena through the crowd of people, with a single thought in my head: "I am going to get you."

TEN

In April 2003, I turned sixteen and was finally old enough to play on the pro tour full-time. I was almost as tall as I would get, but I was still filling out. I needed to get stronger, though, and regain my coordination. I'd seen far too many talented players fade in the third set not to know that. Strength equals stamina, and stamina is everything in the tough matches.

My father traveled with me on the tour. Now and then, my mother would join us for one of the big tournaments, but she just could not stand the stress of the events, sitting in the stands, with no control and nothing to do but watch. She would ask me, "How can anyone hit the net when the net is only a few feet tall and you have the whole sky above?" It was the same with Nick Bollettieri and Robert Lansdorp. Otherwise it was just me and my father, as it had been from the beginning, just the two of us making our way from tournament to tournament, city to city, hotel to hotel, from

North America to Asia to Europe and back to North America. It's a slog. It's endless. It's around the world in eighty days. You visit the entire world but see none of it. You live in a bubble on the professional tour. It's always the same faces, the same rivalries, the same feuds. It's always the same day, again and again.

It took me some time to find a rhythm on the tour, which is probably why I struggled so much at the start of that pro year. The season began, as it always does, at the Australian Open, where I did not win a single match. It felt like I didn't even win a game. All I remember is the long plane flight, the hotel, the losing, and the feeling of emptiness that rushes in like a tide in the aftermath of losing. Did we travel all this way just to live through that bleak afternoon? It was the same with the French Open, the next Grand Slam, played early in the summer. I moved into the hotel, spent days on the practice courts, getting ready, going through my routine, only to get out there and lose. I'd like to say that I at least enjoyed Paris, devoured the museums and restaurants, but no, no, I did not. The fact is, no matter the country, when you lose, you always find yourself in the same bad place. I still had a lot to figure out before I could really compete on the pro tour. I was still a kid, just turned sixteen, learning. I mean, what were other girls my age doing? What lessons were they "taking away," as my coaches told me to do?

"You must try to understand why you lost," my father explained. "You must try to figure out what exactly went wrong. Then, once you've figured it out, you must forget all of it. You must remember it, then you must forget." Remember, forget. Remember, forget. That way, when you find yourself in the same situation again, you will take the same stupid chance, only this time it will work. It's what Robert Lansdorp meant by "having guts." It's what Yuri Yudkin meant by "being tough." Do you turtle? Do you fold up like a card table? Do you become a safe player, relying on high-percentage shots, or do you go right back out there and take the same crazy risk all over again? Do you remember? Do you forget? Meanwhile, I was winning enough matches in the smaller tournaments between the Grand Slams to push me up the rankings. Very quickly, I was in the top hundred. By the time we reached Wimbledon that June, I was ranked forty-seventh in the world.

Wimbledon felt like a rebirth. I've always gotten such a jolt from the pomp of that place. It was a great relief to get out of the hotels and into the perfect little town, where you could lead something like a normal life. It's almost like a village in a train set, a toy town, with gingerbread houses and mansard roofs and narrow attic windows with glass so old it's warped but still reflects the sun, the streets, straight and curved, the clop of horses that makes you feel like you are back in the nineteenth century, the awnings over the shops and the light that comes on in the restaurants at nightfall. And the courts! And the grass on those courts! I loved getting off the red clay of Europe and back onto the English grass. The speed of those grass courts, the way the ball glides low along the court, makes all the difference. I spent my earliest years in Sochi on clay. It was not like the red clay of France, not like that fine loam. It was a hard gray clay in Sochi, and it quickly could turn to muck. On a wet day, you'd come off the court dirty with grime. But I was soon playing almost entirely on hard courts in southern Florida, where the game is so quick you might as well be playing on glass. That's my native surface. But grass, especially the grass in Wimbledon as it was fifteen years ago, soon became my favorite.

I got into the tournament as a wild card, a direct entry into the main draw. They're usually given to players on the rise, young stars, former champions, or local favorites. It gives the agency a certain power. They can wait for a client to slowly climb their way into the big time or they can simply reach down, Zeus-like, and deliver them to the grand stage. It was my first time in the main draw. All my memories were from Junior Wimbledon—junior matches in the junior tournament, the kids' table at the ball, chewing ice as Serena made that grand entrance. I played Ashley Harkleroad in the first round. An American, Ashley was ranked thirty-ninth in the world when the tournament began. I'd yet to win a single Grand Slam match at this point. In other words, I was seemingly out of my depth. And yet everything clicked. I lost only three games in that match. I got stronger with each point, and it was all over in less than an hour.

Apparently, I was really screaming when I hit the ball, so much so that, near the end, someone in the stands mocked me, calling out, "Louder." I don't even know I'm doing it. The noise just rises from some place deep inside me, meets the ball, and sends that ball into the world just as much as my forehand or my backhand. Without my realizing it, this was becoming a thing. In the previous tournament in Birmingham, a couple of weeks before the championships, I was facing Nathalie Dechy. It was on a back court with a few plastic chairs lined up for the spectators, one of the earlier rounds. In the middle of the first set, her husband called over the tournament supervisor and complained that I was grunting too loudly. They told him they couldn't do anything about it. Following the match, which I won in straight sets, Dechy's husband came up to my coach. He apologized, saying I really impressed him and that he would never complain about my grunting again.

After the match against Harkleroad, on TV they described me as a "Russian sensation," which is funny, considering this was the first Grand Slam match I'd ever won. They also talked about all the Russian players who'd suddenly "appeared on the scene." Eighteen of us were at Wimbledon that year. I had felt as if I'd been living my own life and making my own decisions, but apparently I had just been part of a wave, propelled by a force even stronger than my father.

I played one of those Russians in the second round, Elena Bovina, a big girl, over six foot two, with a strong two-handed backhand. She'd already won a handful of tournaments that year, but I was riding a kind of crest, building toward the greatest tennis in my life. I beat her in straight sets, again losing just four games all afternoon. A lot of that match I won with my serve, which, on the grass, was turning into a weapon.

The third round—that was the first big test I faced on the pro tour. I was facing off against Jelena Dokic, the number four player in the world. In 1999, she had famously annihilated Martina Hingis, then number one in the world, on this same court, in straight sets, 6–2, 6–0. As far as I know, that was the only time a number one had ever lost to a qualifier at Wimbledon. She was older than me, more mature, and really in her prime in 2003. She was considered a contender in every tournament she entered. She hit every ball as hard as she could, and they went all over the court. It sometimes felt impossible to keep up. And she had a crazed tennis father all her own, the famous Damir Dokic, who kept pushing Jelena to switch nationality: from Serbian to Australian, from Australian back to Serbian. I was supposed to lose, then be happy and satisfied that I'd made it so far. Instead, to my own disbelief, I won, in straight sets, 6–4, 6–4, which made me even happier. That night, we finally tried the Thai place. It was delicious.

I played Svetlana Kuznetsova in the fourth round. It was tense, even before the match began, mostly because this, too, was Russian versus Russian, and who would be the best, who would carry the banner and so on. Svetlana was a few years older than me, and her father had been an Olympic athlete and an Olympic coach, which is not nothing. She had access to the kind of experience that most of us have to acquire through years of heartbreak and defeat. I had come into the tournament as a wild card, but I surprised her. That was turning out to be the theme of the week. I was surprising everyone, especially myself. It was supposed to be a walkover for Kuznetsova, because she was a counterpuncher and would retrieve every powerful shot I would hit, and I had real problems with counterpunchers when I was young. It was supposed to be a walkover but it turned into a dogfight. You might beat me, but it won't be easy. It came down to the third set. She won the match, but it was one of those rare times I was not crushed by the defeat. In fact, I was encouraged, even invigorated. It was one of those strange matches where the loser actually comes away more satisfied than the winner, thinking, "I can win," while the winner is thinking, "I'm not so sure." Kuznetsova was knocked out by Justine Henin in the quarterfinals. Henin then lost to Serena Williams, who once again beat her sister Venus to become Wimbledon champion.

I had made it into the second week of Wimbledon, which was a huge accomplishment for a sixteen-year-old. Much of the frenzy of the first week has died down by the quarterfinals. As players lose and leave, Wimbledon changes, becomes calmer. My memory of leaving the complex for the last time that year is still vivid. It was quiet, the buildings and the courts and the paths were empty. In the daytime, with all the crowds, you really don't get a good look at Wimbledon; all you see is people. But I saw it now, I really saw it.

It must have been 7:00 or 8:00 p.m. I remember turning around and looking back and just taking in the green ivy on the fences and the brick and the lawns and being in awe of how still and beautiful it was. I was just standing there, the seconds going by, and the mood of the place overwhelmed me. I felt its specialness deep in my bones. I didn't compare it with my expectations, because I had no expectations of Wimbledon—nobody had really painted this picture for me. None of my coaches, not my parents. My father had always told me this is the top, this is where you want to be, but he never really managed to explain why. Likely, he couldn't put it into words. But now I understood what he meant.

* * *

I won my first tournament as a professional that September. It was the Japan Open. Betsy Nagelsen had won the tournament in the first year that women competed, 1979. There was a beautiful symmetry in that. In the final I beat Anikó Kapros in a third-set tiebreaker, suitably dramatic for that first big win. I won the last tournament of the year, too—the Bell Challenge in Quebec—and was named WTA Newcomer of the Year. Winning as a pro turned out to be a lot like my father said it would be. You hold up the trophy and the people cheer, but only for a moment. Then you are right back out on some nowhere court, running wind sprints as the mosquitoes swarm.

There's a short off-season in pro tennis, so short that it's almost a joke. For women, it runs roughly from the end of October to the warm-up tournaments that precede the Australian Open in January. When it comes to actual downtime, you are really talking about two months that run from Halloween through Christmas.

The most I've ever taken off during that time is ten days, because as soon as I hit the last ball of the season, I'm already thinking about how I will improve the first ball of the upcoming season. In 2003, I spent those months in Los Angeles, working with Robert Lansdorp almost every day. I needed to build on this previous season, improve every part of my game, if only by small margins. I also needed to get stronger, much stronger. I was now playing against grown women, though in many ways I was still a kid. Skinny arms and skinny legs. I may have been sixteen years old, but I still looked like I was twelve.

Though I'd finally begun to make some money, it was still a bare-bones operation. My parents and I were staying in a cramped two-bedroom apartment on the edge of Torrance, and we tried to spend as little money as possible. Our only luxury was renting a car so I could get to practice and back. Robert still jokes about it. "I went by that apartment—it was in the middle of December—and I thought, 'What a dump!' Christmas was just a few weeks away. The glittering displays were up in the store windows all over L.A., but your family didn't even have a tree! I was feeling very sentimental at the time, and I thought it was a shame that this child would have no Christmas. So I went out with my now ex-wife and we bought a big evergreen tree and ornaments and presents and tinsel and a star and set it all up when you were out somewhere with Yuri. Your mother let us in. She was looking at us like we were crazy. I don't know if you remember any of this, but we made it perfect, so perfect, so that no matter what you did not have, you would at least have a Christmas tree."

I did not have the heart to tell Robert Lansdorp that we had no tree because we're Russian Orthodox. Our Christmas comes in January.

Lansdorp was not big on strategy or traditional coaching. "Don't fill her head with all that nonsense," he'd say to my father. "Just let her hit the goddamn ball!" Lansdorp was all about instinct, letting me go out and play my game. "The hands will know what to do, even when the brain is not sure," he told me. I always responded best to this type of coaching, which is minimalist, the coaching of no coaching. Less is more. Most coaches love to scout out your opponents and devise some complicated strategy, but I'd rather be the player that gets scouted. Let them devise and overthink. I just want to play. So yes, give me a few tips on how to win the match. Tell me to hit it to her backhand, or to make her run, but more than that and I'm thinking when I should be playing. That's one reason I worked so well with Lansdorp. He was all about the hitting. If you asked him what strategy he had in mind for a particular match, he'd say, "My strategy is to hit until you win."

ELEVEN

A year on the professional tour plays out as a series of seasons. You start in Australia in late December or early January with a tournament or two—if you want to watch them in America, you have to wake up in the middle of the night—leading up to that year's first Grand Slam, in Melbourne.

The year 2004 would turn out to be one of the best of my life. Just two years before, at the end of 2002, I'd been ranked number 186 worldwide. By the end of 2003, I was ranked number 32. My progress on the ranking board was going in the right direction, and this year would continue that trajectory.

The season began with a solid performance at the Australian Open, so much better than my previous washout. In the first round, I beat Conchita Martínez Granados (now that's a name!) in straight sets. I'd come in as the twenty-eighth seed, which meant I was not at the top but was high enough to be scouted and gamed. It was the first time I entered a Grand Slam tournament as a seeded player and not just a wild card. Even then, my best quality was my focus, the steel in my stare. You could beat me by moving me forward, or by making me hit an extra ball, but if you looked in my eyes you didn't have a chance. That comes from Yuri. That game face.

The Australian Open is played in a beautiful facility in Melbourne. It's summer there when the tournament begins, heading into fall, and, now and then, because it's after harvesttime in the countryside, you smell the distant fields burning. If the wind is just right, a fine white ash rains from the sky. If you are playing when this happens, it feels miraculous, as if it's snowing in summertime. By the second round, I'd fallen into a routine. I'd arrive at the venue four hours before my match, go out to the courts and warm up, then meet with Yuri and my coach at the time, Eric van Harpen.

I won the second match in straight sets, beating Lindsay Lee-Waters, who was much older than me—ten years, ages in tennis time. It's a strange thing about this game. Everyone is always arriving or going away. She was going away. I was a kid who had won a few big matches, but the really good things were still in front of me. In other words, I was arriving, still at the very beginning of my career.

Before I looked up, I had reached the third round, losing only eleven games in the process. Everything was beginning to click at just the right moment. It was as if all the things that Robert Lansdorp and Nick Bollettieri and Yuri Yudkin and my father had taught me, in all those hours on all those courts, had suddenly been absorbed by my arms and shoulders. I was consistently hitting the ball low and hard and flat, stepping into my returns, placing my serves into the corners. If anything, I came into that third round feeling a little too good. When you arrive in that way, your opponent will often do you the service of taking you down a peg. In this case, it was Anastasia Myskina, another good Russian player. She was a few years older than me, and really was the better player, although she never felt that she was, because she wasn't powerful or explosive or strong, but she read the game and anticipated the next shot effortlessly, almost like she wasn't trying. No matter how hard or deep the ball would come at her, she had the ability to place it back anywhere on the court with depth and precision. I came to the match on a high—with power and intensity, I felt like I could beat anyone. Maybe I was too sure. Maybe I got too comfortable, and I didn't see how Mysinka's steadiness, her ability to send any ball back, could undo me. Winning a tennis match is a bit like receiving religious faith. You can't get there by work alone. You need grace, and you can't ever take it for granted.

Myskina beat me in three sets, 6–4, 1–6, 6–2. I'd run into her just as she was beginning to peak. It would turn out to be her best year on the tour. She went on to win the French Open that spring and would climb as high as number three in the world. But she would slow down after that. In a sense, I was arriving but she was soon to be going away.

Of course, that meant nothing to me when I gave up that last point and made the sad walk for the sad handshake at the sad net. I hate to lose. I imagine every player feels the same way. It never gets easier, and it never gets old. It never feels like anything less than a death. Over the years, I have developed strategies, ways to deal with the sting of defeat. It starts by "learning the lessons." Every loss teaches you something. The quicker you learn from the losses, then forget about the actual losing, the better off you will be. And do it fast! The last thing you want to do, after losing, is to talk about losing. And be sure to tell yourself that it's just tennis, just a game, though you won't believe it. It's hard to be calm in the immediate aftermath of a big loss. It's not just a game in the aftermath. It's everything. On top of all that, it's embarrassing to lose, so embarrassing. Everyone is looking at you and judging you and asking you to explain what went wrong. So you end up sitting in front of your locker, thinking, "What the fuck am I going to have to listen to at the press conference? Should I call my mom now, or later? And what should I wear? (Maybe a hat to cover my teary eyes?) And what words of wisdom will my grandparents have when they call, which they will do in about, oh, three minutes? They're still going to be down about this match when I see them in two weeks. And I'm going to have to call my mom, and she's going to try to calm me down. And it's not going to work. It's going to take me hours and hours to get through this." No. It's not just about tennis. In those moments, it's about everyone and everything. And you can't stop thinking about all the things you will have to say and do. You have to book a flight, because you are done and must move on. You have to pack and pack fast, but you don't want to go back to the hotel, because everyone at the hotel knows you and knows you have lost and their eyes will be filled with pity, which is the worst. And others', happy you lost, will be filled with joy.

Here's a bit from my diary, which I was writing in constantly in those early years:

Over time, I've developed my own treatment. It's something I call retail therapy. When you feel you need to see a psychologist, go out and buy a pair of shoes instead. If they're really great shoes, all your worries will evaporate. Why pay $300 for some BS talk with a psychiatrist when you can pay the same and end up with a great pair of shoes that will be with you every day. People! It's common sense!

Maybe the best lesson I ever got about loss—and how to handle it—came by way of an example. It was a gift, though the giver did not mean to give it to me. Or maybe she did. You never really know. It was at some tournament in who knows where, and Kim Clijsters, a Belgian player whom I'd always liked, lost and lost early. Very early. But she did not seem upset or embarrassed by any of it. Not at all. I bumped into her right outside the locker room. I looked away, then directly into her eyes, because you never really know what to do in such a situation. Now I was the one with those awful pity-filled eyes. Kim was on her way to the press conference—that is, she was heading into the shit. She's known on the tour to be a smiley, happy girl, but she's tough and ferocious on the court, a real physical presence. If there is a player that everyone likes, it's Kim Clijsters. She had that good-girl image on the tour, could not do anything wrong. She was walking into the media room after losing in the first or second round, and she was so relaxed and so calm. *My God, she actually seemed happy!* I think this happened after she'd had a baby, become a mother. Maybe that had something to do with it. Life experiences beyond hitting a tennis ball can do wonders. Perspective! I looked at her and thought, "Now, that's cool." From then on, whenever I lost, I carried that memory with me, that admirable attitude Kim had after her own defeats. She taught me that every time they knock you down, you should jump up smiling, as if to say, "That? Oh, that was nothing."

I went back to Florida after I lost. I had a few weeks to improve before the start of the U.S. hard court tournaments. I spent them working out at the academy, putting in more hours, trying to keep the sharp edge keen for the tournaments. And it was then, after all that time, that I first faced off against Serena Williams. It was like, yes, finally. It felt as if I'd been circling around her for years. I'd been hearing about Venus and Serena Williams from my father since I was six or seven years old. I'd seen them through the knot-hole of the film shack at Bollettieri's when I was twelve. I'd seen Serena, in a gown, from my seat at the junior table at the Wimbledon Ball when I was fourteen. Now I was seeing her the only way and from the only perspective that really matters—from across the net on a tennis court. It was the Miami Open, April 2004. I got out there first, as the lower-ranked players do, stood around and observed. Then Serena came out. Nothing prepares you for the presence she has on court.

A few years ago, my friend Chelsea Handler flew in to watch me play at the London Olympics. She doesn't follow tennis, and much preferred her Pimm's cup to anything that might happen on the courts. But when Serena comes out to play our gold medal match—and she is 100 percent Serena—Chelsea looks her over, turns to my coach, and says, "What's your game plan there?" And that's exactly how I felt when I got onto the court with Serena for the first time. "What's my game plan here?" First of all, her physical presence is much stronger and bigger than you realize watching TV. She has thick arms and thick legs and is so intimidating and strong. And tall, really tall. I looked across the net, and, no way to get around it, she was just there! More there than other

The genuine smile of my father. And the genuine resting bitch
face I developed at a young age.

Five years old, on a hot summer day in Sochi, practicing on a public park
tennis court. What happened to my shorts?

Our first few days in Bradenton, Florida. Already out on some public courts behind a college. My dad looks like a stud!

May 1994. My first visit to the white sands of Bradenton Beach, wearing a bathing suit my mom packed for me in Russia.

Someone handmade this skirt for me, and I must have worn it five days a week until it ripped. My dad didn't know how to sew it back together.

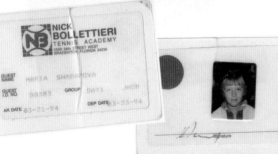

My first ID at the Bollettieri Tennis Academy. My dad had to sign for me, as I didn't have a signature of my own yet.

This was Herald, my boxing coach. I was eight years old, but he didn't treat me like an eight-year-old. I did boxing rounds with him and he would throw a ten-pound medicine ball at my stomach to tighten my core.

With Robert Lansdorp. He's smiling, but he's probably about to make me run side to side until that basket is empty.

First time meeting Mark McCormack with my parents.

Estelle and me, on our favorite trampoline. Partners in crime, forever and ever.

Disbelief. That first Grand Slam
champion moment. At Wimbledon.
Seventeen years old.

(Photograph by Professional Sport, Popperfo
Collection; courtesy of Getty Images)

Arriving at the Wimbledon Ball.
Hair straight, no makeup. I look so
confused, because I am.

(Photograph by Ferdaus Shamim, WireImage
Collection; courtesy of Getty Images)

I was taking my time to get off the
court. I'm guessing they kind of
liked it.

(Photograph by Alastair Grant, AFP
Collection; courtesy of Getty Images)

The first time I beat Justine Henin, and my only U.S. Open championship—
so far. In my favorite Nike Audrey Hepburn–inspired dress.
(Photograph by Caryn Levy, Sports Illustrated Collection; courtesy of Getty Images)

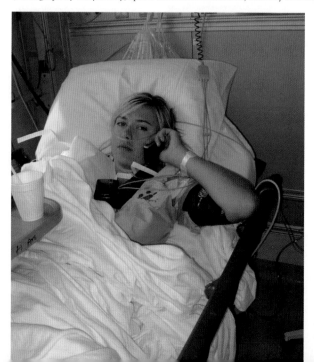

Calling my father
when I woke up from
shoulder surgery. I look
miserable. And felt
even worse because the
journey back had no
guarantees.

Carrying the flag at the London Olympics, 2012. I was the first Russian female to ever do so. I will forever be grateful for this honor.
(Photograph by Christopher Morris, CORBIS Sports Collection; courtesy of Getty Images)

Behind the smile of holding the silver medal in London was the wish to go for gold in Rio. It never happened.
(Photograph by Clive Brunskill, Getty Images Sport Classic Collection; courtesy of Getty Images)

When Grigor and I spoke about which picture of us to use for the book, it was inevitable that this would be our choice. Our first-ever picture together, on our first-ever date.

This smile is why I practice every single day. The trophies are beautiful and rare but the smile is internal.

(Photograph by Matthew Stockman, Getty Images Sport Collection; courtesy of Getty Images)

Leaping into the air after my
first French Open victory.
(Photograph by Art Seitz)

players, if that makes sense. It's the whole thing—her presence, her confidence, her personality. She seemed much older than me in Miami. This was just before I turned seventeen. She was a grown woman, experienced, the best player in the world. It still feels that way. Even now, she can make me feel like a little girl.

As soon as you start playing, you realize it's her confidence you have to deal with. You need to dent it if you are to have any shot at winning. Yes, there is the serve and the ground strokes and the game, but it's also her attitude that defeats you. She looks across the net with something like disdain, as if you are unimportant and small. It's a game face, of course, but it works. I'd met my match in intimidation. Then there is her temper, which can be hot and unpredictable. She is not afraid to scream, throw her racket, bitch at the refs about calls she doesn't like. It's interesting at first, then it gets irritating. Irritating in a way that might be intended—it lets her blow off steam and fills most opponents with rage. She behaves as if she is the only player out there, the only person who counts. And you? You are a speed bump. You are a zero. Many great players have this mentality. Serena Williams just has it more. The best way to deal with people like this—I've learned from experience—is with composure, a maddening composure and a stately calm. It drives them bat-shit crazy.

Serena won that match, but I realized that if I kept working I'd get close to her level. Maybe I also put some doubt in her mind. There were stretches when I felt like I could handle her depth, power, and speed. A spectator new on the scene would have had trouble, on some of those points, telling the champion from the rookie. For me, it was like facing a fear. That's the thing about champions—they rely to some extent on your fear of them.

It's a bubble that protects them. When that is pierced, anything is possible.

* * *

I left for Europe a few days later. I wanted to train and acclimate myself to clay before the European season began. IMG arranged for me to take up a kind of short-term residence at the Juan Carlos Ferrero Academy in Villena, Spain. There were a couple of other pro players, staying in the cabanas and playing on the courts, including the namesake of the academy, a local hero named Juan Carlos Ferrero. In those few weeks, watching Ferrero train, watching him come and go, seeing how he talked and handled himself, how he brushed his hair away from his eyes, I developed a serious crush.

Ferrero—retired now, in his late thirties—was lanky, not too tall, with tousled hair, dark but dyed blond, and warm, mischievous eyes. He'd been playing tennis since he was too young to know if he wanted to play, like the rest of us, but something about him seemed removed, above, calm and cool. He'd won the French Open the previous season, 2003. The picture taken of him after the last point stuck in my head. It was an image of accomplishment, joy, and release. When you win, you finally get to let go of all that tension and stress—that's what it looked like. You finally get to live in the moment instead of in the moment after this moment, when the next shot still has to be returned. I must have seen the picture in the newspaper—on some front page, or tossed behind a seat on some airplane. Ferrero has just won the match. The ball is probably still moving just beyond the frame, rolling lazily toward the vanquished player, Martin Verkerk. Juan Carlos had fallen to his knees and is looking toward the sky, as if to thank whoever up there is in charge of tennis Grand Slams. It stayed with me, that celebration. I always mimic the gestures of the people I admire. I don't mean to. It just happens. Maybe it's a way of saying thanks.

In 2004, Ferrero was twenty-three and I was sixteen. I mean, in most countries, that's not even legal. What can I say? The heart wants what the heart wants. I used to monitor him, watch him come and go. I used to plot and plan. I'd stand at the window of my cabana, behind a closed curtain, peeking out, keeping track of his every move. Here was the big problem. Juan Carlos had a girl-friend! She was probably the nicest girl in the world, but how could I see her as anything other than the reality that undermined my dreams? When they stood together, all cute, I was reminded that I was the silliest thing in the world—a kid with a crush.

Yuri knew none of this. Of course, when I actually got a chance to talk to Ferrero, I was polite and goofy and shy. But he must have known. I later found out that everyone in that Spanish academy in fact did know. I guess I'd been following him around like a lost puppy. I appreciate how he handled himself, the gentle and serious way he treated me, never making me feel anything less than grown-up and important, while also letting me know in his easy way that it could never happen.

There were a number of small tournaments that spring, played to build up our confidence, timing, and endurance. It's all a pre-lude to the French Open, like an overture. You arrive in Paris in May, the best time of year in the city. The grounds of the arena, Roland Garros, are a kind of dream, the intimate stadium of center court, the colorful green banners that encircle the arena contrasting with the red clay, the crowds. I came in as the nineteenth seed. The top spots were occupied by, number one, Justine Henin, and number two, Serena Williams. Henin had won the French Open the previous year. She was one of the best clay court players of all-time, if not the best. It felt like there wasn't a ball she wasn't capable of getting back, especially on clay. She would drive me crazy, the way she kept sending every perfect shot I made back over the net with precision.

Henin did not have height or power, but none of that mattered here. The French Open does not favor power the way the U.S. Open and even Wimbledon do. In Paris, it's all about fitness and finesse. On a dry day, the red clay is hard and cool. The game is fast then, and power can be a factor, but if there is the slightest drizzle or humidity, the clay absorbs the moisture and then everything gets boggy and slow. The surface turns to soup and the points wind down and the clay holds up even the flattest, hardest stroke. Playing in those conditions is a question of persistence and experience. The pros who grew up on this surface feel its rhythm and know when to stop and slide, how to skid into a ball. They excel when it rains or has rained or will rain, which is usually the case at least once in the course of a tournament. The French Open has a way of doing in even great players. Jimmy Connors. John McEnroe. Martina Hingis. Venus Williams. None of them have won the French Open.

I beat Barbara Schwartz in straight sets in the first round, dropping just three games. She was an Austrian who had this one-handed, left-handed backhand that was never fun to play against. Second round? Straight sets again, this time over the Italian Rita Grande. I lost just two games. All the work I had done in the academy in Spain was paying off. I felt stronger on this surface than I'd ever felt before. The third round was a little more difficult. I faced another Russian, Vera Zvonareva, in this round. I might have won that match in straight sets, but something about her game made me uneasy, uncomfortable—as if we might always finish the match deep in the third set. It was straight sets again in the fourth round, this time over the German Marlene Weingärtner, known mostly for her stunning match with Jennifer Capriati at the 2003 Australian Open. She'd been down 6–4, 4–1, and somehow she came back to win. That was her moment.

Just like that, I had reached the quarterfinals—my first time in a Grand Slam—where I'd play Paola Suárez, a smart, tough Argentinian who won on the tour for years and years. Suárez was five foot seven, meaning I towered over her, but, as I said, on clay . . .

Max had turned up in Paris by that time. There was a lot of excitement at IMG. It seemed like maybe, just maybe, this might be my year to make it far in the Grand Slams, to move up in the rankings. I was seventeen and just two matches stood between me and my first Grand Slam final. And all the top seeds—Serena Williams and Amélie Mauresmo, Lindsay Davenport and Venus Williams—had been eliminated. That's clay! For a moment, it seemed like I had a great chance.

Max sat with my father in the hotel bar the night before the match.

Max said, "Tell me the truth, Yuri. Can Maria actually win this match tomorrow?"

Yuri sighed and shrugged. He wanted to lower Max's expectations. My father believes that overly high expectations are just as dangerous as fast living. "If we wake up in the morning," said Yuri, "and there is not a cloud in the sky, then maybe, just maybe, we have a chance."

Suárez was much more experienced than me. When it rains, the clay becomes slower, so you need more strength to really make the ball fly. I needed the clay to play as fast as possible—that was my only chance. So the next morning, game day, I woke up at 5:00 to pee and on my way back to bed I pushed open the curtain for a peek, and what do you think was going on out there? It was like a hurricane, the sky steel-wool gray and the rain lashing down sideways. I lost in straight sets, 6–1, 6–3. I was dejected but not crushed. It helps to have an excuse. In this case, it was the weather. Not me—it was the sky! There's an upside to losing in the quarterfinals. It means at least you don't have to stick around; it means you don't have to put off the healing balm of retail therapy.

After a trip up and down the boulevards with my quarterfinals prize money in my pocket, we headed to England. That's the thing about the tour—no matter how bad you feel, there is always another tournament, another chance to fix yourself, another shot at redemption. You close the page, you open the page. You empty your mind, you fill your mind. We went straight to Birmingham, an industrial city in the Midlands. The Birmingham tournament was a tune-up for Wimbledon. It always felt so good to get off the clay and onto the grass. It was a relief to have that pace back. I remember, at my first practice in Birmingham, taking a slow jog around the courts, just delaying the moment when I finally went out onto the grass, which was soft and so green. I remember just standing there, breathing it all in. Back on grass, back on grass. God, it felt good, so much better than that fucking clay. It was not like that monsoon in Paris, where it felt like my feet were glued to the ground.

I cruised through the Birmingham Classic, won the whole thing in what felt like two games. This is when it started to happen for me. I hung out with another tennis player between matches—back at the hotel or in the city. She was the closest thing I had to a friend on the tour, a Russian girl named Maria Kirilenko. She was my age and grew up in a slightly friendlier version of the world I'd come from. We'd hang out when we could—go to dinner after the matches, shop together, talk. It was with her, back in our junior days—under her bad influence, ha-ha!—that I stole the only thing I've ever stolen in my life. Shoplifting, on a dare. It was peer pressure! "You want it? Take it! Don't be a chicken, Maria! Are you really that scared? Come on!" It was a small round jar of Nivea Body Lotion. I slipped it into my coat and brought it back to the hotel but never could bring myself to use it. It stood with my toothbrush and lip balm in a kind of rebuke. It made me feel ashamed. I threw it away two days later.

I watched the final of the French Open with Kirilenko that year—on the TV in her hotel room in Birmingham. We had both been playing well, so it was as if we were scouting, comparing. It was an all-Russian final in Paris. Anastasia Myskina against Elena Dementieva. Myskina won easily—straight sets—but I did not care about any of that, not really. I cared only that one of these girls would become the first Russian woman to win a Grand Slam. I didn't like the sound of that or how it made me feel. I wanted it to be me.

* * *

We got to Wimbledon at the beginning of June, a week before the first games of the 2004 tournament. The idea is to become acclimated, convince your body that you are a local, that there is nothing special about this place and these games, that it's all part of your routine. Of course, there was no denying the specialness of that town, and how good I felt whenever I was there. The main street lined with boutiques and cafés, the pastry shops and afternoon teas, the crowds, the wide tree-shaded roads at the start of summer. Once again, it was perfect.

We had been booked into a house outside the village, but it did not feel right. The mood of the place was off, the feng shui or whatever. It just felt wrong. I called Max and complained. When you start to win, these are the kinds of calls you get to make. I said, "Please, Max, find us a new place." And he did, quickly booking us into a kind of bed-and-breakfast a half mile from the practice courts. It was a huge old house, all dormers and over-hangs. There was a big beautiful lawn and big windows in big rooms and a big front porch. I just loved it. That house was abso-lutely part of my success at Wimbledon, part of the recipe. It put me in the right frame of mind. We had the entire third floor to our-selves. It was owned by a nice couple with three kids—the youn-gest was two. Having a two-year-old around when you play a big match is great because the two-year-old is interested but does not really care, and that not caring, that happy not caring, reminds you that, in the end, all of this is nothing. There are champions now; in ten years, there will be different champions. It's fleeting, so have fun—that's what you get from a two-year-old. It's a mind-set that gets you playing loose and easy. When you go out there caring, but not caring too much, you become truly dangerous, even if you are only seventeen.

I quickly fell into a routine. Each morning, I had breakfast with my father upstairs on the third floor. Oatmeal. Or maybe just a boiled egg and some strawberries. My father would talk to me about my serve or my return, or who I might play, or where my head should be, or what I needed to do. One of the kids had the great habit of undoing all this strategy by asking silly kid ques-tions, like what's the difference between skinny milk and skinny people? Or, will it rain, and what will that mean for the mud pie situation?

After breakfast, I'd sit on the front porch, watching the entire world go by, thinking or not thinking, then grab my gear and head to the Aorangi practice courts, which were part of the Wimbledon facility. Sometimes my coach met me and we walked together. At this point, I was known in the world of tennis but nowhere else. I was not a celebrity (horrible word), meaning I could go where I wanted when I wanted, without fuss or hassle.

I would stretch on the courts, run a few laps, then start hitting. I worked on each phase of my game at practice, one at a time. Forehands, backhands, first serve, second serve, spending extra time on whatever might need special attention, as some part of my game always does. It's like building a sand castle. As soon as this part seems solid, that part starts to crumble. I usually end up by simulating specific scenarios—down a break, second set, second serve; deuce, first set, you must break her serve, and so on. I'd finish my practice with out-of-the-basket drills, just like I did with Robert. I usually had my coach feed me balls one after another, ten minutes of nothing but hitting, hitting, and hitting, so I could close out on a groove. That's still how I do it to this day.

One day, on my way to practice, I stepped on something. I did not know what it was, only that there was a strange squish, then an extra something on my shoe that felt wrong. When I got to the clubhouse, I noticed the smell, this terrible, terrible smell. A bowels-of-hell kind of smell. I looked accusingly at the other players in the room before coming to a terrible realization . . . I bent my leg and looked at the bottom of my shoe. The treads were packed with what I assumed to be the richest, blackest, most pungent dog shit the world has ever known. I cursed under my breath. So that's clearly what we were dealing with, I thought, the most powerful animal contaminant: corgi shit.

There's a kind of locker-room attendant at Wimbledon. She sits in the locker room, ready to help you with your stuff. She'll wash or stitch your clothes, whatever. I felt bad doing it, but brought her my shoes anyway. "I stepped in dog shit and I'm not really sure what to do," I told her. "I need this pair. Do you have a hose or something?"

"No problem," she said. "It's Wimbledon. It happens with great frequency."

I went to my locker and started to change for practice, digging around for a spare pair of sneakers. As I stepped out of the locker room, this old guy came up to me, a maintenance attendant. He was missing a few teeth, prominent ones, but was smiling anyway. He spoke in some sort of brogue. He said, "Hey there, Maria. I heard you stepped in it out on the lawns."

"Yes," I said groaning. "I stepped in dog shit."

"That isn't dog shit," he said. "I gave it a good look-over. It's fox shit!"

"Oh my God!" I said. "That's awful."

"No," he said, laughing. "The opposite. It's wonderful! Stepping in fox shit is the best kind of good luck. The best! It probably means you're going to win the whole thing."

That was the first hint I had that this Wimbledon was going to be different.

The week leading up to the first match was long and easy. You want to go into the big tournaments with a calm mind, and the hours of doing nothing, or reading, or just hanging around with your working family, are a big part of that. In other words, as hard as I practice, I have learned that doing nothing is just as important as doing everything.

We ate at that same Thai place almost every night. It's where we'd gone the night after I upset Jelena Dokic the previous year, so it became more good luck for us. There is no one more superstitious than an athlete on a winning streak. It got so we did not even have to look at the menu. We could order by number. For me, it was always 8 and 47—spring rolls and sizzling beef with onions. And a side of 87, fried rice.

I spent almost every moment of that week with my team—my father, my trainer Mark Wellington, and my coach Mauricio Hadad. It was Maria and the men! We got so loose and easy, we began playing games and making bets, the sort you make when you know your side has no realistic chance of winning. There was, for example, what I call the bald bet. We were walking to the practice courts one day and out of nowhere I said, "OK, we have to make a deal. If I win, you guys have to shave your heads." At first, they were like, "No way!" Then my trainer said, "OK, but if you don't win—" I interrupted him before he could even get going. I said, "No, that's not fair. You know I'm not going to win." Then we continued on in silence, thinking. Finally, my coach said, "You know what, Maria? If you win this tournament, if you win Wimbledon, we'll shave everything, even our you-know-what." Everyone agreed. Then they forgot all about it. But I didn't.

I was seventeen years old. I'd grown up in tennis, become an adult on the professional tour. I was at the start of my life, but I felt like I was a hundred years old—so much had happened to me already, there'd already been so many adventures, crises, ups and downs, reversals of fortune. I had already played so much tennis, hit so many balls, been to so many towns and cities. It's why a tennis player at twenty-nine can seem like the oldest person in the world. She's been through an entire life span already, from youth to middle age to "get off the court, you're too damn old." A pro athlete really dies twice. At the end, like everyone else, but also at somewhere closer to the beginning, when she loses the only life she's ever known.

Of course, in other ways, I was a typical teenager. I was a girl becoming a woman, prepared for none of it. That year at Wimbledon was the first time I realized I might be pretty. It was nothing anyone said to me, or anything I noticed about myself. It was the new looks that I was getting from the men on the tour, even those men who seemed crazy old.

I wrote about this moment a few years later in my diary, which I quote here without comment:

So all of a sudden I have all these 25-year-old men looking at me and it makes me feel deaf and blind. I couldn't tell what they were looking at. At this point I had to start hiding my blond hair and hiding my long legs. Let me tell you something—it doesn't help! Nothing helps and there's no way out of it. The best part is when they point a finger and yell "There's Sharapova" and the whole village freezes. I might be exaggerating but it's how I felt. I guess they're just too excited to hide it, but please, I was only 17.

Before I knew it, the week was over and I was in the locker room getting ready for my first match. The sky was blue in the morning, but now the wind picked up and it started to rain. That's always a danger at Wimbledon. If Serena Williams doesn't get you, the weather will. I settled in for a long delay. I wasn't scheduled to play till after the men's match and there was no telling how long that would go. Since they play three out of five, you know you're in for a long wait. And of course these guys went into a fifth set, which everyone knew they would—because neither one of them had any consistency. Why even bother playing the first, when you know you're going into a fifth? I was bummed initially, but it turned out to be a good thing because it was during the delay that I found one of my favorite places on the Wimbledon grounds, the Wimbledon's members' locker room. Yes, a locker room that I actually liked!

After warming up and getting a snack, I went to the regular locker room to wait because the players' lounge was a zoo: parents, agents, reporters, and lots of others with questionable credentials. There were only two couches in there, so I took a seat and did nothing for an hour. Maria Kirilenko was waiting for her match, so we chatted and did the Russian crossword puzzles she'd brought. We had about three cups of strawberries in the meantime, without cream. Cream is too heavy before a match. Time went slowly, so slowly. Finally, we got bored and went back to the players' lounge to see what was going on. We found a bench and just sat there, watching the world go by. Lindsay Davenport sat next to us and started talking.

Lindsay is a tall American girl, a top player, with some of the most powerful strokes in the game. I admired the way she played. She had worked with Robert Lansdorp before me. It was, in fact, because my father so admired her game and spotted certain similarities to my own that he first sought out Lansdorp. It gave us a kind of connection. Lindsay spoke to me in a confidential, almost conspiratorial way. After putting in the obligatory time talking about "this crazy English weather," she leaned close and asked, as if I had a secret strategy of my own, "Why aren't you in the members-only locker room?"

"Wait! The what?"

"There's a locker room for the top sixteen seeds," said Lindsay. I had come in ranked thirteen. Lindsay was five. Venus was three. Serena was one. "Didn't you know that?" said Lindsay. "You really should go have a look."

My Russian friend was not ranked above thirty-two. And so I said goodbye, leaving her to her strawberries and crossword puzzles. This is where we must part, I thought, perhaps for only a time, perhaps forever. Then I went up to the members' locker room. And *up* is the word, because it was as if I'd gone up to paradise. I mean, this locker room, the members' locker room at Wimbledon, is the absolute ultimate. When you walked in, you were in a little hallway with paintings from the '80s. To the right was a cozy lounge with two big comfortable couches, and straight ahead was the most beautiful locker room in the world. There were only something like eight lockers in there, but they were the best, like little cabanas you have all to yourself. They have large white wooden French doors and no locks because you don't need locks— it's basically your own private locker room. I maintained my composure, but my insides were screaming with joy.

I was still smiling from this discovery when I finally got onto the court for my first match, which I blew through, defeating the Ukrainian Yuliya Beygelzimer in straight sets. But for me, the real highlight came after the match, after I left the locker room. I was going down a back hall or up a staircase. I don't remember exactly, but the sense I had was of going up—which is why, in my mind, it's a staircase—running into someone coming down, someone who, as we talked, was standing a few feet above me. It was Juan Carlos Ferrero. He'd won his early match and had that cool, pleasant, end-of-the-day-and-nothing-to-do glow about him. He'd just come from his press conference, which, as I've explained, is shit no matter if you win or lose. I was now seventeen and he was now twenty-four and all the other feelings were still there. My tremendous crush on him—in a way, it was not even about Juan Carlos Ferrero but about being in love with love—made everything he said seem funny or important. He smiled at me. "Maria, Maria," he said, "it's so funny to see you here, to see you now. I was just inside with the reporters and they asked me who I thought would win on the women's side and I told them no doubt it would be Maria Sharapova. I put my reputation on the line for you, Maria," he added, laughing, "so don't let me down, or make me look like an idiot."

It was magic to hear Juan Carlos say my name, especially in that Spanish accent of his. It's silly, but I kind of hung on to that memory for the rest of the tournament. It gave me a little extra confidence and motivation. I was not just winning. I was proving that Juan Carlos Ferrero had been right to believe in me.

I played Anne Keothavong in the second round. She was a local player, a hometown favorite, one of the best in Great Britain, but everything was starting to work for me. When I look at films from that tournament, I am always surprised by a few things. First, by how young I am. No longer a kid, but still in the process of becoming an adult, not yet who I am today, sort of half formed, in between. And two, the look on my face, like the person I am playing, whoever that happens to be, has done me personal wrong and now it's payback time. My brow is furrowed and my eyes are hooded. A lock of hair swings across my face. I hear nothing. That's the way you gear yourself up: convince yourself that there's been an injustice and it's your mission to avenge it. In other words, Anne Keothavong did not have a chance in that match that year. Straight sets, 6–4, 6–0.

Now, here's a funny thing. I went on to win Wimbledon that year, and there were many great matches and big moments for me along the way, but I did not play my best tennis in the finals or in the semi- or quarterfinals, though each of those is a highlight of my career. My best tennis was played in the third round, during my first match ever on Centre Court, in front of a small crowd, against Daniela Hantuchová, a Slovakian who, at one point, had been ranked in the top ten. Hantuchová had won the Masters in Indian Wells and had made it as far as the semis at Wimbledon. She was a very good player on grass. This is when you play your best tennis. A good player can push you to make shots that you never believed yourself capable of making.

How's this for motivation? When we met for the coin toss, I realized: *Shit! We're wearing the same dress!* To my horror, Hantuchová and I were wearing the same Nike dress. It was not her fault, but I absolutely hated it, and I'd make sure it never happened again. How? When it came time to sign a new contract with Nike, they included a clause that said I will have an exclusive outfit at every tournament I play—no other girls can wear it, not if they're sponsored by Nike. But the irritation I felt that night added a nice, useful edge to my game.

The points I played against Hantuchová that day, the endless rallies—I still feel them, the pressure of the ball on my strings, the crosscourt winners that barely caught the line. It had been a long trip to this point. I had started off in Spain, played tournaments in Germany and Italy, gotten further than I'd ever gotten at the French, won in Birmingham. I'd put in the time in practice and in matches and now everything was clicking. It felt like the most perfect tennis of my life, by which I mean I made very few errors and executed every shot, the ball landing exactly where I wanted it to land. And it was not just the points or the serves that rang true. It was my state of mind, the intensity of my focus. I'd hit a groove. Remember, focus is not merely about zooming in, it's also about shutting out, eliminating the rest of the world—eliminating and eliminating until there is just this court and this girl standing on the other side of it, waiting to be moved from here to there like a puppet on a string. At such moments, and they come rarely, and you pray for them, you are so sharp, you are dumb. There is nothing but this and this means nothing but this. I won in straight sets—6–3, 6–1—but those numbers don't really capture the great thrill of that match.

I played Amy Frazier in the fourth round—straight sets again, not much more to say. But as soon as the last point was over, my world began to change. I had never gotten this far—the quarterfinals!—on a stage this big: Wimbledon! It was as if, all at once, the entire world, or what felt like the entire world, swung around to take a good look at me. It was as if I were a blank spot that needed to be quickly filled in or explained, a character who wanders into a movie at the start of the third act and you can almost hear the producer calling for a rewrite, shouting, "Who is this? Give us some goddamn background!"

This is when my story started to be told. Of me and my father, Yudkin and the court in Sochi, Martina Navratilova at the clinic in Moscow, the years of struggle—on television, one of the announcers said my father had waited tables to keep me supplied with balls and rackets!—Bollettieri and Lansdorp. It was all written up in the newspapers, told in quiet tones on television as I played. "She's got quite a story . . ." There's nothing like hearing the story of your own life as told by John McEnroe. I recommend it to everyone. Of course, that was a danger, too. That all of this attention would mess up my head, break the spell, destroy that trance of deep focus, and, like a bubble popping in a bathtub of bubbles, this dream would end. I remember sitting with my coach in the dining hall at Wimbledon. Normally, we sat quietly, undisturbed—undisturbed because who would want to disturb us?—eating and talking tennis. Suddenly, it was as if every eye was on us—or was I just imagining that? People kept coming over to congratulate me, and ask how I felt, and give me advice. A group of tennis nuts—I don't know how they got in, but they were from Japan—asked if they could take my picture. When they left, I could see my coach, sort of smoldering. He gripped my wrist. Looking into my eyes, he said, "I understand there is a lot going on, and that a lot of this is new, but you need to do me a favor. For the next five days, you need to put on the horse blinders and look only at the road ahead."

The quarterfinals rose before me like a palisade. Centre Court, television coverage all over the world, the true big time. Of all the hundreds and thousands of tennis players in the world, only eight remained. Among them, my name stood out. It's like they ask on *Sesame Street*: Which one of these things does not belong? The other girls were champions and future Hall of Famers—Serena Williams and Lindsay Davenport. And . . . who? I mean, yes, yes, I was confident and knew exactly who I was and what I could do, but no one else did.

I played Ai Sugiyama in the quarterfinals, a gritty player who could get every ball back, no matter the speed. Playing against her is like playing ping-pong tennis. She stays low for every shot—a huge advantage on grass. And she can stay out there for hours. This match really did me in, wiped me out. I began to tire. Sugiyama was like me in a way—she refused to quit, even when she was beaten. That is, until she actually did quit.

I lost the first set but it was a close thing and I was determined to get back into it. I've seen pictures of my face during the changeover between the first and second. I look bewildered, confused. In a really tough match, there is usually a single moment when everything hangs in the balance—you either redouble and refocus and carry on, or you unravel. Either you break, or she does. When you both refuse to give in, that's when you get the epic matches.

I won the second set 7–5. What made the difference was my serve. I seemed to come up with an ace whenever I was really against it. What's more, even if I did not hit an ace, my first serve was strong enough to set Sugiyama up for a point that did not end in her favor.

Sugiyama almost broke my serve in the first game of the third set. That was her moment, but she let it get away. I hung on, turned around, and broke her serve instead. A three-game swing. That was the match right there. Instead of it being 4–1 Sugiyama in the third, it was 4–1 Sharapova. There was a point at the end of the fifth game when I could feel her buckle and give. She'd been broken, not in her serve but in her spirit. It was all mop up and close out from there. This was, in fact, the first time I felt like I was the fresher player at the end of the third set.

The last point?

I was wearing a white halter-top dress, a gold cross necklace that my parents had given me when I was a little girl, silver earrings a friend had given me for my seventeenth birthday, barrettes in my hair, short white socks, and white shoes. I swayed back and forth as I waited to serve. I walk around a lot between points. It stills my nerves and plugs me into a kind of inner rhythm. I served for the match at 40–0. I pushed Sugiyama back with that serve, grunting loudly as I hit the ball. She got the ball back over, but right into the strength of my backhand. I blazed a return, screaming as my follow-through carried my racket toward the sky. I hit it deep to her backhand. Her return sailed wide, and that was it: 5–7, 7–5, 6–1. I raised my arms, turned my face to the sky, and screamed something like, "Thank God!" I could see my box, where my team was celebrating. My father had his fists in the air, just like me. So that's where I got it from!

Unbelievable. I was in the semifinals of Wimbledon.

* * *

As a rule, the task gets tougher as you get closer to the prize. Each round means higher stakes and more pressure and slimmer odds and fiercer competition.

It was my father who told me that I'd be playing Lindsay Davenport in the semifinals. I don't remember exactly what I thought when I heard this news, but it must have been something like "Fuck." I was a kid. Lindsay was a woman. I was weak. Lindsay was strong. I was stringy and narrow. Lindsay was powerful and solid. As I said, in many ways our games were alike. We went by power, played from the baseline, hit flat and low, without much spin, a style that both of us learned from Robert Lansdorp. She was twenty-eight years old, so far along there was talk of her retirement. She was not number one just then—that was Serena—but had been number one, off and on, for ninety-eight weeks. She was one of the greatest tennis players in the world. In other words, I'd hung on and hung on till I'd advanced myself right out of my league. I mean, how was I supposed to beat Lindsay Davenport? She was just like me, only bigger, stronger, older, and more experienced. She was just like me, only way more.

What's that thing they talk about in school? The pathetic fallacy? When your internal mood is mirrored by the weather? The sky was overcast the morning of the match. Thunderheads were streaming in from the continent. Dark and gloomy everywhere. It rained off and on as I headed to the courts. I went through my regular routine—stretched and ran, then hit for about forty minutes on one of the practice courts—but my heart was in my mouth the entire time. This was the biggest test of my life, what my father and I had been working toward all these years.

Then, a moment later, I was on Centre Court, waiting for the first game to begin. The scene, the pomp and the show of it, dazzled me. I'm a master of high focus, but this was simply too much. For starters, there was the mystique of Centre Court. Every detail of it was like a revelation. The feel of the grass—it's like nothing in the world. How it's kept up and cared for but also left to run down ever so slightly. Parched at the edges, faded green and going brown, dilapidated in the way only rich people allow things to dilapidate. A tweed coat frayed at the cuffs: it does not say you're poor; it says you're sophisticated, evolved beyond green, green grass and other vain perfections. And the way that grass played, the trueness of the bounce and speed—there's nothing in the world to match it.

And the people in the seats, the regular Wimbledon tennis crowd, who, on that day, struck me as the most knowledgeable fans in the world, a swarm of analysts who would x-ray through my skin and see I was a kid and did not belong here. And the Royal Box, where the Queen sat with the aristocrats and retainers. And the celebrities, the legends of tennis past; now I'm thinking of Billie Jean King, who was up there, watching me with eyes that had seen everything in this game. It calmed me down a bit when I looked at my box—each player gets a group of seats for her entourage—where my father sat with my trainer, my manager, and my coach. But it was not enough. Before I realized what was happening, I was through my warm-ups and serving to begin the match. My body felt tight. I was moving so slowly. My arm went up and my racket met the ball and my serve fluttered across the net like a butterfly.

I'd never played Lindsay Davenport before. I'd heard about her power, but there is hearing and seeing at a distance, and then there is being right in the firing line. It's the difference between reading about a person stuck in the cold and actually being trapped in a snowstorm. Lindsay returned my serve like it was nothing, blazed it right past me. I barely had time to react. I went across the court to the ad box and got ready, bouncing the ball before starting into my next serve. There was that butterfly again. A moment later, the ball was behind me and I was down 0–30 in the first game. Something inside me shivered. Something inside me cracked. Something inside me said, "You can't possibly win."

Then, and this proves that even the best moments depend on luck, the dark clouds rolled in and it began to rain. The umpire threw up his arm and we ran off the court and stood beneath an overhang. But it was a short reprieve, as the rain quickly gave way to sunshine and I was back out there getting pummeled as if the first pummeling had never stopped. Davenport broke my serve in the first game—I got one point!—and it was downhill from there.

I was overpowered, overmatched. She was a woman. I was a girl. She was big. I was small. She hit the corners. I hit the net. In that dazzling run of awful games, it seemed as if she did not miss a shot.

What the hell was going on?

I think some of it had to do with fatigue. I'd played so much tennis in the past few months, so many games and points and break points. So many great players. So many marathon rallies. I was seventeen years old and wiped out. Tired. Sore. Aching everywhere. I found out about the existence of certain muscles only because those muscles screamed, "Out of gas, out of gas, out of gas!" At the moment, I did not think I could win. If you think you can't, you can't.

Davenport broke me again, and took the first set before I could figure out what happened. She broke me early in the second set and was on the verge of breaking me again, but somehow I hung on. That was my situation, my desperate situation—down a set and a break in the second set of the semifinal—when the skies opened and the rain really came down. They called for a delay, and it looked to be substantial. I mean, it was pouring. I was such a novice, so new to all this, that I did not even know the protocol. When it rains like that, you have to get your ass off the court, because the ground crew is waiting with the tarp and they need to cover up fast so the grounds aren't swamped. But I was just taking my time—in my mind, this thing was already over—walking to my bag, slowly putting my stuff away, humming to myself, oblivious. When I looked up, there were like twenty men, holding a tarp, glaring at me. There's a picture of this somewhere. They're all looking at me and I'm looking back, like, "What is your problem?"

When I got into the locker room, something inside me gave and desperation made way for glee. I was the happiest person on the planet. Why? Because it was over! I'd made it further than I'd ever made it and now I was finished! In my mind, I was already on the plane, heading home. I asked for a rubdown. Then I was on the massage table and they were working on my leg and my eyes were closed. Then I had a Bounty chocolate bar. It was delicious. Then I sat in a big chair, reading *Hello!* as the rain drummed on the roof. I was thinking: "Is the flight booked for tomorrow? Yup. Is there a good place near the hotel for some retail therapy? Yup!"

Then the sky cleared and the rain stopped. I went to the gym for another warm-up, and ran on the treadmill, getting ready. After the warm-up, you have a few minutes to talk to your team. A few seconds, really. My father and coach stood with me outside the gym, beneath an overhang, rain dripping down. My coach spoke first. He did not have a lot of technical ideas or plans. His advice was simple: "Just get the returns in. It doesn't matter how, it doesn't matter if they're great or if they're shit, just get them in. Make her play. Make her hit a ball. Make her think. She just had two hours in the locker room to think. And what's she been thinking? 'I'm going to be a finalist at Wimbledon.' She's as ripe as a ripe peach. Wouldn't you like to pick that peach? Wouldn't that be fun? And all you have to do is get the goddamn ball over the net. I don't care how you return it, make her hit another. You have a short ball, go to the net. Make her hit a passing shot. She can't hit a passing shot when she's had two hours to think about how nice it will be in the final."

My coach walked away, and then it was just me and my father, as it had always been at the key moments. He was smiling. No, more than smiling. He was laughing.

"Why are you laughing?" I asked.

"Because I know that you will win this match and it makes me laugh," he said.

This might have been the first and last time I had ever seen my father laugh before a match.

"Are you insane?" I asked. "What makes you think I can possibly win?"

"Because it's already happened," said Yuri. "Because last night I saw it in a dream that was more than a dream. It has already happened. You have won the match and the tournament. All you have to do is fulfill what's already been dreamed."

He grabbed my arm, looked deep into my eyes, that hard unblinking stare, and said, "You're going to win this fucking thing, Maria. Now. Win it."

"Excuse me?"

"You heard me. Win it."

"You haven't been watching if you think I can win."

"I don't think, I know. Now go out there and do everything we've talked about and win it."

This made *me* laugh, then it made me angry, then it scared me shitless. But it had its effect. In that minute, I went from feeling like I had absolutely no chance, being beaten before I even went back out on the court, to believing that I'd have the prize if only I could summon the will to take it.

Everything was different after the delay. It was as if I had woken from a trance. The world had gone from foggy to sharp and clear. Suddenly, it was *my* shots that were finding the corners and hitting the lines. Movement was not my specialty; up and back was questionable, and side to side needed work. For years, Max had called me "the turtle." But if you hit the ball hard enough, and with enough depth and precision, none of that matters. And it did not matter after the rain delay. The points were short and crisp. Winner. Winner. Winner. I got her serves back. I made her play that extra ball. I even came to the net, like my coach wanted me to do. I held serve after the delay, then broke Davenport's serve, then held serve again. Three straight games put me right back in the thick of it. As I won, I gained confidence. As I gained confidence, I became aggressive. As I became aggressive, Davenport retreated into a defensive crouch—you're always in danger when you think you have a match won—then she began to fall apart.

I won that second set in a tiebreaker. That was the moment, the exchange that broke Lindsay's spirit. The third set was me on a skateboard racing down a long hill. I broke her early, then I broke her again. Then I was serving for the match. I hit the corner. Lindsay returned it long. It was all over. I went down on my knees. Then I rushed to the net, overwhelmed in the best way. Lindsay shook my hand and said something like "Good job" as if she really meant it. I mean, can you imagine a more difficult moment? There's probably more bullshit phoniness said at the net after a match than anywhere else in the world. But Lindsay was raw and sincere. It was as if she had been playing the match but also watching it from the outside, as if, though she must have been crushed by the loss—you only get so many chances to reach a Grand Slam final—she could appreciate what I had done, the impossibility and importance (for me) of that comeback. She was happy for me. I shook hands with the umpire and waved to the crowd, but I really had only one thought in my head. "I am going to need a dress for the Wimbledon Ball!"

* * *

There was a nice symmetry to the tournament for me. Martina Navratilova played her last professional matches at Wimbledon that year. She was forty-seven years old, and it was her thirty-first consecutive appearance at the All England Club. Astonishing! She was playing for her twenty-first doubles title. How perfect. It was Navratilova who spotted me at that clinic in Moscow when I was seven years old. She picked me out, talked to my father, and sent us on our way to America. And now, a decade later, our paths had crossed again. Does Navratilova even remember that first encounter? To her, it was nothing. To me, it was everything.

* * *

I woke up with a sore throat the day before the final.

I hate to admit it, but this is my pattern. I hold it in and hold it in and hold it in and then at the crucial moment, a day before a big match or event, my immune system breaks down. I touch a railing or shake someone's hand, and bang, I'm hacking up a lung at the worst possible time. I decided to will it away—to make myself healthy, as I'd made myself tall by hanging from that rod in my closet in Florida. "I am in the Wimbledon final tomorrow," I told myself. "It is not permissible for me to be less than a hundred percent in the Wimbledon final. I will therefore be a hundred percent for the Wimbledon final."

I went through my usual morning routine, worked out, then did a press conference, which is required. By the time I got back to the house, my nose was stuffed, my throat was raw, my body ached, and goddamnit I had a full-blown cold.

We called up a doctor, who came over to the house and went after me with every tool in his big black bag. In the end, he shrugged. "What can I say, Maria? You're sick. The good news— no fever, no virus, no flu. It's just a common cold."

"How do I make it go away?" I asked.

"Drink fluids, get plenty of sleep, and don't exert yourself," he said. "The usual. In a week, you'll be fine."

I thanked him, went up to my room, threw myself on the bed, and screamed. Then I called my mother. That's my pattern, too. I act tough and cool in the world, because the world can hurt you, then I call my mom and burst into tears. "Why, why, why?" She shushed and consoled me, then told me to stop feeling sorry for myself. "Tomorrow, you play the biggest match of your life," she said. "Today, rest and think positive. If you do that, everything will be fine."

I spent the rest of the day in bed, reading gossip magazines and drinking tea with honey.

I tried a bit of autosuggestion just before I went to sleep that night. Lying there, beneath the big quilt, in that high English bed, the room as dark as any room in the world, I spoke to my body the way Yuri spoke to me during the rain delay in the match against Davenport. I said, "Listen up, body, in the morning, this cold will be gone and you will be healthy. This is not a request. It is an order. Now do it." Then I turned over, closed my eyes, and tried to fall asleep but couldn't. First of all, there was tomorrow, the television and the crowds, the match, the biggest of my life. Then there was my opponent, the player who would push me more than any other player in my career, Serena Williams. She had won Wimbledon the year before and the year before that. She was trying to become the first player since Steffi Graf to win it in three consecutive years. From the outside she seemed unbeatable, big and fast and strong, a player who could finish off any point from anywhere on the court, perhaps the best to ever play the game. And she was older than me, and had been here before, and knew this, and knew that. And as I thought about all this, as it all went through my mind, I became acutely aware of my throat, which was killing me, and of my nose, which was so stuffed I could barely breathe. And if I couldn't breathe, how could I possibly play? And as I went over it again and again, my heart started to pound. And then I became aware of just how little sleep I was getting because of all this thinking. Of course I needed sleep, but as I was thinking about needing sleep still more time without sleep was passing, and soon it would be morning. Maybe I did sleep a little—maybe I was sleeping when I thought I was just lying there worrying—but, if so, not very deeply and not for very long. At most, I got a few hours—the night before the Wimbledon final.

I felt terrible at breakfast. My father looked at me with real concern. It made me ashamed, and embarrassed. How could I fall apart like this, right at the big moment? It felt like a failure, like weakness. I was angry, but tried not to show it. Yuri made me oatmeal, like he did every morning. I ate that and drank tea and honey, then left for the courts.

I told my coach about the cold the way you might tell someone a terrible secret. To him, it must have seemed like I was excusing my inevitable defeat. You know, "I've got this terrible cold. And I hardly slept last night. So what do you expect?"

He looked at me and laughed.

"What's so funny?"

"You," he said. "That you are sitting here, a few hours before the Wimbledon final, and you are worried about having a cold. A cold. A cold? A fucking cold? As soon as the first point is being played, your cold will be gone. Like it never happened. And not enough sleep? As soon as you get out there, you will be more awake than you've ever been in your life. Ha. Maria is worried because she has a cold!" In fact, I did not have to wait for the first point to lose the cold. As soon as those words were spoken, the cold was gone.

I went through my prematch ritual. Went out on the court, hit for a good forty minutes, came back, went back to the locker room and cooled down, thinking and trying to not think. I was set up in the members-only locker room, plush beyond plush. A few days before, it had been crowded with the other players. Now it was just the two of us, Serena and me. This was my first professional Grand Slam final, so the first time I'd really experienced the spookiness of the last round. Outside, there are huge crowds, fans and reporters. It's a big swarm, a big buzz. But at the center of that swarm you sit in an empty locker room, alone.

Did I sit there, thinking about the long road that had brought me here? Nope. I thought only about now and five minutes from now. That's how you get through this kind of day. You go from task to task.

I went to warm up in the gym. It had turned into a beautiful day, mid-seventies with a slight wind, the world after a storm. The seats were starting to fill. It was early afternoon, but there was a prime-time electricity to everything. I was revved up, excited, ready to go. I could feel that old thing stirring in me, that never-ending desire to beat them all.

I went back to the locker room and waited. Serena was there. I could hear her even when I could not see her. She went through her rituals as I went through mine. She sat alone as did I. It was like we were the only two people on a deserted planet, fifteen feet apart but each behaving as if we were the only person in the universe. Serena and I should be friends: we love the same thing, we have the same passion. Only a few other people in the world know what we know—what it feels like in the dead center of this storm, the fear and anger that drive you, how it is to win and how it is to lose. But we are not friends—not at all. I think, to some extent, we have driven each other. Maybe that's better than being friends. Maybe that's what it takes to fire up the proper fury. Only when you have that intense antagonism can you find the strength to finish her off. But who knows? Someday, when all this is in our past, maybe we'll become friends. Or not.

You never can tell.

There is a great deal of ritual and tradition at Wimbledon; everything has to be done exactly so. The ushers came to take us out to Centre Court, and I went first because I was the challenger; Serena followed a few dozen feet behind, because she was the defending champion, the higher seed. We each had our own escort, a British official in the proper dress, tight-lipped and serious. No joking, no fooling around. I was wearing the same Nike white mesh dress I'd been wearing throughout the tournament, white Nike shoes, and a gold cross on a gold chain. Serena was wearing a white dress with a gold stripe up the side, a white headband, and gold earrings that dangled. She looked like a champion. As we came through the tunnel, I could sense the crowd, all those people. As I said, it was prime time, electric. There is nothing else like it. We were entering the biggest stage in the sport, coming into the court of the Queen. I should have been considering history and empire, life and destiny, tennis and time, but instead, as we made that entrance, as the crowd roared, I had just a single thought on my mind: I have to pee! It was that tea and honey. Why did I drink all that tea with honey?

As soon as we finished our warm-up, I turned to the chair umpire and asked, "Where's the closest bathroom?"

A line judge led me back the way we came, pointing out a door beneath the stands. So that's how it began for me—as soon as I'd made my entrance, I went back the way I came, to pee. It was a fancy members' bathroom right next to the court, with plated handles and silver sinks and real towels instead of paper. "They've got a good maintenance budget," I told myself. I stayed there for what felt like a long time, listening to the crowd, the ambient noise, then went back, got my racket, and started to play.

Serena Williams has an almost arrogant look on the court, a kind of detachment, as if she were viewing you from a great height. I recognize it because I have a similar look of my own. It's gamesmanship—her way of telling the opponent, "You have no chance." Usually it works, and they don't. But it does not always work, especially if the opponent has the same attitude and carries herself in the same way.

* * *

Maybe, if you work long enough and hard enough, you will be given a single perfect day, a few hours when everything clicks and even the moves that seem wrong at first turn out for the best. For me, that was the Wimbledon final, July 2004. I served the first game, and held. Serena served the second game, and held. But even on the points I lost, it was clear that I was looser than my opponent. Some of it probably had to do with just where we were in our careers. Serena was number one in the world, a returning champion. Everyone wanted something from her. Everyone expected her to win. If she did win, she'd therefore be doing nothing more than what had been expected. There was little upside and an abyss of downside. How could she lose to . . . what's that girl's name again? And me? I was no one from nowhere. I was supposed to go down in straight sets. Just being here, years ahead of schedule, was my victory. I was lucky to be on the same stage, with John McEnroe calling the match from the broadcasting booth. In other words, while Serena had everything on the line, I had nothing to lose.

I think this dawned on Serena in the fourth game of the first set. She was up 0–30 on my serve. This is when, in the normal course of events, she begins to put players away. Instead, I returned each powerful shot with a powerful shot of my own. On this point, I blew the ball past her and she fell down. People made a lot of it, but she did not need to fall down. I love the way she plays—she's an incredible athlete—but there's a lot of drama in her game. It's like she's acting, showing everyone in the world just how she feels. Is stumbling when she doesn't need to her way of telling the world, "Oh, I could have gotten that if the grass wasn't so fucked-up"? It doesn't feel real. She got up fast but I won the point, held my serve, and won the game. Serena suddenly knew that I would not quit and would not break. And even if she did break me, she was going to have to break me again and again. Now she knew that she was in for a fight.

In the fourth game, as we played points that went on and on, I felt something shift. In a moment, Serena's look of confidence, which she carries like a racket—it's almost as important for her game—gave way to something else. At first, I could not tell exactly what sort of look it was, though I knew I'd seen it on the faces of other girls before. Then, amazingly, as I went on to break Serena's serve in that first set, it hit me. Fear. Serena looked afraid. It was as if she'd suddenly realized how upsetting it would be to lose to this skinny seventeen-year-old kid in front of all these people. I did not lose another game in the first set.

Still, for a moment in the seventh game, it did look like Serena would get back into the set. I was down two break points and battled back to deuce. We went in and out of deuce for what seemed like hours. Serena is a great champion, and great champions are toughest to beat when it comes time to put them away. They grow stronger the closer they get to defeat. They will not go down easily. Game and set point: I finally managed to put a ball exactly where I wanted it, skidding across the baseline. Serena got to it, but her shot was weak and ended up in the net. First set: Sharapova, 6–1.

I sat during the changeover, drinking water and staring straight ahead, trying hard to think about nothing. The changeovers are short reprieves, like the blissful break a boxer gets between rounds, without all the blood. I wiped off my face and took a bite of a banana. I stared into the crowd. Everywhere I looked, people looked back, smiling as if they knew me. I looked and looked till I located my box. My father was up there with my coach and my trainer. Not my mom—she was back in the States. It made me feel good seeing my father, knowing he and my coaches were with me all the way. And yet, at the same time, the presence of these people, so close and still so far away, reminded me that I was really all alone. Tennis is not a team sport. It's not a sport where the coach

whispers to you on the sideline between plays. You are surrounded at nearly every moment of the day by coaches and partners and friends, surrounded right up till the first point is played,
and then you are alone—as alone as you can possibly be, which
is alone in a crowd. Surrounded but apart, with no one to help
you or hold your hand. The bigger the game, the more alone you
will feel.

I passed by Serena as I went back out on the court. It's a strange
moment—the changeover walk-by. You come close enough to brush
shoulders, but do not acknowledge it. You are entwined with this
person, as close as you can get to another player, yet cannot acknowledge each other.

Time had gone by. The light was changing. I had won the first
set. I had one more to get. It was the middle of an unbelievable
day. Serena would try to bring real pressure—this was her moment. She needed to break me early in the second to flip the plot.
She held her serve in game one, then pushed me to break point in
game two, but I hung on.

Something interesting happened in game three of the second
set, the sort of thing that does not show up in statistics or on
charts, yet that can mean all the difference. We both came to the
net in the middle of a rally. She hit a hard shot, but I hit it back
even harder. It caught her flush on the nose. I won the point, and
she seemed at first irritated, then angry. There was a flash in her
eyes. It's humiliating to take a shot in the face on Centre Court
at Wimbledon, with the TV stations showing it, then showing it
again in slow-mo, then again in super slo-mo, then from a reverse
angle. A thing like that can be exactly what a player needs to
get going, to reverse the momentum. Serena won that game, then
pushed hard to break my serve. I hung on, but she played with a

new fury in the games that followed. I did not win a point in the fifth game, and in the sixth she broke my serve.

Just like that, Serena had seemingly turned the tide. We were deep into the second set and she was ahead 4–2. Another possible future opened up before me, a future that fit the common pattern: Serena Williams wins the second set 6–2, goes on to win the third, and secures her third consecutive Wimbledon championship, cementing her place as the number one player in the world. They would say I should be happy to have made it so far, winning a set in the final before Serena took over. You could feel it in the crowd—it was how things were starting to look, that it might be Serena's day after all. It can happen a dozen times in the course of a single match. Fortunes shift, fates change. The minute you accept it, you're finished. At such moments, here's what you say to yourself: *Good! I need to be down if I want to be known for making an amazing comeback.* In other words, it was the gut-check moment.

Do I fold and give in, or do I stand and fight?

As I've said, it's my defining characteristic. I'm a fighter. I do not quit. Just because you're beating me 4–2 does not mean I will roll into a crouch for games seven, eight, and nine. In fact, that's the time to counterpunch, just when that other girl is starting to believe in her own victory. So what did I do? I took the force of Serena's serve—now and then, it hit 120 m.p.h.—and turned it right back on her. She broke my serve? I broke her serve, then hung on to win the next game. Now it was 4–4 in the second set. That was the crucial swing. It set up the all-important ninth game of the second set. This was where I'd have to take it. Serena was serving. I watched her bounce the ball, take a second, bounce it again. She was the same old Serena Williams, yet something had changed.

Something in her seemed diminished, faded. Maybe she knew that she was going to lose. She'd already seen it in my eyes. And she knew how bitter it would be. And still, because she is such a fierce competitor, she would fight every step of the way going down.

That ninth game—the sixteenth game of the afternoon—was epic, the whole match in miniature. It went on and on and on. I pushed Serena to break point four times. Each time, she hung on and pushed back. Finally, on the fourteenth point of that game, racing toward a ball that I'd put in the back corner, Serena slipped and fell, but it looked phony. Does she do this to take that point away from her opponent? "It's nothing that you did," she seems to say. "It's just my bad luck." In other words, she does not miss the shot because she's fallen down; she falls down because she's going to miss the shot. She scrambled to her feet and got to the ball but, once again, it ended up in the net.

I was now serving for the championship, all momentum with me. I lost the first point, which is never a good way to start a championship game. I hit an ace on the second point, then a great serve to get it to 30–15. Another return error by Serena and I was a point away from winning it all. I served to her backhand. The return came back faster than a Ping-Pong ball: 40–30. Then, getting ready for the next attempt, I remembered something my coach had said earlier that day. "Do not serve to her backhand. That's her strength. Make her beat you with her forehand." So that's what I did. Serena returned it, but it was weak. I quickly set up, shuffling my feet around my forehand, and hit the ball as it was starting its rise from the grass, hit it with my own forehand right to hers, screaming as I made contact, reversing my follow-through over my right shoulder, a stroke that capped every stroke I'd ever made. I ended with my arms and eyes pointed skyward.

Serena's return did not make it over the net. I dropped to my knees and put my hands over my face and exulted. Even as I was doing this, I was aware that this gesture—everyone has their own way of punctuating a big win; some pump a fist, some point to God—was not my own. It was exactly what I had seen Juan Carlos Ferrero do when he won the French Open. I'd like to say I did this intentionally, that I was thanking him for the confidence he'd shown when he (ridiculously) picked me to win the tournament, or that I was sending him a coded message, but in fact I did not know what I was doing. I was just living in the moment.

I jogged to the net. I'd expected Serena to reach across and shake my hand. That's what you usually do, shake hands and exchange the bullshit pleasantries. But she came around and hugged me instead. It was a surprise. I remember thinking, "Is this the protocol? Is this what you're supposed to do when you lose a Grand Slam final?" Then: "Well, if it's a hug she wants, it's a hug she's going to get." Serena squeezed me and I squeezed her right back, although I was really looking past her into the stands, trying to locate my father, trying to make eye contact with him for the first time as Wimbledon champion. Serena said something like "Good job." And smiled. But she could not have been smiling on the inside.

There is a tradition at Wimbledon—a new tradition, it turned out, but it seemed old to me—of winners climbing into the stands to celebrate with their families. Being seventeen, I wanted to taste everything, have all of it. So I hopped the rail around the photographers' pit and went up into the seats toward my father. It had been him and me then, and it should be him and me now. I love to look at the film and see Yuri at that moment. My father is not an emotional man. It's there, under the surface, but he does not show it. In fact, the only time I've ever seen him cry was when my little dog had to have surgery the day after we got him—that's another story. You can see him, on that film, trying to make his way to me as I am trying to make my way to him. It's like a silly old movie. He finally got to me, grabbed me, and endlessly hugged me. Everything was in that hug, all the struggles and all the dreams.

A minute later, I was back on Centre Court, where everyone had assembled for the awards ceremony, which takes place immediately after the last point. They were waiting for me, but, just as I began to make my way over, I suddenly remembered my mom! *I have to tell my mom!* "Hey," I screamed to my father—he was twenty or so rows up—"I want to call Mom!" Yuri, without thinking, got his cell phone out of his pocket and tossed it to me. Perfect throw, perfect catch. I dialed as I walked toward the television camera to do the postmatch interview. I dialed and dialed again, but I kept getting either voice mail or a fast busy signal—oh, the dreaded fast busy signal! Here's what I did not realize: my mom was on an airplane, flying from Florida to New York on JetBlue, where I would meet her after the tournament. But she was watching all this on TV. She was calling over the flight attendant and explaining and laughing and holding up her phone but nothing could be done. Everyone in the stadium was laughing, too. I still had the phone in my hand when someone stuck a microphone in my face and said, "Can't get a signal?"

I stood next to Serena a few minutes later when they gave out the trophies. Losing on a big stage is tough—believe me, I have come to know. You have to appear warm and gracious while everything inside you is screaming. Wimbledon is especially torturous, as it's the only Grand Slam where they make the loser walk around the court with the champion, as she showcases her trophy to the public. It's one of the toughest moments any player ever faces on the tour. You've left every piece of yourself on that court, expecting to win. And somehow you lost! Now you have to stand out there in public and on TV celebrating the person who took all that from you. It's torture.

The runner-up gets a commemorative plate and a thank-you. The winner gets a silver salver, also called the Rosewater Dish—it was first awarded in 1886—and close to a million dollars, plus plaudits and love. The trophies were handed out by Prince Charles and the head of the All England Tennis Club. Serena got hers first. She really did handle it beautifully—when the television reporter asked about her feelings, she spoke only of my accomplishment—but behind all the smiles and nice words, you can see that she is suffering and can't wait to get the hell out of there, just as anyone would. On TV, I thanked everyone I could think of. I thanked Nick Bollettieri and Robert Lansdorp. I thanked my parents. I talked about my cold and I alluded to Juan Carlos Ferrero, though I did not say his name. I didn't think I'd ever share that until writing this page. At some point, I looked up at my box and, smiling at my entourage, made cutting motions. This was me reminding my father, my coach, and my trainer about our bet. "If I win, you have to shave your heads." In the end, I did not hold them to it. For one thing, if my father cut off all his hair, it would probably never grow back.

I went to the locker room alone. Serena had left the court as soon as she could without making a scene. I did not notice it and wouldn't have thought about it if not for what was going on when I got to my stall. Having your own private stall means that, even though you cannot see your opponent, you can hear her. And what I heard, when I came in and started to change clothes, was Serena

Williams bawling. Guttural sobs, the sort that make you heave for air, the sort that scares you. It went on and on. I got out as quickly as I could, but she knew I was there. People often wonder why I have had so much trouble beating Serena; she's owned me in the past ten years. My record against her is 2 and 19. In analyzing this, people talk about Serena's strength, her serve and confidence, how her particular game matches up to my particular game, and, sure, there is truth to all of that; but, to me, the real answer was there, in this locker room, where I was changing and she was bawling. I think Serena hated me for being the skinny kid who beat her, against all odds, at Wimbledon. I think she hated me for taking something that she believed belonged to her. I think she hated me for seeing her at her lowest moment. But mostly I think she hated me for hearing her cry. She's never forgiven me for it. Not long after the tournament, I heard that Serena told a friend—who then told me—"I will never lose to that little bitch again."

✳ ✳ ✳

The next few dozen hours went by in a delirium. It was the culmination of everything that we had worked for and planned. Victory really only lasts a moment, and then you are right back out on the practice court. But what a moment!

The morning after the final I went out to find a gown for the Wimbledon Ball. Winning Wimbledon changes everything—there's no denying it. Every other time that I wanted to get a new dress in London, I had gone to my favorite store, looked through the collections, gone into the dressing room, and so on. But on this occasion, when I said that I wanted to head into the city to do some shopping, an official Wimbledon town car materialized at my front door. It carried me across the country and into the city like a magic carpet gliding over streets and rooftops. They were waiting for me in the showroom at Louis Vuitton. I was surrounded by salespeople who were waiting to help me in and out of the most gorgeous dresses you have ever seen. Red and gold and silver. I walked away with a unique cream double-figure dress with a pleated skirt underneath.

I was in the dress that night. I had dried my hair straight and wore barely any makeup because I had no clue what to do with makeup. I was nervous and shy and there were more cameras than I had ever seen. The flashbulbs hurt my eyes. I was seeing spots and wanted to get past all this and run inside. Official escorts stood at either side of the grand entrance. The doors opened and I floated in and continued to float all the way across the floor, following the same path that Serena had followed three years before. Back then I was watching, but now I was the player at the center of the action. The people in the room stood and began to applaud. A standing ovation. I went by the junior table, stealing a quick look at the girls I knew I'd have to defeat in the coming years if I wanted to stay in this perfect spot. The night flew by. It was a fantasy. All those gowns. All those colors. All that music and wine. It was 8:00 p.m. Then it was 2:00 a.m. I was back at the house, making my way up the stairs, shoes in hand, wanting nothing more than to tell my father about everything that had happened, all of it, but he was not there.

As important as winning Wimbledon had been for me, it had been, if anything, even more important for my father. He'd had his mind fixed on this goal ever since Yuri Yudkin first pulled him aside and spoke to him beside the courts in Sochi. Everything he had done, everything he had sacrificed, he had done and sacrificed to reach this moment. And here we were. Whatever came after this would be wonderful and terrific and everything, but, for my father, and, in a sense, for me, too, it would never be better. This was the destination, the true peak. What came later would just be our lives. This was a dream. And my father was going to celebrate it and mark it properly. He was not going to do that by going to a tea party or fancy ball. He would not do it by wearing a tux or dancing with a duchess. Nope. None of that bullshit. Yuri Sharapov wanted to celebrate in the old way, in the traditional way. He went out and got drunk. He stayed out until the night itself had been defeated. He went into a pub in the dark and did not come out till it was light, drunk and exultant. He woke me up when he finally got in. It was five in the morning, and he was carrying a tower of newspapers.

I sat up in bed. "What's that?"

"The newspapers," said Yuri, smiling. (I can't remember if he was speaking in Russian or English.) "I went to that little shop on the corner. It wasn't even open when I got there. I sat and waited. And waited. The goddamn sun was coming up! The guy who owns the place, he finally comes in with the keys. He's stacking up the papers. I take a paper off the pile and, my God, Maria, you are on the front page! The front page! And I show it to the guy and I point to the picture and I ask him, because I am still not sure if this is real, I say, 'Do you know who this is?' And he smiles and says, 'Of course, that's Maria! She won on Saturday.' Maria—even the newsagents know you by your first name! I said, 'I am Maria's father.' And this guy, he was so excited for me, he starts going all around and gathering up every paper with your picture, and look at how many!"

He dropped the pile on the floor and began going through them. I went back to sleep, but he stayed up, reading all the articles in the living room. He later said that it was only by reading those articles, which had the statistics and the history and the fact that I was one of the youngest players to ever win Wimbledon, that he realized just what a big deal this win was. A few days later, he ran into Conchita Martínez somewhere. Martínez is a Spanish player and a former Wimbledon champion. She and my father got to talking about Wimbledon and she told him, "Yuri, your life is never going to be the same."

I had been invited by Mayor Yury Luzhkov of Moscow to some sort of event in that city—the invitation came after I won the final. I'd already committed to something in New York, but my father offered to go in my place. The mayor sent a private jet. Yuri later told me the drinking resumed as soon as he took his seat on the plane. In other words, he marked my first big win the Russian way. Finally, completely exhausted, he met his brother in the mountains, where they had spent so many important days as kids. They hiked and talked and all of a sudden the whole thing finally seemed real to my father. Something about going back to the place where you started—you can see things more clearly there.

Meanwhile, I was also sensing life had changed. As I stepped out of the car at the airport, heading to New York for a promotion commitment, I was met by a crowd of reporters and photographers, paparazzi, the cameras going flash, flash, flash. People suddenly cared about me in a way that was cool, but also kinda creepy and disorienting. The reporters kept yelling, "Maria, Maria, Maria." I, the rookie, was thinking, "Take it easy, guys, I'm two feet away from you." It was the start of a new life—good and bad.

Losing. I know what losing does to you. I'd learned its lessons on tennis courts all over the world. It knocks you down but also builds you up. It teaches you humility and gives you strength. It makes you aware of your flaws, which you then must do your best to correct. In this way, it can actually make you better. You become a survivor. You learn that losing is not the end of the world. You learn that the great players are not those who don't get knocked down—everyone gets knocked down—they are those who get up just one more time than they've been knocked down. Losing is the teacher of every champion. But winning? On this level? It was entirely new and I would have to learn its lessons, which can be devastating. In short, winning fucks you up. First of all, it brings all kinds of rewards, which, if seen from the proper perspective, reveal themselves for what they really are: distractions, traps, snares. Money, fame, opportunity. Each laurel and offer and ad and pitch takes you further from the game. It can turn your head. It can ruin you, which is why there are many great players who won just a single Grand Slam, then seemed to wander away. They simply lost themselves in the thicket of success. And then there is what winning does to your mind, which is even more dangerous. It completely distorts your expectations. You start to feel entitled. When you win Wimbledon, you expect to win Wimbledon every year.

I had begun my journey by picking up a tennis racket on that clay court in Sochi when I was four years old. My ability to hit a ball off the back wall of those courts brought me first the attention of the locals, then of people from all over the world. My father and I followed that attention from Russia all the way to America. It was an adventure that we shared, a dream that was a quest. It had a beginning and a middle and an end. It started in poverty and ended in fame. It led to a kind of city shining on a hill. The fabled city of the big win. In the weeks after Wimbledon, we looked at each other and almost whispered, "So the legends are true." It was happy, but of course it was also sad. The end of a journey, the end of a quest, is always sad. There is a loss of altitude and of direction. Do we simply do again what we've already done, or is something else expected of us? My first existence—the days of me and my father alone, the two of us against the world—was over. And I had not yet figured out what would happen next.

TWELVE

A nd so began the crazy first days of being famous. The telephone rang, the agents called, the offers poured in. Everything was perfect and everything sounded great. How do you say no when the world is on the line? I would eventually become a great pitchperson, a master of selling products, a name in the corporate world. But it really began with a single company—Motorola.

It was the Wimbledon final that did it, not the match but what happened immediately after. I took my father's flip phone and tried to call my mom but could not get a signal. From there, the ad wrote itself. It would be me on a tennis court after a big match, wanting to call my mom and this time finally having the right phone for the job. Motorola called IMG the day after Wimbledon, and we did the shoot. The ad shows me, racket in hand, chatting on the new Motorola RAZR phone, which wasn't even out yet. They gave me some kind of prototype to carry around. It was so cool, superthin and sleek. I went from having a piece-of-crap phone to being like James Bond, flashing the newest piece of high-tech hardware. I remember eating lunch at a sushi place in New York right around this time. I was holding the RAZR phone, and a businessman was eyeing me, and the RAZR, like a hawk. Finally, he came over and said, "Excuse me, how did you get that phone?" I told him that I knew someone at Motorola. But I wanted to say: "Because I won Wimbledon, that's how."

They made me the face of Motorola, which itself became a story: that I was just a kid and yet was representing a huge brand, with ads everywhere. People assumed I was making millions of dollars, but it was really not a huge deal. Max's idea was to go with a cool, quality brand—we'd gotten bigger offers from competing phone companies—and let other work flow from that. "We don't want to tarnish your name by going downscale," he explained. And he was right. The offers flooded in after Motorola. I was soon working for half a dozen blue-chip companies. TAG Heuer. Land Rover. I'd had a sponsorship deal with Nike since I was an eleven-year-old junior, as many tennis players do, but now I actually started doing commercials for the company. *Bleacher Report* put together a slideshow of my greatest commercials. They've got Nike on there, Canon, Head rackets, and a funny thing I did for ESPN. I never planned to become a big pitchperson or public face, it just happened. It was more like a side effect of what I was doing at the tournaments, but it made me famous. All of a sudden, writers were more interested in my life off the court than on the court. I went to the beach, someone snapped a picture of me in a bathing suit, and the next day it was all over the Internet. How crazy is that? And there were rumors. Ridiculous rumors. Every day, they had me dating someone else. It was weird. Irritating. Everyone thinks they want to be famous, but let me tell you, a little goes a long way, especially for a seventeen-year-old girl.

And your life changes. It's not the money or the fame, but the way the money and the fame separate you from other players. They see it as a zero-sum game. We are all competing for the same dollars, so this reasoning goes, so if Maria gets them, they don't. If you are a certain kind of person, you will really dislike me for that, though you never will admit it to my face. Jealousy became a new thing I had to deal with on the tour. If they resented me, it was not because I was beating them on the court, or because I was a better player, but because I was getting all those goddamn ads. It drove some girls crazy. Elena Dementieva, a Russian who traveled with her mother, was always giving me dirty looks, laser beams. Then, one day, her mother complained to my masseur, a Russian who worked with a lot of Russian players. She told him, "Elena can't get any deals in Japan because Maria has taken them all."

* * *

How does the world change when you win Wimbledon?

Of course, the most obvious thing is the money. At some point, and it must have been later, I heard a reporter say that I was the highest-paid female athlete in the world. I don't know if that's true, or has ever been true. I have never cared enough to look into it. But things did change, and fast, after I beat Serena Williams. I first became aware of it a few weeks after I got back from England. I was in Florida, shopping at the T.J.Maxx in Bradenton, standing there alone in the aisle with my cart, looking at all those discount pants and shirts, and I had this sudden realization. I thought, "My God, I can buy whatever I want." A few years back, standing in this same store, I'd actually thought, "Wouldn't it be cool to be able to buy anything in here?" And now I could. I could probably buy the whole store!

Then, a few weeks later, we went to Los Angeles so I could get back to work with Robert Lansdorp. There's always something else to work on, prepare for, improve. Even the biggest win gets you just a moment of celebration, then it's right back at it. The wheel never stops turning. Stay off too long, you'll never get back on. I'd usually stayed in a crappy hotel in Torrance, a motor court, a roadside ruin. Max did not even tell me that he'd switched hotels, just gave us a name and address. It was the Beach House in Hermosa Beach, which—well, Hermosa Beach is like heaven, miles of boardwalk and stores and shops beside the Pacific. The room itself was much smaller, and there was no kitchen, but the view! It was ocean till the water met the sky, and then the sun went down, and the moon came up, and the stars came out. I could stand on that balcony for hours and hours, thinking about nothing. And the bathtub! It actually had a little yellow rubber ducky next to it! I called up Max as soon as I'd unpacked. I was laughing. I said, "Max, winning Wimbledon is the greatest thing in the world!"

Not long after that, we bought our first home. My parents and I chose a house in Longboat Key, Florida, because that's what Yuri loves—the shoreline, the harbor where the sharks swim at night.

A year later, we bought a house in L.A., for all those trips to see Robert. My crappy hotel days, the days of motor courts and dorms and second bunks in shared rooms, were over. It was an upgrade—not just in room or class of hotel, but in life.

Yet, at the same time, seen in a different way, things did not change that much. It was still tennis, tennis, tennis. It was still practice, practice, practice. It was still run, hit, play, stretch, run, hit, sleep. Or else it was life on the tour, the endless merry-go-round of airports and hotels and buffets in the lobby, the same tournaments, the same girls, only now they had an extra motivation when they played me. If they won, they'd not just be beating a girl from Russia, they'd be beating a Wimbledon champion.

Life on the tour is strange. It's a hermetically sealed bubble, beyond normal history and current events. First of all, you are in all these different towns and cities, the most beautiful places in the world, but, unless you now and then force yourself out of the bubble, you see none of it. You are in cities but not in cities. You are in the world of tennis, where the rooms are filled with the same people and the same energy, no matter where you happen to be. Second, it's very difficult to have any sort of personal life on the tour. You are under a microscope, being watched by other players and coaches and reporters all the time. You can't have much of a social life, and forget about a boyfriend. I mean, you're never home, so the only way you can have a relationship is either with another tennis player, a player also on the tour, or with a person who gives up his life to travel with you, becoming part of your entourage. And who does that? Someone without a life of his own? That is, someone you'd probably not want to date in the first place. These sorts of characters do exist. You see them in the players' lounges or carrying bags. Not the coach, not the parent, but the boyfriend. By definition, any relationship you have is going to be long distance, which amounts to a kind of telephone buddy or pen pal. Not terribly exciting.

Of course, after you win, life on the tour does change. Because you have won, you are treated better. You're given all kinds of extras, like your own driver at tournaments and better practice courts. The atmosphere in the tournament venues and at the press conferences changes, too. It turns chilly, intense. Suddenly, the world, the only world you have ever known, is filled with girls who dislike you. They're jealous of the money and fame. They want what you have and the only way to get it is to take you out. Every match becomes a big deal—if not for you, then for her. There is no more sneaking up and taking a player by surprise. Everyone has scouted and studied you, probed your weaknesses and come up with a plan. Everyone is waiting.

It's the first big test of a long career—yes, you can win, but can you win again? That's an even tougher task. The history books are littered with the names of athletes who got that single big win but never got a second Grand Slam. One-hit wonders. Not because they were not great, or won by luck. But because they never figured out how to adjust after everyone else has made their adjustments. They never figured out how to play as the favorite, which is another thing altogether. As the weeks go by, the pressure mounts—you've got to win that second Grand Slam. Only once you've done it will you have proved you are something more than an asterisk. What's on the line? Not just that second Grand Slam but, in a weird way, the first one, too. Only by winning again can you prove that the first Grand Slam was something more than a fluke. This feeling was new and never went away. It was pressure. There was much more on the line after I'd won Wimbledon. But I welcomed the challenge. I wanted to prove myself again and again and again. I wanted to beat them all. I was eighteen years old, the reigning Wimbledon champ, with nothing but time in front of me.

THIRTEEN

I started the 2005 season by playing an exhibition tournament in Hong Kong, a tune-up for the first Grand Slam of the year, the Australian Open, in Melbourne. It was winter in most of the world, even California. In West Hollywood and Manhattan Beach, the shops were filled with Christmas trees and mistletoe. In the windows of the toy stores, the model trains went around and around. The lights in the houses on the hills above the sea glowed at sundown; the sounds of families on the boardwalk, voices unclear because of the breakers, kids on school break living the childhood you never had a chance to live. That's the moment, when the whole world seems happy and all you want to do is sit in your house in sweats and watch movies, that the coach calls to remind you it's time to pack up and get going, back on the road, back to the tour, the match that's always waiting, the young player who is determined to shut you down and take it all away. It's always hard, starting up again.

The heat was an issue from the moment I arrived in Australia. I was not adjusting well to the conditions, and the sun just sat up there, pounding me. I won the first round in straight sets, but struggled at times as the tournament went on. I beat Lindsay Lee-Waters in three sets, then beat Li Na of China in straight sets. In the quarterfinals, I faced my nemesis Svetlana Kuznetsova, who I finally overcame, 4–6, 6–2, 6–2. It was a victory but it was grueling. Which was important because, by the time I'd reached the semifinals, and it was a big deal to get that far, I'd already played a whole lot of tennis. I felt fatigued, which is not really how you want to go into a match with Serena Williams.

I got off to a quick start in that semifinal. Serena was a little off her game at the beginning. Maybe she cared too much. Maybe she was playing tight. Her forehand deserted her at a few key moments. I took the first set 6–2. I kept pushing. I quickly found myself 5–4 in the second set, serving for the match. Then something happened. I can blame it on the heat—that match against Svetlana Kuznetsova had taken a lot out of me—but of course Serena was playing under the same sun. Or I could blame bad breaks or fluky plays, but in fact all that really evens out in the end. It was just Serena. She cranked it up, lived up to her vow—she said she'd never lose to me again—and just like that she battled back. I dropped three straight points, then went into the third set dejected. The worst part: I had my chances. What were they? Three match points! When you have your chances, you've got to convert them. That's the story. Make the shot when the shot is there. Because how many times in your life will you have a chance to win a Grand Slam? You make that shot, or you don't. That's your career. Serena won the match point she had and I did not win any of the three I had. I battled to the very end, though. That's how I salvaged a losing effort; that's how I could walk away disappointed but not unsatisfied. I lost 8–6 in the third set. The match lasted close to three hours. This was tennis at its most grueling: just the two of us out there, on our feet the entire time, and the ball never stopped coming. We shook hands at the net but really said nothing. Serena Williams beat Lindsay Davenport in the final. You can tell a lot by reading the score, 6–2, 3–6, meaning both of them had a chance to win right up until the third set, which Williams took 6–0.

After the match, I told the reporters that I was not discouraged, which could not have been true. Not after a match like that. The first part of the next day I spent in my hotel room, with the curtains down, flat on my back, watching movies. At some point, I realized I had to get out. I remember walking to Bulgari and looking in the displays and seeing this beautiful ring and calling my mom and asking permission to buy it because it was pricey. And a Chloé bag with a chain handle that I still have and will probably never use again. Then I had a nice lunch in the sun by myself. And as I sat there, I began to let go of those three blown match points. Because what else can you do?

That's how I began one of the great consistent stretches of my career. Two years—2005, 2006—when, as far as I'm concerned, I played some of my best tennis. That's when I became number one.

Why did my game get so good?

I'd like to say it's because I'd added a new skill, or improved my serve, or got stronger or faster, but I really don't believe any of that was the case. In fact, I think the reason I got better had mostly to do with my growing knowledge and acceptance of my own game. For the first time, at age eighteen, I finally began to really understand how I played: what I could do and, just as important, what I could not do.

What could I do? What were my strengths?

I could hit the ball hard. And flat. And deep. I could push the other girl around the court by taking the ball early. I loved returning an opponent's serve, especially her second serve. There's nothing like taking a few steps in from the baseline for that second serve. I already had big-time power, even as an eighteen-year-old. Now and then, my forehand could get a little dodgy, but, thanks to my coaches and opponents, it's improved a lot over the years. But my backhand was—and is—my money shot, backhand down the line, the one I love to hit. Maybe because by nature I'm (probably) a lefty, I can hit that shot all day. And my serve—it was a great part of my game back then, a crucial weapon. I could hit a hard serve exactly where I wanted it. It would change—but more on that later. And stamina. And focus. I had a surplus in all those categories. And my greatest strength is probably my will. I will not quit.

What couldn't I do? What were my weaknesses?

Speed. I didn't have it. I wasn't a fast person, wasn't a great runner. I didn't have a quick first step running to a drop shot, and I could be sloppy going from side to side. I was not terrific moving up to the net. It was like something was keeping me away. And even when I got going, it was one step forward, two steps back.

Knowing and accepting these weaknesses turned out to be the most important part of my development. It meant that I could

UNSTOPPABLE

steer matches away from my deficiencies and toward my strengths. After so many years, the coaching and strategy made absolute sense. With a good plan, I could dictate with my strengths. It was during that 2004 season that I really began to put it all together. I'm not sure why it happened at that particular moment—maybe that's just how the mind works. You don't get it, and you don't get it, and you don't get it, until one day: you get it. That's when I began winning match after match. That's when, and this gave me special satisfaction, I beat both Serena and Venus Williams in the same year.

I played Serena in the final of the WTA Championship at the Staples Center in L.A. It was the end of the season. We played on a blue court. I'd begun to relax. Maybe that's why I did so well. This was some of the best tennis of my life. I lost the first set but I won the match. Not many people will remember it—it aired, on the East Coast, in the middle of the night—but I will never forget it. What do you get to keep when you quit the game? Trophies, some money? It has to be memories of those few perfect matches, those days when everything went just right—when every serve landed exactly where you wanted it and every ball hummed. Even now, that's what I feel when I close my eyes at night and wait to fall asleep. The jolt that goes all through your body when you hit it just right, the happy exhaustion of the endless rallies, the last few shots and the winner that ends it all, and how you felt when you got back to the locker room knowing that whatever reserves you'd had in physical and spiritual strength had been spent on the court and your mind was empty and your body was drained and satisfied.

I remember walking off the court after the last match of the

209

season. My friend Sophie was waiting and she smiled and said, "Do you realize what you did this year? You won Wimbledon and the season-end championship."

In the summer of 2005, not long before the start of the U.S. Open, I learned that my father's dream had come true. When the new rankings came out, I was number one in the world. I knew I was getting close, that I had a shot, but still, you never believe it until you wake up on that Monday morning and pull up the new rankings list on the tour's Web site. The rankings are based on a system. All year, as you travel on the tour, you accumulate points. A certain number for reaching the round of sixty-four, a certain number for the round of thirty-two, for the round of sixteen, and so on. These numbers are amped up during major tournaments. Reach the quarters or semifinals of a Grand Slam, you are talking about serious points. Win a Grand Slam and it's like the cherries on the slot machine line up and out pour the coins.

A new ranking list is published every week. It has to do with how well you've performed, and also how many tournaments you've entered, and how well other players have performed. In other words, I never really know. It's a complicated system. You'd need a doctorate from MIT to understand exactly what's going on. I'd been ranked as high as number four, and, really, the difference between number four and number one might be the difference between flying to Japan to compete in some small tournament and laying off for a week to rest your shoulder. From the beginning of my career, I've planned schedules that I believed would best prepare me to peak at the Grand Slams. I never thought of adding tournaments to that schedule to gain extra points for a better ranking. And that continues to be the way I plan—Grand Slam–focused, not rankings-focused. And yet hitting number one is special and thrilling. I was surprised by my reaction. I didn't think I would care that much, but I was wrong. I couldn't stop thinking about it. As long as I held that ranking, I was the best female tennis player in the world.

All these years, this is what I'd dreamed about and what I'd been working toward, and now it had happened. Number one. Think of all the great players who'd held this spot before me! Billie Jean King. Martina Navratilova. Steffi Graf. I was now part of an elite club—that could never be taken away.

But the feeling did not last. Maybe just as long as it took me to finish breakfast, look at my phone, and head out to the courts. There is always another tournament, another winner, and another reckoning of points. There is always another girl, a crowd of other players, working, at this moment, to take your place.

As happy as I was, and I'm not entirely sure that this *was* happiness, my father was ecstatic. Number one? It was something he'd dreamed about and worked for since those first afternoons in Sochi, when Yudkin, crazy czar of the clay courts, told my father I had it in me to be among the best in the world. "But what are you willing to give?" Yudkin had asked my father. "Because this will mean giving up everything and changing your life."

What troubled me was that I was still missing that essential thing—a second Grand Slam championship. It kept eluding me, making me sort of jumpy and nuts, aware everyone was looking at me, thinking, "Sure, she won once but it might have been a fluke, an accident, even luck. Can she win that big again? That's the question." As I entered the 2006 season, it was about the only thing on my mind. Being ranked number one is not enough—I had to prove that I deserved to be ranked number one. I had to win that second Grand Slam.

* * *

I had my game face on when I reached Melbourne for the 2006 Australian Open. I wanted to get going immediately. I wanted to shut up the skeptics, gossips, and doubters. I wanted to earn my top rank right there at the start of the season. I flew through the early rounds, defeating each of my opponents—Sandra Klösel, Ashley Harkleroad, Jelena Kostanić Tošić, Daniela Hantuchová— in straight sets. I faced Nadia Petrova, a Russian girl who'd always given me trouble, in the quarterfinals, and beat her. I was like a sprinter flying down the track. Nothing could stop me—until I ran into the wall, as eventually happens to everyone, even sprinters. In my case, it was the small, tough, relentless, mosquito-like Belgian player Justine Henin.

My game had not matched up well against Henin. She exposed my weaknesses better than any player. She makes you move, move, and move. No matter what you hit, or where, she anticipates its direction and gets it back, which is why I've compared her to a flying, stinging insect. You slap it and think you've got it, but when you look down you realize she's gotten through your fingers and here comes another ball. I always keep my philosophy basic: *I do not have to be the best player in the world to be the best player in the world. I just have to be a little bit better than the other player on that particular day.* Henin's philosophy is seemingly simpler still: *If I just hit the ball at her one more time than she hits the ball at me, I win,* which can make for a long, grueling match. And that one-handed backhand slice! Even when I've beaten her, she's made me look bad and worn me out. I would go to sleep with her one-handed backhand staring me down. Before she retired in 2011,

Henin spent 117 weeks ranked number one in the world and won seven Grand Slam titles, which puts her among the all-time leaders.

I believed I could beat her, but I knew it was going to be tough. Before every match against her, I knew she'd be ready to play for three hours, and I would end up in an ice bath. And that day she just hung in and hung in and hung in. On point after point, I'd hit what I believed to be a winner and she'd somehow hit it back even better. In fact, it was one of the cleanest tennis matches I felt I have ever played—so few errors. It was also one of the toughest physically. Henin is a nightmare to play. She is small and tough and will not relent and will not quit. And she looks like a robot when she plays, no expression on her face at all. And that ponytail! It swings back and forth like a metronome. If you are not careful, you'll be hypnotized. She was just so hard to finish off—that's what really annoyed me. I edged out the first set 6–4, but her tiny legs just kept going and going, along with that expressionless face and crazy determination.

I lost 6–1 in the second set, then lost 6–4 in the third. But maybe I had done more damage than I'd realized. She had to pull out of the final after winning only a single game, complaining of stomach pain. Sometimes, the real final is not what's played at the end of the tournament.

Losing hurts. It is so painful. It can also be the best thing. It prepares you for winning. In this case, it taught me how to play Justine Henin, which would prove vitally important just a few months later.

✳ ✳ ✳

The U.S. Open is the last Grand Slam of the season, and it comes as a kind of relief, a cool evening after a hot day. My recollections of it tend to be intimidating nighttime memories, of traffic and billboards, Arthur Ashe Stadium under the lights, the sound of the crowd, the highway to the Billie Jean King National Tennis Center, the people and energy and excitement of the city. I have said Wimbledon is the ultimate prize, but a case can be made for the U.S. Open. There's nothing like winning in New York City.

I came into the 2006 U.S. Open ranked third in the world. Justine Henin was number two. Amélie Mauresmo, an outstanding French player, was number one. A few weeks before, I'd filmed an ad campaign for Nike. The commercial was released at the end of August, a few weeks before the start of the tournament. It was shot like a documentary, a film crew following me through a typical competition day: me waking up, getting ready, leaving my hotel—the Waldorf-Astoria in midtown Manhattan—and heading to Arthur Ashe Stadium. Along the way, I run into people, each of whom sings a line from the *West Side Story* song "I Feel Pretty." "Oh so pretty and witty and bright." The ad ends with me on court, hitting a backhand winner in the final. A jinx? Well, the idea was to turn that commercial into reality. It was shown during every commercial break of the tournament.

One of my first serious challenges in the U.S. Open that year came from the top seed, Amélie Mauresmo, in the semifinals. She had a tricky one-handed backhand and was great at the net, which was far from my strength. Her game was smooth and resilient. I'd never beaten her in a tournament. She'd already won two Grand Slams that year: the Australian Open, where she prevailed because Henin had to withdraw, and Wimbledon, where she beat me in the semifinals and Henin in the final. Here, we played on center court at sunset. You had to drift between the shadows, eagle-eyed, the ball moving in and out of the light. And there was wind—a lot of it. I was wearing a lilac dress that night, and silver shoes. I was nineteen years old, working toward the peak of my career.

I took the first set without losing a game, 6–0. She beat me in the second, 6–4. Was there a moment of doubt? Maybe. The conditions we were playing in took away all the confidence a player might normally have had. During the changeover, I first looked up at the score on the jumbotron, then I looked up into the box. There was my coach Michael Joyce. There was my father. He held up a banana, then a bottle of water. I took a moment during the changeover to visualize it: winning. I was consistent, solid. Did the right things, played the right way. I did not lose a single game in the third set. Finally! I was back in a Grand Slam final for the first time since I'd won Wimbledon.

They interviewed me on the court after the match. They wanted to know what I thought of Justine Henin. We'd be playing in the final on Saturday. I had faced her four times in the past two years, and lost all four times. But that didn't faze me. "I'm not done yet," I told the crowd. "I haven't beaten Amélie in a competition match before; I beat her today. I don't have a great record with Justine, so, you know, I mean, it doesn't really matter. It's a new match, new opportunity." Looking back and writing these words, I can't believe how confident I was.

I wore that black Audrey Hepburn dress to the final, determined to turn that Nike commercial from fiction into fact. The crowd seemed especially close to the court that night—the stadium was just electric. Camera flashes and movie stars. Now and then, you feel less like you are living your life than like you are watching it being lived. Like you are someone else, somewhere else. You need to snap out of that before the start of the first game. You have to be present to win. In other words, I came at it slightly removed, which is nerves. Henin broke me right away—took the first two games before I even woke up. The crowd was muttering, mumbling. I could feel that they were for me—they wanted to lift me up.

The key was my serve. That was one of the best years for my serve. I began to hit it again and again. It was precise, consistently placed where I wanted it to be. In the corners, on the lines, delivered with force. When you do that, you control the point even when it's not an ace. By knowing my weaknesses, I was able to direct the action toward my strengths. I began to impose my will. On some points, I moved Henin like she was a puppet on a string. I moved her the way she had moved me in our four previous meetings. It got in her head, which meant that even when she stepped on the line to serve, she knew she was in for a long rally. After a bad start, I went on to break her twice in that first set. I took it 6–4. It was more of the same in the second. My serve set up my backhand, which determined the course of the night. I broke her in the eighth game of the second set—and sometimes you only need that one break.

As we neared the end, I could feel the energy build. The crowd, the shouts and the screams of New York. At this point, it was all about my focus. I had it in this match as I'd never had it before. The tournament rested on my serve. It was a good one. Henin played it to my backhand. Big mistake. I hit the ball with pace, power—she couldn't handle it. It ended up in the net. And that was it. At that moment, I dropped to my knees and put my face in my hands, then ran into the stands to hug my father. Then I ran back onto the court for the trophy, a silver cup, which I raised up so fast, the lid fell off. Typical of me. I couldn't stop laughing.

I knew I'd win but still couldn't believe it. That impossible second Grand Slam, won right there, in New York City, with everyone who cheered for me and everyone who cheered against me watching. Life can be sweet. At that moment, it seemed like it would always be sweet. Of course, whenever you think that, whenever you are so sure of anything, you are probably wrong.

FOURTEEN

As a famous singer says, "Some days are diamonds, some days are rocks."

The year 2008 was not a diamond. It was bad news followed by bad news. It was one damn thing after another. It started with Robert Lansdorp, who'd become such an important part of my team and my life. He was crazy; he was a pain in the ass; he was difficult and he was weird—but I loved him. Apparently, my father did not. Apparently my father could no longer stand to work with him, or vice versa.

The story?

It depends on whom you ask, and what time of day you ask it.

My father will tell you that things change, that time passes, that people grow apart. We had taken what we had needed from Lansdorp, he will say, and Lansdorp had taken what he had needed from us. It was no one's fault. It was just over. It was just time to move on. My father believes that it's important to change coaches and routines every few years—it keeps you learning and it makes life interesting.

But Lansdorp will dismiss all this talk of natural endings and people growing apart as bullshit. He cites a specific incident instead, a specific day.

I was playing Nadia Petrova, a Russian girl who I didn't think much of. It was just something about her. Maybe it's more intense when you're facing another Russian. It's like you're playing for the love of the same parent. That intensity can feel like hatred. I assume, when I stop playing, that everyone will be able to forgive me and that I will be able to forgive everyone, but as long as I am in the game, I need that intensity. It's never really personal. It's never really about the other girl. It's fuel. I need it to win. The match was getting nasty, and all eyes were on my father, who was sitting with Lansdorp in my box. Yuri had become a famous tennis parent by this time. He did not give interviews, did not comment in the press, did not do any kind of grandstanding, which made him seem mysterious and interesting. Before he knew it, he'd become a caricature in the tennis world, a cartoon of the crazy Russian father, pacing in his hoodie, frowning, grumbling, keeping to himself. The crowd picked up on this, and the mood around the Petrova match turned stormy. Finally, right in the middle of things, someone in the stands threw a tennis ball onto the court. I had one ball in my hand, and was preparing to serve, when here comes this other ball, arcing down from the sky. Everyone started to hiss. Then I heard my father's voice, booming over everything: "Just finish the point!"

The press played it up. Another outburst from the wild Russian. A reporter called Lansdorp and asked him what he'd thought of the episode. Lansdorp did not say much, but what he did say, and what the newspaper published, infuriated my father. Lansdorp, in essence, said that he did not believe that Yuri should be yelling down from the box. At the next match, in Lansdorp's version, my father was daggers and laser beams with Robert. They sat side by side in icy silence. Tension, tension. I began to fall behind on court, and the worse it looked for me, the more evil the mood became. Finally, after I lost a point, my father turned to Lansdorp and said, "See? That's what you get when you don't yell down from the box."

How did Lansdorp respond?

Well, if you've ever met Robert, you probably know.

He said, "Fuck off, Yuri. Don't give me any shit."

And that was it—the end of my time with Robert Lansdorp. He never coached me again. It was a bigger loss than you might imagine. It was not just the flat shot or the repetition that Lansdorp gave me. It was friendship, confidence. It was a kind of stability and balance you rarely encounter. It's not a surprise that so many great players cite the role that Lansdorp played in their success. And it's not technical stuff they mention. You can get that from anyone. It's the intangibles, the relationship, the sense he gives you that, no matter what sort of slump or hole you have fallen into, you will survive because you are a champion. Want evidence? Well, would he be at your side if you weren't? It was something that I'd miss over the years, but especially in the months immediately ahead. In other words, Robert Lansdorp bugged out at exactly the wrong time—just as I was about to enter one of the most difficult passages of my career.

❋ ❋ ❋

The year wasn't all bad. I did win my third Grand Slam. This was the Australian Open. It was some of the cleanest tennis I've ever played at a Grand Slam. I remember everyone talking about where Lindsay Davenport would end up in the draw because she had been injured and wasn't seeded. It turned out she was going to be my second-round opponent. I didn't like that. It doesn't matter how well you're doing or how high you're flying, if a great player has a great day, there's a good chance it won't be a great day for you. And Lindsay Davenport was a great player. So I prepared for that match like nothing else mattered even though I still had a first-round match to win. It was the toughest draw I've ever faced in a Grand Slam. After Davenport, I had to beat Elena Dementieva, Justine Henin, and Jelena Jankovic, all world-class competitors.

I played Ana Ivanović in the final. It wasn't my best tennis of the tournament. I was better against Davenport and Henin. It was pretty close in the first set. Ivanović had a few chances to lead. That all turned around during a particular rally. She tried to hit a drop shot in the middle of a rally that didn't really need it, and the ball bounced in front of the net. That's when I saw it in her eyes. Fear? Nerves? It's a tell. It said she was not up to the task. From that moment, I took over the match mentally even more than any-thing else. I beat her 7–5, 6–3. It was a big deal—winning my third Gland Slam. I'd won all the majors but the French Open.

One of the first calls I made after I won at the Australian Open? It might surprise you. It was Jimmy Connors.

It was Michael Joyce who first made that introduction. This was back in 2007, during our prep season training for the new year. Joyce suggested we go see Jimmy Connors in Santa Barbara. Have him be part of our practices, go to dinner together, benefit from his experience. I immediately agreed. As an athlete, being in the presence of champions is humbling, inspiring. You listen to their every word, inspect their every move. Michael and I drove up to Santa Barbara, where Jimmy resided, in early December, listening to U2's "Where the Streets Have No Name" the whole way. It was Michael's favorite song, and soon became mine. We spent four days practicing alongside Jimmy. I was nervous. To miss a ball, to say the wrong thing, to not have an answer to his questions. He had a calm, mysterious demeanor and spent every water break talking about his mother's influence, her guidance, and her no-bullshit attitude.

He had me jump rope at the beginning and end of practice until my arms were ready to fall off. He explained that in the old days they didn't do any of the gym bullshit they do now; it was all practical, simple stuff. So jump rope it was. I liked his approach, and I liked the feeling I left Santa Barbara with even more. I don't remember the particular U2 songs on our drive home, mostly because I was dead asleep in the passenger seat, emotionally and physically drained from the hours of practice. It occurred to me that, although Michael was still running the practices and we were doing similar drills to those we had been doing for years, having Jimmy Connors on the sidelines watching my every move—silently, like a hawk—adds another gear of concentration, and desire. I didn't want to miss a single ball in front of Jimmy Connors. I didn't want to let any winner get by me. I pushed myself, scrambled, laser-focused.

About a month later, the night we were celebrating my Australian Open victory, I called Jimmy during our celebration dinner. I thanked him for spending those days on court together; I told him that they had inspired me. He told me he was happy for me. But he also said to make sure I don't only call him when I win, but also when I lose. That stuck. And continues to be a very important quality I look for in people I come across. Will they want to hear from me when I lose? When I'm down?

It was strange, those days right after I won the Australian Open. Big things were happening, but not in a good way.

The first big thing: I separated from my father; I separated from Yuri. Not as a father of course—he and my mother will always be closer to me than anyone else in the world—but I separated from him as a coach. My father had always said you need to change it up, get together with new and different people every few years, because it adds energy and revitalizes routine and vanquishes boredom. Boredom, routine—those can be the most deadly foes of all. Eventually, and there is irony in this, Yuri's advice led me to the conclusion that I had to separate from Yuri himself. For the first time, I could glimpse the end of my professional career. The players I'd made my name against were beginning to call it quits. Younger and younger players were coming up behind me. So this was the time: If I wanted to prove that I could do it on my own, win on my own, be a fully functioning player and fully functioning adult on my own, I had to do it now. By firing my father—that really is too harsh a term—I would be taking control of my life.

I sent him an e-mail because I felt that was the best way I could express my feelings. My father did not take it hard. He did not scream or throw a vase or overturn a table. In fact, he got it. He understood it. He said, "Now, Maria, yes, you have to live your own life." Maybe he was ready to get off the road, to quit the endless rounds of airports, hotels, and arenas. My father has since dedicated himself to a life of serious active leisure, the beach and the mountains, skiing and exercising, reading and thinking about his beloved Tolstoy. He works out as if he were training for the senior Olympics. The grace with which he stepped away was his last great act as my coach. I continued on with Michael Joyce as my coach. Everything remained the same, and yet it was of course entirely different. Which might have been the only thing on my mind that year, if not for the second big thing that happened after I won the Australian Open.

It was a small thing at first—an ache in my shoulder when I served. But the pain got worse and worse. It reached the point where I did not even want to play, it hurt so much to serve. I cried after some matches, the pain got so intense. I tried to play through it, then to change my motion to alleviate the pain, which only threw other parts of my body into disarray. I was falling out of rhythm, losing my feel and confidence for the game.

Meanwhile, my trainer was treating me with ibuprofen and exercises and rubdowns, but none of it helped. The pain was always there, especially on my serve and high backhand volleys. If I played a point without pain, I was overjoyed. Then the pain roared back, and when it did, I was plunged into a panicky gloom. I became moody. My father finally said, "Look, Maria has always had a tremendously high threshold for pain. If it's this bad, it must be something more than just the normal wear and tear."

We went to see a doctor. He said it was tendonitis. The right rotator cuff. The tendon is like a big rubber band there, made of many small strands. These can become inflamed, even frayed— that's tendonitis. In my case, he said it was probably caused by the repetitive motion of my serve. He told me to take it easy but to keep on playing—if you don't move the tendon, it can get stiff and even lock. He told me to ice my shoulder after each session and take an anti-inflammatory. It might take a few weeks, he said, but the pain will fade.

"The pain will fade."

Do you know how many times I heard that line? Too stinking many. I played and iced and took anti-inflammatories, but the pain did not fade. In fact, it got worse. I went to see another doctor. He took the same pictures and did the same tests and came back with a different diagnosis. It might've been tendonitis, but now it's bursitis, he said. Without going into a lot of detail, suffice it to say bursitis is an inflammation of the tissue beneath the tendon. I was told to stop playing for a few weeks, put ice on the shoulder, and take anti-inflammatories for pain. Given time, they said, my shoulder would heal. In the worst-case scenario, there would be cortisone shots.

One day, after I'd done all that—didn't play for two weeks, took anti-inflammatories, applied ice, even tried the cortisone shots—I laced up my shoes and went out to play. I hit some balls from the baseline—so far, so good. But as soon as I lifted my arm to serve and made contact, there was the pain, waiting for me, and worse than ever. I did not feel it when I hit a forehand. I could volley just fine. And I did not feel it every time that I went up for a serve, which was confusing, but I did feel it most of the time. It was right at the top of my shoulder—a sharp pain that sort of mellowed into a dull ache that lasted maybe ten seconds. While it was happening, I could think of nothing else, which made it impossible to play out points. I was devastated. When you are an athlete, your body is everything. When it fails, it's so painful. It feels like you're finished.

Someone recommended a doctor on the Upper East Side in

New York, Dr. David Altchek, an orthopedic surgeon who'd seen everything that could happen to a shoulder. They said he was the best in the country. It took him about five minutes to know that I had a serious problem. He did a lot of tests—X-rays and MRIs—then sat me down in the waiting room. The news was not good. The bursa was not irritated. The tendon in my shoulder was not inflamed—it was torn. I had been playing for weeks with a torn tendon, which is why I had all that pain. It was probably a result of my serve, the repetition of that same violent motion. My shoulder rotated till my hand reached the middle of my back, exploding forward to meet the ball high in the air. Once, a few years before, a baseball coach who'd seen me serve took my father aside and said it was a motion he'd seen only in certain pitchers. He admired it and said it generated tremendous power, but warned my father that it could also cause tremendous injury later on. My father had forgotten all about this exchange, but remembered it now. He thought, "I knew she should be playing lefty."

The doctor said I needed surgery. The tendon would have to be reattached, sewn back together. The sooner, the better. It was a serious operation for a tennis player. He did not sugarcoat it. Several tennis players had had shoulder surgery in the past, but none had made it back to the top. "You can overcome it," he said, "but you will not be the same player."

I sat there, staring at my feet, taking in these words. I was twenty-one years old. At first, it did not register. I did not believe him. Later that night, when it did hit me, I fell into a kind of black hole. I'd finally made it, gotten my game and life just where I wanted it to be, and now I was going to lose everything because of one small split tendon? And what if my career did end there? How would I be remembered? As a flash in the pan, just another sad story, a cautionary tale? No. I refused to believe that this is how it would end.

✳ ✳ ✳

I was in the hospital a few days later, prepped for surgery, and in that gown that has been in and out of the washing machine so many times. I went to New York with my mother, Max, and Michael Joyce, who'd now been coaching me for several years. I'll never forget Max's face. He was saying all the right things, and being encouraging and calm, and it's no big deal, every player, and so forth and so on, but his eyes were red and it seemed to me that he'd been crying. He was so shaky that it made me shaky, but mostly I was touched. Max and I had been together for so long, been through so much. Without realizing it, we'd become family.

The details of the operation had been explained to me. I understood it on an intellectual level, but the thought of someone cutting into my shoulder and playing around with the ligaments and nerves was terrifying. It's a big part of the makeup of any athlete—being in control. *My* serve, *my* plan, *my* game. And now, when it came to the most important game of all, I was giving up all control. A complete loss of autonomy. When the big plays were made, the plays that would affect my own body, I'd be less than a spectator. I'd be unconscious.

Here's what bothered me most: various people, nurses and doctors, came into my room and asked me a question that had already been asked many times before. *Which shoulder?* Is it this one, or that one? Are you sure it's not the left shoulder? I felt like saying, "Hey, have you ever watched a tennis match? Have you ever seen me serve? I serve with my right arm, my right shoulder! Which is why it broke down, which is why I'm here!" Finally, someone came in and drew a big X on my right shoulder with what looked like a Sharpie. An X surrounded by all kinds of helpful arrows. Operate here!

At some point, after they'd shot me up and wheeled me in, a man put in my IV . . . I was gone. When I opened my eyes, and it seemed like a moment later, my shoulder and arm were swaddled like a newborn baby and my thoughts were as thick as syrup and I was being wheeled down a long linoleum hallway. Fluorescent lights. The hum of rubber wheels. Then I was back in my hospital room, surrounded by three familiar faces. Thirty minutes later, I looked at Max and said, "I don't belong here. Get me out of here."

Then I sat up and, as I did, vomited all over the floor. It was from the anesthesia. I guess I wasn't ready to leave the hospital yet, but that's when I began my long journey back.

I started rehab in Arizona soon after. I did most of that work with Todd Ellenbecker, a specialist in shoulder recovery based outside Phoenix. I would fly to Arizona each Monday with Michael Joyce, then back to L.A. on Friday. Every week, on Monday and Friday, that same bag of peanuts on that same Southwest Airlines flight. I could have stayed in Arizona, but the work was hard and tedious and I don't love living in a hotel, so I went back to L.A. each weekend.

We started with stretching and strength exercises. It was as if I had a brand-new shoulder, still stiff from bubble wrap and tape. I had to regain power and mobility. Of course, I had known about all this and was prepared. But what I was not prepared for, what took me by surprise, was the pain. The incredible pain. It hurt like hell to lift those little half-pound weights and do those little drills, but I could not rest and could not whine. It went on for days and days. And every day seemed the same. Hours of gray skies and bad moods and afternoon showers, and meanwhile the world was going on without me, the matches and the finals and the trophies raised at center court, all of it continuing as if my presence did not matter, as if I'd never been born. It was like being shut out of your own life, or locked out of your own house.

They brought in various trainers and strength coaches to work with me and still it hurt like hell and still the progress was slow. They'd cut me open in October 2008. I was back on the court, hitting balls (badly) by Christmas. But everything felt different, and by "different" I mean wrong. It hurt and was ugly. My strength was gone. My flexibility was gone. And my range of motion. When I tried to serve, I could not get my arm back far enough to generate any power. I would eventually learn to hit the ball again, to emerge from this pain and funk, but as a different player. I'd never have the same kind of serve that I'd had at seventeen. Not as consistent, not as free, not as loose. Not as powerful. Not as accurate. My motion had to be shortened. I knew that, but could still not get it quite right. I did not feel comfortable on the court, or in my body. What was I doing out there during all those miserable mornings in the winter of 2008? I was learning to play tennis again. I'd have to rely more on canniness and strategy. I'd have to rely less on my serve than on my return of serve. In some ways, I'd be a better player as a result. In other ways, I'd be worse. In either case, I had to learn to win in a new way.

My father set up a few practice matches. These did not go well. I lost to inferior players. It sent me into a kind of panicky moodiness. Nothing made me happy. I became obsessed with my shoulder, my future, my game. And did I mention my shoulder? It made it impossible for me to enjoy the other parts of my life—my friends and family, food, shopping, a sunny day.

My parents were worried about me. And so was Max. Not about my tennis—they claim they always knew that I'd find my way back—but about my spirit, my state of mind. Despite the large amount of support and love I received from people in my life, I felt so lonely and small. And nothing they said could make me feel any better. So I decided to resume my childhood habit of writing in a journal, putting my sad thoughts on paper. As days went by, that paper became my best friend, the only friend I could trust, the only friend I could share with.

It would be a crucial part of my recovery. I came to believe that the physical act of writing can reeducate your brain. By writing, you access certain thoughts and feelings that might otherwise remain hidden. You can bring them to the surface, where they can be understood and then dealt with. It's like turning on a light in a dark room. What you had believed to be a monster is revealed in the light to be little more than shadows. Boom, you're back to your old, less freaked-out self. I also came to believe that you can plant positive thoughts in your psyche in the same way. Put it on paper and in it goes. Which is why, if you look through those diaries, which I have saved and used to help write this book, you will see pages given over to nothing but positive phrases in the nature of "Yes, you can. Yes, you can. Yes, you can." But mostly I am talking myself through my injury and frustration and pain.

A typical entry:

I am completely flustered! You see I can't even write. It's been God knows how long since I started (I believe eight weeks now) and I'm still all the way in the bottom of the ditch somewhere in the middle of America. Basically I don't feel like my shoulder is getting any better. It's a constant battle. I'm doing everything I can possibly do for it. Yet I constantly have a hollow feeling inside me. I know that it will get better and I am going to play and serve without any pain but I also feel like I'm fooling myself for no apparent reason. I walk into the clinic every single day and do what? Get stronger? Will that take the pain away? How long will it take? It's these constant questions that I myself cannot answer.

I missed too many tournaments while rehabbing my shoulder. My ranking, which had been near the top, fell into the high double digits. I'd had to skip the Australian Open, meaning I could not defend my 2008 title, which really stunk. It meant I wouldn't get to walk through that tunnel and see a picture of me holding up the big trophy beside all the previous champions.

I did not begin really playing again until March 2009. I started in the dregs. My shoulder hurt, my body disobeyed my mind, my serve did not exist, and I tired easily, but I was determined to scrap my way back into the game. Nothing makes you want something more than having it and losing it. Until I got that top ranking, I hadn't realized how much I'd wanted it. Now, more than anything, I wanted it back.

The French Open was to be my reemergence on the scene. That's what I was training for, but I felt just awful. The bottom came in May at a small tune-up tournament in Warsaw, Poland, on the worst clay courts I had ever seen. I did not want to play in it, but I had to get through some matches. I couldn't go into the French Open cold turkey. I won maybe two matches, losing in the quarters, in a match I could've won convincingly at any other point in my career. The winner was Alona Bondarenko, a Ukrainian. After the match, I watched her give her press conference.

I remember every word she said, like it was yesterday. *Maria has lost the speed on her serve; Maria has lost her power; Maria has lost her game; Maria is not what she used to be; blah blah blah.* I remember seeing those lines run across the bottom of the screen on CNN. That was just the fuel I needed. That's the kind of thing that gives you motivation. Of course I wanted to win the French Open and Wimbledon. But now it was more than that. It wasn't just that I wanted to win. It's that I wanted to make Alona Bondarenko eat those words.

The French Open was a disaster. That's how I remember it, anyway. When I look back at the stats, the story seems a little more complicated. The fact is that in my first Grand Slam postsurgery, I made it to the quarterfinals, playing some good matches and beating some good players to get there. But I tend to really remember only how things ended. Were you playing on the last day, or were you already in the next town while the focus of the tennis world was on someone else? I lost a terrible match in straight sets. I managed to win only two games. I should have been all right with the result, as it was just my second tournament back, but I wasn't happy with the tournament and I was very unhappy with that final match. It was a low point, utterly deflating. After a match like that, you go back to the locker room and scream.

My diary:

Ever since the Open, I am walking around with a huge doubt on my shoulders. I go into my press conference and the first question is . . . "People are saying you're not making progress. Why is that? Do you think you need a new coach?" Seriously, why the fuck do you care, why does anyone care? It's as if these people were scientists, that they think they know everything! Get a life!

I eventually made my way to Wimbledon. I was hopeful when I arrived in town because Wimbledon had always been a magical place for me. Whenever I'd been down, that town and those grass courts and that tournament had always brought me back up. It had been like pixie dust. Well, not this time. It was an upside-down world. Whatever had been good turned out bad. This was the real rock bottom. Maybe I wanted it too much. Maybe I had pushed too hard. I made it through the first round, beating a qualifier but having to work hard to do so, and lost in the second round to an unranked Argentinian player named Gisela Dulko. It was one of my quickest exits from a Grand Slam ever. Before I had even unpacked my bags, I was back on the plane, heading home. The sportswriters were busy writing obituaries on my career. I was twenty-two years old. It had been a good life, but now it was over.

As soon as I got in from the airport, I took out my diary and began to write:

Well, I am finding myself back home on a Thursday the first week of Wimbledon. Yep, it pretty much sucks. To be honest there's such a mix of thoughts and feelings. On the one hand it's pretty amazing to think that my arm has held up as well as it has. I really didn't believe I was ready to play at such a tough level, four tournaments in a row. And yet for some reason I feel like someone kicked my dog. Of course it's Wimbledon, and I don't like to lose. Then I'm at the airport this morning buying one of those stupid gossip magazines with every paper staring me down with my face on the cover, the headlines saying, "It's All Over for

Sharapova"! Fuckers! Then I get on the plane and they're asking if I want a paper every two seconds. Then the lady in front of me is reading the sports section. And there it is again. "It's All Over for Sharapova." All of a sudden women decide to start reading the sports section on that particular day?

FIFTEEN

Who can you turn to in such a confusing time? For most people, it's friends from work, all those people in the office, but I am not friends with many people from my "office." Not because I do not like them, but because in our world, it's very difficult to be friends with another player. These are your opponents on the court, and being friends with them is giving away one of your advantages. If I like you, I'll have a harder time putting you away. I don't believe I'm the only player who feels this way, but I am one of the few who will admit it. When I see two players all buddy-buddy on the tour, I know that friendship will always have its limits. I'd rather live honestly and be truthful than put on a phony show for the press. In the tough times, it's my family I turn to, and to the few genuine friends that I have made over the years—not my rivals.

Of course, there's also the comforts of boyfriends. When I look back at my diary, I see, scattered between the positive-thinking exercises and dark ruminations, the constant discussion of crushes and would-be boyfriends, as well as my general thoughts on romance. In my early years on the pro tour, I was amazed by the way I seemed to attract the attention of grown men. It was funny to me, probably because I still felt like a kid.

I was always interested in the question of what sort of guy would best suit me: "Who would I consider *the one?*" I wondered in my diary as a teenager.

First he has to understand and respect the business I'm in. And he has to have his own purpose in life. He has to be down to earth meaning if he has millions of dollars then you wouldn't be able to tell. He has to have a sense of humor because I love to laugh. He has to be affectionate, caring, and sweet. He has to be open-minded about things like telling me the truth, because I hate people who have secrets. And most importantly he has to love me for the person I am on the inside rather than on the outside. But I still like the bad boys. Even though I know it's trouble. I want to fix them and take them home. I love challenges.

I didn't date seriously until I was nearly twenty-two years old. It was the end of 2009. A friend of mine was preparing a casual barbecue at her house on a Saturday, and she called me up a few hours beforehand to say I needed a distraction, could she invite someone to come who might have potential?

I said "Sure," not really understanding her intention.

He walked into her house in the middle of dinner with hair still wet from the shower, in sports gear, ice wrapped around both

knees. I liked him immediately. Saturday night, and he'd just finished practice? That's my type of person.

His name was Sasha Vujačić. He was a Slovenian basketball
player in his fifth year with the L.A. Lakers. That night we ate
grilled fish fillets and talked, then exchanged numbers.

The next morning I was on a flight to Napa Valley with my
mom and some close friends. This was my postseason vacation.
I told her about Sasha.

I said, "He's tall and European."

She said, "Masha, no. Basketball players rarely have a proper
education."

Well, I didn't have a proper education either. And besides, he
grew up in Europe, and has traveled around the world. He must
have picked up something along the way.

She shook her head. She didn't want to hear any more.

I didn't think that was fair. I wouldn't disqualify someone
because their athletic lifestyle had prevented them from going to
school. I decided to give him a chance.

We formed a bond, a closeness and understanding that I
thought at the time only athletes could form. And we made sense
together. He had a home in Los Angeles and was a professional
athlete, he had the height, he had an Eastern European mentality,
and he was close to his family. All good on paper.

But there were signs of trouble even in the early days. For one
thing, he always insisted, when we were in L.A., that we stay at his
place, even though my place was much bigger and much nicer
than his place, and just down the street. It was a man thing, or
maybe it's just an Eastern European man thing. He always had to
make it clear that he was the center of the action, that it was his
place and his world and he was in control. He did not like to be

reminded that I had a career of my own, a bigger place, and a bigger income. I couldn't care less about those things, but they mattered to him. The fact that I was probably more successful in my world than he was in his was not something we could ever talk about or acknowledge. So we stayed at his place and did not talk about it. We just went on.

About a year into the relationship, we got engaged. It was less like a traditional plan to get married—I was definitely not ready for that—than a statement of commitment. Like going steady. I think this was also an Eastern European or Slavic thing. Like pledging your love. It was a way of telling the world that for me there was only him and for him there was only me. He gave me a ring, a huge rock, which I took off only when I played. I'd just stare at it in disbelief, thinking, "Am I really engaged?"

The tennis world is small and gossipy and my news quickly spread everywhere. Some of the other girls congratulated me or asked about my wedding or my honeymoon plans. One day, around this time, Serena Williams pulled me aside in the Wimbledon locker room. I was about to play my first match of the tournament and was trying to get into the mental space you need to reach when it's time to play—players tend to leave each other alone in the hour preceding a match. Serena did not know or care. She was too excited and wanted to talk about my engagement. She'd just come back from an injury. I hardly ever talked to Serena, but she came on like we were old friends.

I said, "Hi, Serena, I'm glad you're back."

"I heard you got engaged," she said, excited. "Sorry for that. HA! HA! HA!"

Then she just stood there, laughing and laughing at her own joke.

I just stood there, too. I mean, what was I supposed to say to that? I laughed with her. As I said, it was just an hour until my match. I was already in my dress, about to start my warm-up. She had to know that. She was done playing for the day, so what did she care? She saw me in the members' locker room, sat next to me, looked around, as if checking for spies and eavesdroppers, then whispered, but it was one of those loud stage whispers, the kind you use if you really want to be overheard, saying, "You know, I got engaged, too! And I haven't told anyone but you."

Think about it. This was a person I've never had a real conversation with in my life. Our talk had never gone deeper than the sort of pleasantries you exchange at the net after a match. Still whispering, she said, "You won't believe it, Maria, but I'm dating a guy. I have been with him such a long time. And he asked me to marry him. But I don't know what to do. I want to get married, but I don't think it's the right time."

I looked at my watch. Forty-five minutes till my match. First round of Wimbledon.

I said, "That's interesting to hear, but now—"

She talked right over me.

"I've got to show you this," she said, reaching into her bag and pulling out a little pouch with a clasp. "I have the ring right here," she said, then dropped this big diamond into my hand.

"So are you engaged?" I asked. I didn't know what else to say, what else to do.

"Yes and no," she said, taking back the ring. "Or, well, yes. But nobody knows. My father doesn't know. My mother doesn't know. Only you. You are the only one who knows."

I just sat there staring at her. I did not know what to say. Why was she telling me this? Then I went down and won my match.

Afterward, when my coach and team rushed up to congratulate me, I said, "You will not believe what happened just before I got out here."

Then, one day, Sasha was traded to the New Jersey Nets. It would be his chance to get more game time, or that was his plan. Hoboken, New Jersey, his new home: Where the hell was that? He told me it was just a ferry ride to one of my favorite cities in the world. I was skeptical. I started looking it up, searching for local coffee shops where I could sit while he was at practice. All I could find was a place called Carlo's Bake Shop, apparently made famous by the reality TV show *Cake Boss*. If people are lining up outside a bakery to buy cannoli in Hoboken, I asked myself, how bad could the place be? Pretty bad. Even worse in February when the rivers are ice, the ferry is off-limits, and the traffic is so congested that the city I really wanted to be in felt like it was a million miles away.

Many months later, as the NBA was heading into a lockout, Sasha was considering a few financially appealing offers he'd received from abroad, deals I never thought he'd accept until, one day, he did. He signed with a Turkish team. Goodbye Hoboken, hello Yesilkoy. Another town I didn't know anything about. I struggled with the idea, then struggled even more with the reality.

We were now apart for months at a stretch, which gave me time to really think over the way we were struggling in our relationship. He so badly needed to be the man in the relationship, and my own career made it hard for him. The fact that I was more successful in my world than he was in his was something he could never acknowledge. My success, my fame, and my wealth were evidently becoming a struggle for him. Maybe it was always there, but our time apart really opened my eyes to it. Or maybe I just never wanted to admit it. Now it started to really bother me. It made me feel closed in, claustrophobic and trapped. In the months before the 2012 French Open, I started to withdraw from Sasha emotionally.

When I got to the locker room after winning the final of the French Open, with the trophy sitting in my lap, I dialed his number. He answered the phone, but I could hear the shot clock ticking in the background, players on the basketball court in the middle of practice. His coach had told him I'd won my match. He congratulated me. I was so excited, so emotional, that I then began thanking him. For being there for me during many challenging moments. For encouraging me when I was down. For pushing me, believing in me. He seemed genuinely moved, upbeat. It was more than I'd had from him in months. But when I called that night, his mood had changed. He sounded aggravated, almost angry. I asked him what was wrong. He said he'd watched my match when he got home, then the trophy ceremony. Now I knew exactly what was on his mind. He was mad that I hadn't thanked him in my victory speech. That's all he could think about it. For many months, I had been waiting for some sign from him, some hint. Now I had it. In just one sentence. Our relationship was over.

I've often asked myself what I want in a relationship, or what it is that I think I want—other than height. Well, I guess I want a partner who is also a friend. An equal. I want the house and the kids, but that seems so far in the future that it's hard to imagine, because my life is just city after city after city; because it's such high highs and such deep lows and there are very few men who can take being second to whatever is happening or not happening to a player on the court. As I said, the man wants to be the man. If you are on the tour, then you have to be the man, no matter your gender. If you have a boyfriend on the tour, he's most likely sacrificing his career to be with you, and who wants that? Or, and this is the other possibility, he's going to be another tennis player. And I've tried that, too.

* * *

I get a text from my agent Max after every match I play: "You are a champion." I can tell how much he means it by the number of exclamation points he puts at the end. It has become so automatic, I wonder if he just copies and pastes the message. Does he say that to all his clients? I don't even want to know. In October 2012, as I walked off the court after my quarterfinal match in Beijing, I checked my phone and there was the message from Max. "Thanks," I typed back, just as I do every time.

Ten minutes later, I got a second message, which surprised me. Max was in Miami, and it was 4:00 a.m. there. Shouldn't he be asleep?

"Grigor Dimitrov wants your number."

I looked at my phone surprised, and may I say excited? The phone went back in my pocket, and I went through my ten-minute cooldown on the bike, followed by fifteen minutes of stretching while my coach was in my ear, talking to me about the match. But my mind wasn't really with him, which is nothing new, because Thomas Högstedt—he was coaching me just then—talks too much after a match, more than anyone needs. I took my phone out, and now I had a new text message from Max. It was the same thing: "Grigor Dimitrov wants your number."

Why two messages? Did Max think the cell service was bad in Beijing?

I typed back: "For what?"

Max: "For what? Are you fucking stupid?"

I googled Grigor's name to find his age. Was he even legal?

Twenty-one. Barely.

"Give him my e-mail."

I remembered noticing a kid walking through Wimbledon village, tall, skinny, and carrying a type of good-looking grin that says he knows he is good-looking. I remembered telling my coach, "Thank goodness he didn't exist in my generation, that would have been dangerous. Dangerously distracting."

A few back-and-forths with e-mail, and Grigor asked for my number.

I played hard to get and gave him my BlackBerry messenger PIN. Then my cell number. Our messages turned into phone calls, our phone calls into Skype calls. It was very simple and genuine. I didn't think too much of it until, after one of our phone conversations, he dialed me back thirty seconds later and said, "I'm sorry, but I miss your voice. Can we speak for a few more minutes?"

I didn't know his ranking at the time.

Our Skype conversations continued. My mom started calling them my therapy sessions because, at the end of each, I always had a smile on my face.

Something about Grigor's tour schedule confused me—he was getting to Paris too early for an indoor tournament in Paris. It didn't make sense to me.

What would he be playing before the main draw began? I quickly opened a much-dreaded application I have on my phone called Live Scores, which has live scoreboards from every tennis tournament being played around the world, including all the tournament draws. I spent way too much time on NBA.com during my three years with Sasha, searching for minutes played, point percentages. I wasn't ready for another round of that, not so soon. And yet here I was, again.

I checked the main draw. Grigor's name wasn't there. I moved on to the qualifying draw. There he was. Ranked sixtieth in the world. Next thing I knew, I was peeking at the live scores of qualifying matches.

It was all long distance until one night he arrived at my doorstep with red roses and a giant teddy bear.

We spent a lot of time together over the next few weeks.

Within days he asked me if I would be his girlfriend. It caught me off guard. I wasn't ready for anything like that. He said he would wait until I was ready.

"Who is this person?" I asked myself.

I looked at him, wonderingly: Why is this handsome guy, who could be playing the field, waiting for a woman who is not ready to be in a relationship?

"OK," I said, "but I don't know when I will be ready. It might be months."

"OK," he said. "I'll wait. I know what I want and I want you."

Weeks rolled into months and there was nothing that could stop us. I watched him grow, triumph, suffer setbacks, recover. Up and down. I loved watching him play so much. I would find myself sitting on a rubber chair, on Christmas Day, watching him practice. Just me; my best friend, Estelle; him; and his hitting partner on a sunny California day that felt nothing like Christmas.

I watched him climb through the ranks. I watched him go from dumpy hotels by the highway in Madrid—the sort of hotel even the rats avoid—to a suite at the Four Seasons in Paris, the Carlyle in New York. I watched him go from being a kid who was reluctant to spend a little extra on an upgrade to economy-plus while flying to Australia, to being a man boarding a private jet provided by a new billionaire friend. After one of my matches in Brisbane, he gave everyone on my team a white crisp collared shirt with a note wishing that one day he could have a team like them. And before we were through, he did. I watched him grow into his own person, a person who makes his own decisions; I watched him shift into manhood.

Grigor has been called the next Roger Federer, the next this, the next that. He's been ranked as high as eighth in the world, and has so much potential. He has beautiful strokes. The way he hits the ball, then slides, even on hard courts, is inspiring. He can do amazing things with his body. It's a gift and also a curse. It's gotten in his way, this need not only to win but to look beautiful doing it. It has to be perfect or he does not want it at all. It has to be unbelievable or forget it. That's why he's yet to fulfill all that potential. What sets the great players apart from the good players? The good players win when everything is working. The great players win even when nothing is working, even when the game is ugly; that is, when they are not great. Because no one can be great every day. Can you get it done on the ugly days, when you feel like garbage and the tank is empty? That's the question. I've been close to flawless on a few lucky afternoons—I can count them on one hand—but it's usually a question of figuring out how to win with whatever I've got. There are so many matches that I've won just by figuring out how to sneak by. Grigor has yet to learn how to do that. It's like if it's not easy, if it's not perfect, he does not want to do it.

Grigor recently told me—we were talking on the phone after he'd reached the semifinals of the Australian Open—that one of the worst things in life is when you have the right thing at the wrong time. It made me think of an evening we spent before the 2015 Wimbledon tournament. He had reached the semifinals the previous year by beating Andy Murray; he lost to Novak Djokovic in four sets in that round. He pulled out a book that Wimbledon puts together of previous championships. He quietly flipped through the pages of the book until he found a picture of me, in his box, watching his match.

He looked at me, sad—I thought I saw tears in his eyes—"Did you see this? This means everything to me. Seeing you in my box next to my mother."

It was then, at that moment, that the emotional pull I had been fighting came to an end. I knew, and so did he, that I couldn't be that person at this time of my life. I was supposed to be focused, getting prepared for my own matches, my own triumphs and defeats, on the largest stage of my career. I had been watching his match that day only because I'd lost early at those championships. So his good memory was my bad memory. What meant everything to him happened only because I had lost. Like he said, you can have the right thing, but it might come at the wrong time.

SIXTEEN

Meanwhile, I was playing tennis. A lot of tennis. Nothing but tennis. I was no longer young, but not yet old. Twenty-five, twenty-six, twenty-seven. I was in the dead center of my professional career, past the excitement of the early days, but still with many days and years to go.

I wonder if the middle years are the toughest. You are past the initial eagerness that drove you on to the first triumphs. Many of your goals have been fulfilled. You have lost and you have won. You have raised the trophy at center court and also faced the morning after, when you must get right back to work. You are no longer a novelty to the analysts and reporters. You have been looked at and discussed until the shine has worn off. In any other world, you would still be at the start of things, new enough to be a rookie, but here, in tennis, you are beyond all that. You have been injured and repaired and injured again and again. Your body has worn out and broken down. Once upon a time, not very long ago, you identified and marked the great players of the game, the established stars you would have to defeat to get where you wanted to go. But to the new crop of player—and they never stop coming, churned out by the Rick Maccis and Nick Bollettieris—you are the star, the monument, the established player who must be defeated. Every player comes into every game against you with maximum energy, maximum motivation. Beating you will mean something more than just beating you—it will be the sort of highlight that can redeem an otherwise bad year. But what's going to motivate *you*? What are *you* playing for? You've already reached number one, already won Grand Slams, Wimbledon and the U.S. Open and the Australian Open. Winning them again, going around that same big track one more time . . . is it really enough to get you out on the practice court morning after morning?

The idea of legacy and of greatness—is that enough? Will that do it? Probably not. That's just abstract bullshit, for writers and fans. For me, the best motivation has always been small rather than big, personal rather than universal. The record book? Posterity? Fuck that. Did you hear what that girl said about me at the press conference? That's what gets me going. Make them eat their words. No matter how many seasons and tournaments go by, I want to win.

I had been working with Michael Joyce since 2005. He was a great coach and an even better friend. We'd been together through everything, all the good and all the bad, but we hit a kind of wall. I think we became almost too close. Over time, he felt less like a coach than like a brother. And you know how it is—at some point, you just stop listening to your brother. Our practices lost their spark. We fell into a rut. We decided to bring in a second coach. We would not fire Michael, we'd just get him an additional voice instead. We hired Thomas Högstedt, a Swedish former player and coach who brought great energy to my practices, planning drills and workouts that put the fire back in my game. But he was not so great at being a co-coach. This became clear at our first tournament together, the first time Högstedt and Joyce had to work side by side at an actual match and not just practice. Högstedt quickly took over, bossing around and otherwise dominating poor Michael Joyce. As soon as the tournament ended, we knew what we had to do. With great sadness, we sent Michael away. It was one of the toughest choices I've ever had to make. I don't like to use the word *fired* because, as I said, he was less a coach than a sibling at this point. It was just that we could no longer help each other as much as we needed to. In the end, it did not work out with Högstedt either, but that's another story.

My shoulder was not like it was when I was seventeen, but it was as good as it was ever going to get. I'd found a new way to play. It relied less on the serve than on the return. It was still about hard, flat strokes, still about power, but now with a bit of variation and spin thrown in. As you get older, your game has to evolve. That would be the case even if my shoulder had never been hurt. You have to learn to do consciously what you once did without thinking. You have to find little advantages and small ways to get a jump. Read the serve, move early, adjust your game around your abilities, which are always changing. If you don't do this, you won't have a very long career. If you do, you can actually get better as you get older. That's why the careers of the great long-lasting athletes, and not just tennis players, can be broken into various phases, in the way of great painters. As there was a young Picasso and an old Picasso, there was a young Agassi and an old Agassi. The young athlete knows how to pour it on, how to play. The old athlete knows how to conserve, how to win.

I had been on the tour for ten years. I was doing well. I'd won a lot of tournaments and was usually ranked in the top five. Still, it had been a long time since I'd won on the biggest stage of all. It had been a long time since I'd won a Grand Slam, not since the shoulder surgery. And that's what I needed. Another Grand Slam title. For my own sense of well-being and for my own sense of accomplishment, but also for the story of my career. It was the only way I could prove I'd made it all the way back. Without that, my career would be told as a story of before and after, as in: she was still a great player after the surgery, but not great enough to win a Grand Slam.

I came close at the 2012 Australian Open. I was ranked fourth coming in. I flew through the early rounds, losing only four games on my way to the group of sixteen. I dropped the first set to Sabine Lisicki in the fourth round, but quickly righted myself, winning the next sets 6–2, 6–3. My first really tough match came near the end of the tournament, against Petra Kvitová in the semifinals. A Czech player a few years younger than me, Kvitová's always dangerous. She's a lefty who hits big, dominating ground strokes that get you moving from side to side, and she has a tough serve to read. I mean, this was one of the best players in the world. I'd lost to her in the Wimbledon final the year before, which was all the motivation I needed. That was the first time I'd made it back to the Wimbledon final since 2004, and Kvitová had spoiled the story. She came in as the second ranked and would be a challenge.

She wore purple; I wore a white dress and played in a fluorescent green visor. I had trouble with my serve all afternoon. *My shoulder. My timing.* I double-faulted ten times in the match, half of those coming in the first set. Yet I was still able to be savvy and to bluff and hit my way through. It was all about will. Who was going to impose and who was going to get imposed upon. I took the first set 6–2. She took the next 3–6. On the best points, I was able to take her pace and turn it back on her. The day went on, and the plot revealed itself. I started to read her patterns, the directions of her serves. I had not felt this way in years. I was getting into my groove. I broke her serve to win the match.

The final was a letdown—for me. I lost quickly and disappointingly to Victoria Azarenka, a Belorussian. It was a terrible loss. The whole thing was finished in just over an hour. I won the first game, then started to tumble. Nothing felt right that whole evening. I won three games in the first set, and did not win another game for the rest of the match. It was one of the most lopsided finals in the history of the Australian Open. This is why athletes, if they want to survive, have to have a short memory. It's important to remember, but it's more important to forget. When you lose a close match, you learn what you can and remember what you've learned. When you lose like I did at the Australian Open that year, it's best just to forget.

I came into the 2012 French Open as a strong favorite. I really felt like this was the moment, this was the time. It was going to happen. That final of the Australian Open? That was just me burning off whatever I had to burn off. I was healthy and playing well when I reached Paris. They told me that if I won, I'd probably get back that number one ranking. And there was this small detail: the French Open was the only Grand Slam I had never won. That would be absolutely huge! Getting them all—that really was something to aspire to; it was a marker, special and rare. It put you in the history books. It's called a career Grand Slam. Only nine women had ever done it. Three Americans who dominated in the 1950s: Maureen Connolly Brinker, Doris Hart, and Shirley Fry Irvin; Margaret Court, an Australian who won her Grand Slams in the 1960s; and the others are Billie Jean King, Chris Evert, Martina Navratilova, Steffi Graf, and Serena Williams. In other words, I went into the tournament in exactly the right frame of mind.

I'd had trouble on clay in the past. It's a surface that suits mobility and patience, neither of which had been my strength. At one point, following a match I really struggled in, I told a newspaper reporter that, playing on clay, I felt like a cow on ice. But I'd been working at it. And working at it. In fact, the clay season that led to the French had been one of the best I'd ever played. I had won twelve clay matches coming into the French Open, winning the titles in Stuttgart, Germany, and in Rome. I'd even taken some French classes. Speaking French might not help me win, but it wouldn't hurt if you found yourself holding a trophy on the podium with a microphone in your hand. Nearly four years had gone by since my shoulder surgery. It had taken me eleven Grand Slams to get back to a final, at Wimbledon, the year before. And I was still waiting for the big win.

I dropped only five games in the first three matches of the French that year. But the fourth round was tougher. I took the first set 6–4, and Klára Koukalová, a Czech player, won the second set in a tiebreaker. But I took the third set 6–2.

The score sheet might not show it, but my most difficult match of that tournament was probably the semifinal against Petra

Kvitová. She'd played some of her best tennis against me in previous Grand Slams. Plus—the weather. It was one of those late spring days when you'd love to be walking down a Paris boulevard in a big floppy hat, looking in store windows, stopping for a coffee and croissants, but it was hell on the red clay, because of the wind, the bluster. It can hold up even the best shot, push it off course. It can wreak all kinds of havoc. So for me, in many ways, that match was really the final. If I got past this round, I knew I could take it all. I got it done in straight sets, 6–3, 6–3. The bonus for winning that match? I regained my number one ranking.

I played Sara Errani in the final. If you're playing Errani in a Grand Slam final, you could say it's a good draw (especially when you see her eating a Mars chocolate bar an hour before the match). But that's dangerous thinking. Everyone knows how an athlete competes as an underdog. Errani is an Italian player, around my age. She was just breaking through to the first serious success of her career, coming to be known for her finesse. But what can I tell you? It was just my day. I was wearing a black Nike dress and a black visor. Every shot I hit landed precisely, every target I marked, I found. Every now and then, it happens like that. It was overcast, with dark clouds rolling in, but that had nothing to do with me. All I had to do was keep things simple. Simple, yet smart. The first set seemed like it was over a moment after it began, 6–3. I was deep into the second, rolling downhill. Then, just like that, I was all alone out there, wind riffling my hair, serving for the tournament. Errani returned my serve and off we went, chasing down that last great point, back and forth, back and forth. I finally got the ball just where I wanted it, deep in the corner, just inside the line. She got to it, but could only manage a weak lollipop lob. I waited and waited for the bounce. For a long moment, the ball just seemed to hang there. And the stadium was quiet—so quiet. It was the sort of quiet only a crowd can make. Then I brought back my arm and struck the ball with a two-handed backhand, the shot carrying my racket above my shoulder and toward the sky. Errani ran and ran but did not get it back over the net. The crowd exploded into cheers. I dropped to my knees and put my face in my hands. Then I looked for my father. And looked and looked. It was the first time he had not been there at a Grand Slam victory, watching from the seats. It felt strange not finding him, like something crucial was missing. It felt wonderful, too. Then I went to the net and shook hands with Errani. Then I smiled. Then I jumped up and down. Then I turned circles in the center of the court, arms raised. I realized what this championship meant to me the instant it was over.

It was a perfect capper to my career. At the beginning, so much came so fast for me. I won Wimbledon when I was just seventeen years old. I became a star. Sponsors picked me up. I was the center of ad campaigns and jealousy. I won the U.S. Open in a black dress at night. And then, one afternoon, when it seemed like nothing could go wrong, everything did—the tendon in my shoulder snapped and suddenly a sport that I loved meant defeat and pain. My shoulder was cut open and repaired, but the recovery was long and difficult. For stretches, it seemed like I'd forgotten how to play the game, like I'd never get back what once came so naturally. I was lost. I wandered. Then slowly, bit by bit, and by working like I'd never worked before in my life, I began to find my way. I learned to play the old game in a new way. I realized there's more than one way to win a match. And now, eight years after I took that first Grand Slam at Wimbledon, I'd made it all the way back. I was in the same place, in the same world, but I was not the same player and not the same person. I saw it all again with new eyes and truly appreciated it for the first time. It gave people a new way to understand my story. It's exciting when a kid wins on the biggest stage. That's new life, that's spring. But how much sweeter when a player who once had everything loses it all, and then, miraculously, gets it all back.

SEVENTEEN

That summer, I played in the Olympics. London, 2012. People often ask me: Are you Russian or American? I could be American and speak English like an American and get all the references and all the jokes because I really grew up in Florida and was raised by my parents and my coaches but also by movies and television, by the scrappy counterpuncher and the evil bullies in *The Karate Kid* and by the all-knowing wisdom of Mike and Carol in *The Brady Bunch*. My humor is less Gogol than Seinfeld, and my smarts are less Dostoyevsky than *Full House*. But I never stopped and never will stop feeling Russian. When I'm down a break point deep in the third set of a match, I am Russian. But more—it's deep in my soul, in the history and the heritage of my family. I feel it every time I go back to Gomel in Belarus to see my grandparents, or to Sochi to see old friends, or to Moscow to play in tournaments. It's the language, the sound of the people on the street, not just the voices and the words but the mannerisms, the mentality, and the assumptions. It can be hard to define home, especially when you have led a life as crazy and all over the place as mine, but you know it when you're there. It's where you feel most grounded, most understood, where you don't have to explain. It's where they get you. I am a Russian. I have always known that, every minute of every day. Which is why the request, or the offer, or whatever you want to call it, meant so much to me.

It came by text—not exactly a handsome rider on a handsome steed carrying a golden scroll, just a few words that popped onto the screen of my phone. It was from someone at the Russian Tennis Federation. It mentioned the upcoming Summer Olympics in London, then asked if I'd be interested in carrying the flag for my country in the opening ceremony, leading the Russian athletes into the arena as the whole world watched, standing for and representing my country.

At first, I thought it was a joke. At first, I think everything is a joke, especially if it comes from the Russian Tennis Federation. There's no way! No fucking way! Someone is teasing me, making sport of me. I showed it to my mother. She read it over carefully, then read it again through narrowed eyes. Handing back the phone, she said, "Well, Masha, this seems to be pretty real."

As soon as she said that, I got the chills. Goose bumps.

It turned out to be one of the greatest honors of my career. I was the first woman to ever be given that honor by Russia, so it was a bit of a controversy. When they came to fit me for the outfit— a burgundy coat, wide-legged trousers—I could not stop smiling. You can go back and look at footage of the event itself. I am walking in front of four Russian men who wear blue coats and Panama hats. Behind them, the rest of our team, in burgundy coats, smiles and waves. I wear a straw hat of my own, and I cannot stop grinning. As we walked, all I could think about was watching the Olympic opening ceremony as a little girl. I wore a white beret, and walked circles around my bed, as if I were one of the athletes in the parade on TV. And now I was really here.

The Olympic matches were played in Wimbledon, which— well, you know how much I love that place. I made it all the way to the final, which was played on Centre Court on a windy day. I was beaten—I won only a single game!—in the final by Serena Williams. Of course, I'd like to have performed better. For myself, and for my country. But the story seemed to be less about Russia and America than about me and Serena Williams. What's going on? A player can beat Serena, and I can beat that player, but I don't beat Serena herself. My career record against Serena? It's not pretty. I've beaten her only twice, both times before my shoulder surgery. Of course, a lot of that lopsided record is explained simply by her excellence as a player. Her game—her serve and power, her ability to move her opponent from side to side—matches up well against mine. Serena's strengths are like puzzle pieces that snap into my weaknesses. And then there's my serve—when I lost that first serve, I lost a serious weapon. Maybe it gave her the edge. Yet that cannot be the whole story. There must be something else at work, there just has to be. I think Serena has an extra motivation when she plays me. She wants to beat everyone, but she wants to beat me more. Why? Because I beat her at Wimbledon when I was a kid. Because I took something from her, that first flush, which you can never really get back. Because I happened to walk into the clubhouse at exactly the wrong moment and so heard her crying and witnessed her low and vulnerable moment. And I don't think she's ever forgiven me for it.

I stood on the platform after the final, staring straight ahead, as Serena was covered in gold. A moment earlier, I had been given the silver medal. Silver is beautiful, but silver is not gold. I had only a single thought in mind: I will get her back at the Rio Olympics in 2016. Of course, that wouldn't happen.

That's the last part of my story.

EIGHTEEN

I'd had several coaches in the course of my career.

My coaching days with Thomas Högstedt were coming to an end in the summer of 2013. That year's Wimbledon was our last tournament together. Thomas came in at the perfect time in my career. He got me motivated after shoulder surgery. Brought back so much energy to my practices that I began looking forward to practice instead of dreading the constant repetitions, same drills, nonstop. But off the court? The most challenging individual I have ever worked with. But I couldn't focus on that, because what he was bringing on the court outweighed everything else, and one of my greatest strengths was knowing how to separate the unnecessary from what really matters. Until I just couldn't. I had to stop working with him. Abruptly. It felt like the right decision until I realized I would have no coach and didn't know or couldn't think of anyone else.

Max sent me a list of possible coaches. I grimaced at everyone on that list, until I saw Jimmy Connors on the bottom of it. I liked it. Was this even an option? Max called his manager. Jimmy was interested, but his interest came with a very expensive price tag. I had never seen numbers or bonuses like that for a coach. I knew that Andy Roddick had worked with him previously. Was Andy paying him that much money? I never found out. But I didn't have other options, so within days it felt like Jimmy had my bank information for unlimited withdrawals. He would drive down every day to L.A. from Santa Barbara. I offered him a hotel room so he didn't have to drive, but he said he liked listening to the radio. It must have been a good station because he spent more than five hours a day driving back and forth.

What I thought would be the same experience as back in 2007 was completely the opposite. The difference was that Michael Joyce was no longer leading practices. Jimmy was. There was no structure, no thought-out plan for the practice, no particular drills or things we would work on. I would hit in the center of the court for hours at a time. No patterns, nothing. He said to make sure I didn't let any ball get by me, no matter if it's in the court or not. He did this drill where he would stand with a basket of balls at the corner of the net and basically play fetch with me. He would feed the ball high and loopy toward the baseline, and I would have to run to it, catch it with my hands, and bring it back to the basket. Endlessly. Until I couldn't run any longer.

I thought maybe this was just the beginning, that he was learning about my game, getting to understand me better. But weeks went by, and nothing had changed. The moments I enjoyed most were during water breaks, when he would talk about his career, his experiences, what his mom was like, his mentality. All the things that had nothing to do with my game. And that was the problem. This was one of the very few times in my career where I would drive to practice feeling miserable. I remember it so clearly: it would be around 9:00 in the morning, I'd be pulling up to the country club tennis courts, and in my gut I would know it wouldn't work out. I called Max. I was holding back tears and cried as I got off the phone. I told him I didn't think this was going to work. Max asked me to give it some time, things would fall into place. That I would understand Jimmy's structure, his way of communicating. I knew Max was wrong. But I also knew I didn't have any other options at the time so I was going to have to suck it up.

We had already announced our partnership, and our first tournament together was going to be in Cincinnati. I met Jimmy at the airport; he came to the check-in desk wearing old-school faded blue jeans and a cream sweater vest. He carried a large suit bag. He mentioned he liked to watch matches wearing button-down collared shirts and suit jackets. I didn't know he packed them so well. He said all the other coaches in their track suits and baseball hats looked like clowns. I wasn't used to that attire, but if he wanted to dress the part in the stands, I didn't really care.

Arriving at our first practice together at the tournament felt very uncomfortable. Everyone watched our every move. Fans shouted both our names at the end of each practice. Jimmy waved and signed autographs. It felt like being part of a circus act when all I wanted was to do my work on the court, take some pictures, sign a few autographs, and quietly slip out the back door. With Jimmy, it felt like so much more.

He deserved that recognition more than anyone practicing on

those courts, but it didn't make me feel any better. And I couldn't quite understand why.

I played Sloane Stephens in the first round. Jimmy sat in my player box wearing an ironed white button-down shirt. I lost in three sets. But nothing about the match, the way I played, or the result mattered to me. All I could think about was that this partnership had no future. How was I going to get out of it without hurting his feelings? How would I tell the world I am firing Jimmy Connors after just one match?

The walk back to the locker room was painful; the talk with Jimmy was even worse. He said I had played well. "Don't put your head down. It's a long road ahead; we have the U.S. Open coming up." Except it wasn't. Not together, at least.

I was quiet, just nodding to his postmatch delivery. My first few words came out at the drive-through of a Wendy's a half hour later. When all things are going wrong, there's little that a spicy chicken sandwich can't fix. Milk shake. Fries. I ordered it all. And finished it in the car way before we pulled up to the driveway of the house we were renting. That night, we sat at the dining room table until 4:00 a.m. It was me, Grigor, my hitting partner Dieter, my fitness coach Yutaka, and my physical therapist at the time, Juan. Nothing about that evening felt promising. We were in someone else's house, in the middle of nowhere in Mason, Ohio, sitting there with only one thing on our mind: How were we going to tell Connors?

The truth is, there is no nice way or right way to say we are finished. I am not sure how he felt about it. He must have been furious, but we did not have a close enough relationship for me to find out. I knew it was the right decision.

The match against Stephens ended up being the last of my

season that year. My shoulder was becoming a problem again: there was that unavoidable pain. Those few months off, they gave me a chance to settle down, to look for the right person. I also didn't have to face journalists and answer their questions about Connors. My shoulder problem proved to be a blessing in disguise.

In 2013, I began looking for a new coach. You interview the coach, but the coach also interviews you. You have to be on the same page, be chasing the same thing, have the same sort of plan and goal in mind. In the end, one candidate stood above all the others: Sven Groeneveld, a Dutch pro who, after his own career, had coached a handful of excellent players, including Monica Seles and Mary Pierce. I first met Sven in the lobby of a New York hotel during the U.S. Open. I'd withdrawn because of a shoulder injury. He was ten minutes early, which didn't really work in my favor—I walked into the lobby holding a vanilla ice cream cone with sprinkles that I'd just bought from the ice cream truck around the corner. I am sure he assumed I was going to throw the rest of it away as we began speaking about the possibility of working together, but nothing gets in the way of my vanilla cone with sprinkles. So I kept going at it, mumbling questions and replies. At the time, he was running a player development program on tour. It was a good job and a good life and he was making good money, but he missed the competition of the game. He wanted to get back into the thick of it. I had to make sure he could help me, give me something new, and he had to make sure I was in it for the right reasons, that I was ready to do what I had to do to win, that the fire still burned, before he hitched his career to my own. He was worried, he told me later, that I was already thinking of the end, the graceful bow-out. He did not want to quit his own life just to be part of someone else's farewell tour.

When I sat down with Sven for this book, I asked him exactly why he'd decided to come aboard. He laughed and said, "Well, Maria, I was in fact concerned. I said to myself, 'Here is a player who is not all that far away from thirty, and, you know, the average tennis career, for women in this sport, can end in their late twenties. And here's a player who has already done everything. Won every Grand Slam, been the top rank in the world. So what's she still doing it for?' I asked you exactly that, and I was afraid you'd say you wanted to secure your legacy, or win one more Grand Slam, because that's how it is with most players. But that's not what you said. Do you remember? I asked, 'What are you playing for now?' And you said, 'Because I want to beat them all.' Right then, I said to myself, 'I'm in!'"

I've worked harder with Sven than I've ever worked in my life. That's how it has to be when you get a little older. You need to go twice as hard to look half as natural. You need to double your effort to get the same result. In other words, practice is everything. If you have a bad practice, you will have a bad match. If you let up for one day, you will most likely exit your next tournament one day early. In other words, you pay for everything. If you take a day for yourself here, you give up a day on the courts.

Sven and I clicked immediately. He's become more than just a coach. He's a confidant, an advisor, and a friend. How do you tell a real friend from a fake? Those who stick with you in the bad times as well as the good are your friends. The others fall off when the water gets rough, and good riddance. Sven has stuck with me through it all. Our partnership reached a real high in the spring of 2014 at the French Open. The clay, often a problem in the past, suddenly seemed to favor my game, the new game I'd slowly put together in the years after my shoulder surgery. This was a game built around the power of my return, those hard, flat backhands that could end a point from any place on the court. I'd actually come to love playing in Roland Garros, on the red clay of center court, with the colorful pennants that fly in the wind high above the stadium, the knowledgeable crowds, and of course Paris itself, which waits patiently to embrace its winner. I came in ranked at number seven. Serena Williams, who'd won the tournament the year before, entered at number one. But Serena went down in the second round—a huge upset. She lost in straight sets to the Spaniard Garbiñe Muguruza (who would also beat Serena in the final of the French in 2016, when I was out of the game). I cruised to the quarterfinals, where I faced, you guessed it, Garbiñe Muguruza. She won the first set, but she really did not challenge me the way she had challenged Serena. I beat her 1–6, 7–5, 6–1.

It didn't get any easier from there. It took me three very tough sets to beat Eugenie Bouchard in the semifinals. Then I faced Simona Halep in the final. The match went on and on—over three hours. It seemed like we'd been trading ground strokes for our entire lives. At times, it felt like I was playing my best tennis. Other times, it felt like nothing was working for me. My serve deserted me for long stretches. Twelve double faults! No matter how hard I hit the ball, Halep seemed to find a way to hit it back. Ball after ball—they just kept coming. We traded the lead—back and forth, back and forth. And the heat! It was one of those matches that comes down to will. Who wants it more? Who refuses to quit? It was not going to be a question of who was better but of who was going to hang on, who was going to get up one more time than she'd been knocked down.

In other words, I simply refused to give in. I finally found myself serving for the match and the tournament at the end of a very long day. Halep returned my serve, and I hit a hard, flat shot, just the sort I had learned from Robert Lansdorp in another life, into her backhand corner. She got her racket on the ball, but barely, and the result was a pop fly that I watched and watched as it turned in the sky. It finally came down on the red clay, a couple of feet outside the line. I fell to my knees, put my face in my hands. If this was my last Grand Slam championship, then perfect! What better bookend to my first Wimbledon? I was so young at Wimbledon, too young, too new to the scene, to really understand what it all meant, and everything felt so easy, winners falling as naturally as rain on a tin roof. At the French in 2014, I was mature and the matches were hard. It was all struggle. It took so much work to overcome Halep, an opponent who, like me, refused to go away and die. If things had played out differently, she might have won the match. Then it would have been Halep holding the trophy at center court, but, on that day, it happened to be me.

NINETEEN

Where was I in the winter of 2015? Not physically, but mentally? I guess I was in retrospection, thinking about the past. I had begun this book. I was imagining my retirement; subconsciously, I was probably planning it. I was thinking about my life after the game. I would play through the winter and spring, appear at the Olympics in Rio that summer, then begin my last professional season. Maybe one more turn around the circuit, with this book appearing on shelves a few weeks before the 2017 U.S. Open. That was the idea. I'd tell my story and take my bow and say goodbye. I remember sitting with Max in a hotel room and talking about my thirtieth birthday. I told him I wanted to celebrate it like a normal person and not be in some locker room in Stuttgart when it came around. We talked about a party. We talked about this and that. In other words, I was full of plans. And you know how the saying goes: Man plans, God laughs.

The year 2016 began, as the year always does, with me in Melbourne for the Australian Open. I got through the early rounds, only to meet a familiar fate. Serena Williams beat me in the quarterfinals, 6–4, 6–1. It felt like a decent start to my twelfth professional season. But, as sometimes happens in nightmares, what felt like the beginning turned out to be the end.

A few weeks after the Australian Open, when I was back in Los Angeles, training and rehabbing my left wrist, practicing and preparing for the American hard court tournaments, I got a funny-looking e-mail. It was from the ITF, the International Tennis Federation, the body that governs our sport. The messages I get from the ITF tend to be in the nature of mass e-mails, announcements with attachments, the sort of e-mail that is hardly alarming. But this one was different. It was addressed to me and to me alone. I clicked on it and read it, and as I read it my heart started to pound. It said that the urine sample I had given in Australia had been flagged and tested and had come back positive. In other words, and I had to read this again and again to make sure I was not hallucinating, I had failed the drug test. What? How? I'd always been very careful to treat my body right and to follow the rules. I searched for the name of the drug. What the hell could it be? I took nothing that was new, nothing that was not legal and prescribed by a doctor. There it was at the bottom of the note. It was called meldonium. OK, obviously this was a mistake, I told myself, relieved. Who had ever heard of that? I copied the word from the note and pasted it into the Google bar and hit search, just to make sure.

Then I understood. I knew meldonium as Mildronate, the brand name. It was a supplement. I'd been taking it for ten years, as had millions of other Eastern Europeans. Mildronate is an over-the-counter supplement in Russia. You don't even need a prescription. You just grab it off the pharmacy shelf. In Russia, people take it the way people take baby aspirin in America: for a heart condition, for coronary artery disease. It is used by people with any sort of heart issue. It's so common that you don't think of it as a drug, let alone a performance-enhancing drug. I'd first been told to take it when I was eighteen years old and I was getting sick a lot and having an issue with irregular heartbeats and abnormal EKGs. A cardiologist told me to take Mildronate as a precaution during high-intensity training and matches, along with vitamins and minerals. I was not unfamiliar with the supplement, because my grandmother also takes it for *her* heart condition.

For seven years I had written confirmation from a WADA-accredited lab that all the supplements I was taking, including Mildronate, were permissible. In fact, I think the system I had in place for checking new supplements was better than the system used by just about any other athlete out there. I was careful—extremely careful—but I got too comfortable with the idea that the supplements I'd been taking would stay legal.

WADA—the World Anti-Doping Authority, which sets the policy followed by the ITF—grew concerned about meldonium not because it improves performance but because it was being taken by so many athletes from Eastern Europe and Russia. WADA's thought process seemed to go something like this: if so many hundreds of athletes are taking it, they must think it gives them an edge.

At first, WADA put meldonium on a watch list. Then, as of January 2016, it was banned. How were we informed? Meldonium was included in a catalog of banned substances that the ITF sent out to players. It was viewable by clicking through a series of links in an e-mail. I never followed those links, and didn't ask any member of my team to. That was my mistake. I was careless. But the ITF didn't draw any attention to the fact that they were suddenly banning a supplement that was being legally used by millions of people. That was their mistake.

An issue that could have been easily resolved became a crisis instead. I felt blindsided by the ITF's poor notifications, trapped, tricked. The whole thing seemed like a misunderstanding. I figured all I had to do was explain myself and it would be fixed. I mean, meldonium had been banned for what? Four weeks? So, at worst, I had inadvertently been in violation of the ban for less than twenty-eight days, along with hundreds of other athletes. And this coming after twelve years on the professional tour. It should've been easy to clear up. But I soon realized that I was running into a brick wall. First, I'd have a hearing before a panel selected by the ITF. If I failed to win my case at that hearing, I could be banned from the game for up to four years. Four years! It would be the end of my career, the end of everything. All that I had worked for and built would be washed away, just like that. And for what? An honest mistake.

The news had not yet hit the press, and I did not know how or when it would. That scared me. I stayed strong on the outside, just hoping this would all get resolved quickly, but on the inside every cell of me was crying. Then I thought. And thought some more. Then I rallied. I asked myself, "Why just wait for the news to break? Why not go out and explain to the world exactly what happened? If I tell the truth, nothing can hurt me. If I tell the truth, everyone will understand and this nightmare will be over."

I called a press conference less than a week after I got that e-mail. I wrote a statement, then got ready. I had told no one but my parents, Sven, and Max. There were few people I could talk to. I did not tell anyone else because I did not want the news to leak. I wanted to be the one to tell it, at my own time, in my own way. It was the only thing I could still control. I was relieved that I'd finally be able to tell the members of my team, my friends and the people I worked with, what was going on. As much as anything else, this week had been isolating and lonely. Who did I tell before everyone else? My friend who also happens to be a hairstylist. I called him a few hours before I went in front of the cameras for the press conference, and asked him to come over with his gear. When I explained what was going on, he said, "You mean, all this time, we could have been doing really great drugs, and this is what you chose? Honey, next time you need to ask my advice before you go pharmaceutical shopping."

It was the first real laugh I'd had in days. I could not tell marijuana from cocaine. Or anything from anything. That's what made the whole thing so bitterly ironic. They always nail you for the things you don't do, for being the person you are not. The people who really do the drugs—my guess is they know how to protect themselves, so they don't get caught. My test flagged red because I took the pills and went in for the sample without thinking. I'd been taking those pills for years, they'd tested me for years, without any problem because they were completely legal, so why all of a sudden should I go about my routine differently? It's like if they suddenly changed the speed limit from 55 to 35 but did not post the change. It would be no problem for the speeders—they've got radar detectors or whatever to beat the cops. It's the rest of us who go 55, believing we are well within the limits, who get nailed.

There were maybe fifty reporters and TV people at the press

conference. The room was filled with unfamiliar faces and camera crews. There was speculation that I had called everyone together to announce my retirement. I stood before them in a black shirt and a Rick Owens jacket. I felt like I was dressed for a funeral. I had written notes. I looked at them as I tried to explain what had happened in the most direct words I could find:

> I wanted to let you know that a few days ago I received a letter from the ITF that I had failed a drug test at the Australian Open. I did fail the test and I take full responsibility for it. For the past ten years, I have been given a medicine, Mildronate, by my family doctor. And a few days ago, after receiving the letter, I found out that it also has another name of meldonium, which I did not know. It's very important for you to know that for ten years this medicine was not on WADA's banned list and I had been legally taking the medicine for the past ten years. But on January 1 the rules changed and meldonium became a prohibited substance, which I had not known. I was given this medicine by my doctor for several health issues that I was having back in 2006. I was getting sick a lot. I was getting the flu every couple of months. I had irregular EKG results, as well as indications of diabetes with a family history of diabetes. I thought it was very important for me to come out and speak in front of all of you because throughout my long career I have been very open and honest about many things and I take great responsibility and professionalism in my job every single day. And I made a huge mistake. I let my fans down. I let this sport down—this game, which I've been playing since the age of four and love so deeply. I know with this I face consequences and I don't want to end my career this way and

I really hope I will be given another chance to play this game. I know many of you thought I'd be announcing my retirement today. But, if I ever did announce my retirement, it would probably not be in this downtown Los Angeles hotel with this fairly ugly carpet.

I felt so relieved exiting that room. I had nothing to hide and I have nothing to hide. I wanted my friends and fans and even my enemies to know exactly what had happened because it was an inadvertent mistake and I believed they would see it and understand.

I was wrong. Mostly. I mean, yes, some people came to my defense, or at least said, "Well, let's not rush to judgment. Let's wait and see." But the newspapers really went after me, called me a cheater and a liar and compared me with famous cheating athletes. In the course of two news cycles, everything I had ever accomplished had been tarnished. My image, all that I stand for and believe in, all that I have worked for, had been ripped up as if for sport. What does it matter if you are exonerated in the end if you have been destroyed along the way? That's what people mean when they say the trial is the punishment. Worst is the way this bogus charge made me doubt the world and the people around me. Until now, I had not paid much attention to what was said about me. I had not cared. I figured, "I'll do my thing, I'll work hard and play my game, and the rest will take care of itself. The dogs bark, but the caravan rolls on." But the firestorm that followed the press conference made me doubt that. It was like a worm in my brain, just the worst kind of mindfuck. I'd never felt that way before. Suddenly, no matter who I looked at, I found myself thinking, "Do they know? And do they believe it? Do they think I'm a cheater? Do they think I'm a liar?" For the first time in my life, I was worried what people thought of me.

It really hit me a few hours after the press conference. I was sitting at the kitchen table in Manhattan Beach, talking to my mother, who was making dinner. My phone rang. It was Max. He sounded grave. He had just gotten off the phone with Nike. He did not go into great detail, but simply said, "It was not a good conversation, Maria." (Anytime Max uses my name something has gone wrong.) Two hours after that, Nike put out a statement, and it was brutal. It was about me, and trust, and role models, and we're so disappointed. They said that they were suspending me, which I didn't understand at first. They were a sponsor. They were either affiliated with me or they were not. There was no such thing as a suspension in my contract. Was this part of the shameful scramble of certain businesses and certain so-called friends to put distance between themselves and me, to cover their asses and get clear? When the shit hits the fan, that's when you can separate the actual friends from the mere acquaintances. Those who flee, let them flee, I told myself. Those who stick, love them. That was a silver lining of this nightmare. It taught me the real from the fake.

Maybe I should have given my sponsors a heads-up before I held the press conference, but I was so determined to not let the news leak, to break it myself. I think what really hurt me was the fact that I had been with Nike since I was eleven years old. They knew me better than any other sponsor in my life. They knew me as a young girl, an athlete, a daughter, and yet their statement was so cold. A few days later, Mark Parker got in touch with Max, who called me to say they wanted to have a conversation. I told Max it was still too raw for me, and that I would call him back when I found the strength.

I was sitting in the kitchen, eating the rice pilaf my mom had made for me (when my mom can't decide what to do, she makes rice pilaf). I was in a funk, a deep funk, feeling so low I'd have to reach up to touch bottom. A castle made of sand. A house made of cards. That's what I was thinking when my phone started to buzz. It was a text from my old coach and friend Michael Joyce. I clicked on it, expecting a show of friendship and solidarity, but it was immediately clear that this message was not meant for me. It was probably meant for his wife, but he must have hit my name by mistake. It's the sort of mistake that makes you think Freud wasn't so crazy after all. It was just one line—"Can you believe that Nike did that to her?"—but it cut to the quick. It was not just the information, that Nike had suspended my contract, but the tone and the sense I suddenly had of people everywhere, people I had known all my life, speaking about me behind my back, coldly, without affection or warmth, even with a kind of amusement. The fork dropped from my hand. My mom looked up. I wanted to tell her what he'd written, but nothing but sobs came out. That was the moment, the bad moment, the freaked-out vertigo spin moment. I ran upstairs to my room, crying hysterically. I sat there on the floor holding on to my bed for what felt like hours, sobbing. I called Max. He said, "Shhh, shhh, shhh." He said, "Calm down, Maria, calm down. It's OK. No, no, no. Nike did not drop you." My mom spent the rest of the night holding my hand. For the next two weeks, she didn't let me go to sleep alone.

The next morning was the hinge moment. Either you curl up in a ball, the covers pulled over your head, or you get out of bed and carry on. I'd signed up for an 8:30 a.m. spinning class not far from my house. I was going to meet Sven there. I'd called him at 7:30 and said, "Forget it. I can't do it. I can't go." My eyelids felt heavy. My body felt heavier than it had ever been, even though I'd been losing weight. But something told me I had to go. I had to get out of bed and get dressed and go, make myself do it, or I'd never get out of bed again. This was the moment. Stay down, or get the fuck up. Ten minutes later I sent Sven a text: "I'll see you there at 8:20."

I put on some clothes and dragged myself to the car. There were two paparazzi outside the house. Those goddamn Priuses, I never liked that car! They followed me as I drove myself down the hill to the plaza. At the studio, everyone was staring at me, or maybe that was just in my mind. That's the thing. You start to go nuts. Your own mind turns against you, tortures you. I just got on a bike in that dark room, put my head down, and made myself pedal. Left. Right. Left. Right. I was a mess, a goddamn mess. I cried through the entire class, but I did what I had to do. From that moment, I knew it was going to be awful and unfair but that I'd get through it. Somewhere, deep down, I knew I'd survive.

We began preparing for the hearing right away. I was getting my papers and records in order, and researching meldonium. I wanted to know everything about it. Meanwhile, I had been provisionally banned from competition. I was already missing tournaments: Indian Wells, Miami. There was no way to predict the future. In the moment, it felt like I'd never make it back, yet I kept training. This was not only for my physical health but for my mental health, too.

One afternoon I found myself really struggling at practice. Sven sat me down and said, "Maria, when you go to that hearing, I want you to be the fittest person in that room."

I gave him a look. "Well, that's not going to be difficult."

"You know what I mean," he told me. "I want you to be so strong physically and mentally that they can't hurt you."

In those weeks, I worked as hard as I ever have. I could've gone out, that June, and played at the French Open. I was in that kind of shape. I practiced on a clay court behind someone's house in Palos Verdes every day. Normally, I practice on a side court at a country club. It's the most private court I can find, but it's still visible to everyone walking by. What I needed now was privacy. But there really was no escape from my own terrible thoughts. I was afraid to look at my phone, but I could not keep my eyes away. It was like the ring that ruins Gollum in *The Lord of the Rings*. It was "my precious." It seemed to vibrate whenever I looked at it—it flew into my hand whenever I thought about it. Who knew what terrible news I was going to get next? I was afraid when Max's name popped up—my heart was in my mouth—because "what happened now?" And yet I needed to talk to him. All the time. His calls caused anxiety that only his calls could relieve. In the end, I did not even know what I was afraid of. I just knew that I was afraid. All the time.

The first hearing was in June in an office tower in London. I remember waking up in the Rosewood hotel near Covent Garden. The bed was so big and comfortable, and for a moment I was happy because I had forgotten why I was in that city and in that hotel and in that bed, and then I remembered. Downstairs, they asked if my family had come with me and I laughed. My family hardly ever came when I was playing in a tournament. Why would they come for my trial? The hearing was held in a kind of boardroom. On our side, it was me, Max, and my two lawyers. On their side, it was ITF's antidoping head and their lawyers. We gave our testimony to all three members of the panel.

The whole process was set up to make me fail. All three members of the panel had been selected by the ITF. The chairman of the panel had actually been copied on the original e-mail that set off the whole nightmare. In other words, the case, brought by the ITF, would be decided by the ITF, too. How can such a hearing be impartial, fair? Simple answer: it can't. That's why my lawyer told me not to expect justice or even a fair outcome in this round. We have to lose here, he said, so we can get to the next panel, where you actually will get a fair hearing. I was shocked. "You mean I'll have to go through this twice?" I couldn't stand the thought of it. I had to testify for hours and hours. Then, when I wasn't testifying, I had to sit and listen to the other side call me a doper and a cheat. But there was one thing that gave me confidence. I knew that I was telling the truth. I did not try to claim there had been a mistake on the test or that I had not taken the supplement or had taken it only before the ban. I admitted to taking the supplement in January 2016. But it was a mistake. Wasn't that obvious? I didn't know the supplement had been banned, or that there was any issue with it. It did not enhance my performance or make me a better player. I had been told to take it for my heart, so I took it for my heart. As far as violating a ban, that was just a stupid oversight. But the ITF took a hard line, delivered in an aggressive tone. What a sad, infuriating joke. Why were we even fighting? I screwed up. I didn't do enough to check the revised prohibited list. But they screwed up, too. They should've been much clearer about the changes to that list. They should've flagged the ban, shouted the change to the hills. How about at least making some phone calls to some agents and giving the players an advance warning? Instead, they expected a player to comb through that long list and find the change. Considering meldonium was on the monitoring list throughout 2015, they should have known it was in my system. I'd been giving urine and blood samples for years. Why not let me know what was happening? It seemed like a setup, a trap. Not a day went by when I did not wonder if someone was trying to do me in.

Despite all that, I came away from the first hearing optimistic. I thought I'd explained myself well. The truth seemed so clear. Which is why the decision, and the report, which was issued a few weeks later, came as such a shock. The three-member panel agreed that I had not intended to violate the rules—that it was indeed a mistake. Those lawyers admitted there was no intent to cheat on my part. I was happy about that, but the rest of it? The report? It was just a screed of lies, an endless attack on me. They killed me, ripped me to pieces. It was so opinionated, so brutal, and so mean. I was horrified by it, disappointed and stunned. The ban was set at two years. When the word came down from Mount Olympus, I drove to Ojai, California. My team and I rented a home there. It felt good to be somewhere beautiful when something bad was happening. But it hurt badly. Two years? OK, it was not the max, it was not four years, but two years? Would I be able to come back after a two-year hiatus? When I'd be thirty-one years old? I felt like a ninety-year-old man who gets sentenced to ten years in prison.

My lawyer called me aside and explained. He said, "Look, this panel is not really the one that matters—it's prejudiced and unfair. Famously unfair. That's why so many of their decisions have been reversed on appeal. The last six have been overturned! But that's the process. We needed this ruling to get to the next panel, the one that really decides. So stay strong, and keep training and be optimistic. I promise you: this will not be the last word."

And so we began preparing for the second hearing, which

would be heard by the CAS, the Court of Arbitration for Sport. The CAS is an international quasi-judicial body first established by the Olympic Committee in 1983, but its role has grown. It's become the court of last appeal for cases like mine. It's a truly neutral body. I hoped to clear my name at the CAS, but of course a tremendous amount of damage had already been done. Many of my sponsors distanced themselves from me and my ranking was dropping by the week. I'd miss the Rio Olympics. And my reputation? Look at the damage that was being done even before I got to make my case. The trial felt like the punishment. In May, in New York, as I was coming out of the Bowery Hotel, catching a car to my first Met Gala, a crazy man started screaming at me in the street about steroids. A few weeks later, while I was talking to a landscaper in front of my house in L.A., a car drove by and a boy who sounded no more than fourteen years old shouted, "Dope ho! F.U., Maria!" How did I feel? Bad for the landscaper! He was nice and seemed so upset and embarrassed that I just wanted to tell him everything would be OK.

Welcome to my life. What a nightmare.

In the meantime, I kept training. During one practice, I got frustrated. "Why are we doing this?" I asked Sven. "What are we training for?"

Right then, I realized I needed to do something else, something more. This was a question of sanity. I have always been interested in business, so I enrolled in a two-week summer program at Harvard Business School. I worked with brilliant professors and students, most of whom couldn't care less about my tennis problems. They made me feel normal. And stupid. That was a relief. Just to be out of that pressure cooker. Just to be raising my hand and asking questions. It was a vacation from my trouble. I learned so much in that program, and it was fulfilling—this notion that I was not wasting time. Though I was going through this ordeal, I was still growing, still trying to become a better version of myself. When that was over, I wrote an e-mail to Adam Silver, commissioner of the NBA. I'd never met Adam, but I had long admired his work. I told him about my respect for the league, the players, and the teams, the way that the product was promoted and presented to the public. He invited me to New York, where he set me up with a kind of internship. For three days, I shadowed him, watching Adam Silver do his job, learning. We did a lot of talking; he gave me his thoughts on my situation. He didn't need to or have to but he did. I cannot tell you how comforting it was. Not just the internship itself but the very fact of it. I felt like the whole world was against me, that I'd become an outcast, a pariah. Looking back on it, the fact that Adam Silver brought me in and showed me around and told the world, by bringing me in, that there was in fact no shame in working with Maria Sharapova—it was a tremendous feeling. All I needed at the time were small doses of happiness that added together and got me through this. I'm a much better athlete, much better person, when I'm inspired. And those experiences inspired me. They made me feel good about myself, like I was learning and growing.

The CAS is headquartered in Lausanne, Switzerland, but the second hearing was held in an office building in New York City. Once again, we made our case before a three-member panel. Only this time, the three were not chosen by the ITF. One was chosen by the ITF, one by my team, and the chairman by the CAS itself. The process was very similar to the first hearing, except we all walked into that room like it was a war. Their lawyers went first. (Oh, how I hate those lawyers with their suits and crooked ties.) Then it was my turn. I spoke for another three hours. I had mixed feelings when it was over. I felt like I'd made my case and the facts were clear, but that's how I'd felt after the first hearing. So I tried to keep my expectations in check. I almost wanted to feel like shit about it so I'd almost force a different outcome. I do something like this before certain tournaments, too. I spent the next several weeks training, keeping the date of the decision forever in my mind. October 4, 2016. I eyed it like a hawk.

It was a different kind of training than the sort you normally do. When you are competing, you train like a boxer, working your way toward a specific goal, peak performance, which should be reached the day before the fight or tournament. But I had no tournament, which meant I had no such goal. I never wanted to peak, or get too high. I just wanted to maintain, lock myself into a holding pattern that would be broken only when I really knew what the future would look like. In a way, my long, forced hiatus actually helped me. I'd been suffering from all sorts of nagging injuries, aches, and pains. I'd been struggling with my wrist during the first few months of the year, and now it could heal. I'd been playing tennis almost every day since I was four. I'd never simply let my body get better. Now, for the first time in years, I actually began to heal. It was funny. I was banned from competition, but, as a result of that ban, I felt better and more ready to compete than I had in years.

I was in my bedroom in Manhattan Beach when the verdict finally came by e-mail. It arrived at 9:21 a.m. Pacific Standard Time. I knew it was coming, which meant I could not really sleep the night before. I was either running to the bathroom, or tossing and turning, or staring at the ceiling, or willing the hours to pass. I could not stand to read the report right away—I was just too nervous—but the first line in my lawyer's e-mail gave me a hint. It said the CAS had knocked the ban down from two years to fifteen months. And I'd already served much of it. I screamed when I read that. My father was in Belarus, visiting his mom, but my mom was downstairs. I shouted to her in Russian, "I'm coming back! I will play tennis again. I'm coming back!" Then I called my grandma. Then my father. I was overjoyed, relieved. It was not perfect—nothing is. But a huge weight had been lifted from my shoulders.

The wording of the report was even better than the verdict. They cleared my name in just a few paragraphs. I felt like I'd gotten my air back. My lawyer copy and pasted and highlighted the key paragraphs of the report into the e-mail:

[The] Player did not seek treatment from Dr. Skalny for the purposes of obtaining any performance enhancing product, but for medical reasons.

No specific warning had been issued by the relevant organizations (WADA, ITF or WTA) as to the change in the status of Meldonium (the ingredient of Mildronate). In that respect, the Panel notes that anti-doping organizations should have to take reasonable steps to provide notice to athletes of significant changes to the Prohibited List, such as the addition of a substance, including its brand names.

The Panel wishes to emphasize that based on the evidence, the Player did not endeavor to mask or hide her use of Mildronate and was in fact open about it to many in her entourage and based on a doctor's recommendation, that she took the substance with the good faith belief that it was appropriate and compliant with the relevant rules and her anti-doping obligations, as it was over a long period of her career, and that she was not clearly informed by the relevant anti-doping authorities of the change in the rules.

Finally, the Panel wishes to point out that the case it heard, and the award it renders, was not about an athlete who cheated. It was only about the degree of fault that can be imputed to a player for her failure to make sure that the substance contained in a product she had been legally taking over a long period, and for most of the time on the basis of a doctor's prescription, remained in compliance with the TADP and WADC. No question of intent to violate the TADP or WADC was before this Panel: under no circumstances, therefore, can the Player be considered to be an "intentional doper."

I flew to New York. I was in the city when the findings became public. I had not done an interview in nine months. No comments, no popping off in the media. That press conference had been my last word on all this. I wanted to wait until the last legal word was typed. Now it had been. I went on the *Today* show and *Charlie Rose*. I did a big interview with *The New York Times*. I guess I wanted the ITF to acknowledge their mistake. Instead I got hedging and hems and haws. But that's OK. It's something experience has taught me: there is no perfect justice, not in this world. You can't control what people say about you and what they think about you. You can't plan for bad luck. You can only work your hardest and do your best and tell the truth. In the end, it's the effort that matters. The rest is beyond your control.

Here's another good thing that's come from all this: I heard from so many fans, so many young girls, who had been inspired by my example and my life. I had never thought of my influence on other people before, how all the work I was doing might pave the way for the next generations, as others had paved the way for me. But I saw it now, and it inspired me. It made me happy and it awed me and of course it made me really want to get back out there and play my game. It's interesting. Before all this happened I was thinking only about the finish line. How it would end, how I would make my exit. But I don't think about that anymore. Now I think only about playing. As long as I can. As hard as I can. Until they take down the nets. Until they burn my rackets. Until they stop me. And I want to see them try.

ACKNOWLEDGMENTS

My mother. There are not enough pages in a book to describe how special you are. For my sixteenth birthday, you bought me a pearl bracelet. A pearl is everything you stand for and bring to my life. Elegant and bold. Your love of literature inspired me to write this, although I am not even close to the level of the legendary authors you embrace. There was a time you hesitated about my desire to write this book, but I do hope that one day you will read it.

Father. You paved the road for me that I continue to walk on every single day. You never told me I had to be a winner. You never told me I didn't. You simply guided me to be a *champion*. Not only did you take me to my destination, but you were there along the whole journey. Your stories are incredible, although your storytelling needs a faster pace. You can still be slightly annoying, and no matter how many times you tell me to put my phone away while eating, that will never change. I'm too old for that. I promised you I'd serve and volley once before you die. It's coming. You're still young.

Rich. I believed you were going to help me write this book seven years ago when I read one of your earlier works. I am so grateful for your humbling talent. And beyond grateful for your patience with all the male figures in my life. Thank you for living and breathing my life for this chunk of time. These pages would be a hot mess without you.

Estelle. I love you. Your name should be next to the words *best friend* in the dictionary. I will forever look forward to writing and receiving endless Christmas and birthday cards from you. And I know they're not getting shorter anytime soon.

Max. Nineteen years and this is just the beginning of what we will accomplish together. I know you had more hair, fewer chins, and a more attractive waistline before you became my agent, but those are things money can pay for, right?

Jennifer. You believed in this book way before I ever did. Your confidence is contagious—a boss in capital letters! I want to be like you when I grow up.

Sarah. The passion with which you worked on this project is unforgettable. You believed in my life story from the very few paragraphs I put down on paper. No questions, no requests. You simply gave me the freedom to write this thing. Thank you!

A Note About the Author

Born in Nyagan, Russia, Maria Sharapova moved to the United States when she was six years old. At seventeen, Sharapova beat Serena Williams to win Wimbledon. She reached the number one world ranking at eighteen, and has held that ranking a number of times since. To date, she has won five Grand Slams. She lives in Manhattan Beach, California.